Paul Ricoeur between Theology and Philosophy

Indiana Series in the Philosophy of Religion

Merold Westphal, editor

Paul Ricoeur between Theology and Philosophy

Detour and Return

Boyd Blundell

Indiana University Press | Bloomington and Indianapolis

This book is a publication of

Indiana University Press

601 North Morton Street
Bloomington, Indiana 47404-3797 USA

www.iupress.indiana.edu

Telephone orders 800-842-6796
Fax orders   812-855-7931
Orders by e-mail iuporder@indiana.edu

⊗ *The paper used in this publication meets the minimum requirements of the American National Standard for Information Sciences—Permanence of Paper for Printed Library Materials, ANSI Z39.48-1992.*

MANUFACTURED IN THE UNITED STATES OF AMERICA

Library of Congress Cataloging-in-Publication Data

Blundell, Boyd, date
  Paul Ricoeur between theology and philosophy : detour and return / Boyd Blundell.
      p. cm. — (Indiana series in the philosophy of religion)
  Includes bibliographical references and index.
  ISBN 978-0-253-35465-5 (cloth : alk. paper) — ISBN 978-0-253-22190-2 (pbk. : alk. paper) 1. Ricœur, Paul. I. Title.
  B2430.R554B58 2010
  194—dc22

                                                                 2009041086

          1 2 3 4 5 15 14 13 12 11 10

In memory of George Schner, SJ, who, in his
all too short time with us, taught so many
that most authentic expression of grace:
tireless effort on behalf of another's project

CONTENTS

CONTENTS

PREFACE AND ACKNOWLEDGMENTS

Philosophical hermeneutics has as one its central features an awareness of the effective history that moves under and through every conversation, so it seems appropriate that I identify the effective history that runs under and through this project. The motive force comes from my first sustained encounter with Karl Barth in a graduate course with the late George Schner at Regis College in Toronto. After much warning about how hard it was to understand Barth when reading alone, I found it surprisingly easy to absorb Barth's rhythm of expression. I did not grow up in the Reformed tradition, so this was puzzling to me. I had received other such warnings about other philosophers and theologians, and did indeed have trouble understanding them without some guidance. It was only later that I realized that I consistently used the hermeneutical language of Ricoeur that I had acquired as an undergraduate when trying to articulate what I thought Barth was saying. This in turn led me to recall that I had had a similar experience with Ricoeur, and I realized that my natural affinity for Ricoeur came from my reading, under the guidance of Gary Madison, a great deal of Gabriel Marcel before reading any of Ricoeur. Marcel had been a revelation to a young philosophy major raised in a Canadian evangelical tradition that suffered from many of the effects of what Wheaton's Mark Noll has eloquently described as "the intellectual disaster of fundamentalism." That someone who was committed to his Christian faith could do that kind of philosophy gave me hope that intellectual sophistication and Christian faith were not mutually exclusive concepts.

Schner was an oddity as a theologian, a Jesuit postliberal, and his distaste for Tracy's theological model shone through brightly. But amongst the postliberals, I saw similar hostility toward Ricoeur's hermeneutics, and could not figure out why. The things they objected to in Tracy's revisionist theology seemed to have nothing to do with Ricoeur's philosophical hermeneutics as such, which I eventually came to see that they neither understood nor cared to understand, content to dismiss it as a general theory of interpreting texts that threatened orthodox biblical interpretation. Their commitment to an ad hoc approach, with a view to restraining philosophy's influence on theology, struck me as a serious impediment to doing any constructive Barthian theology, for such conceptual work cannot avoid a philosophical vocabulary. An ad hoc approach to that task can result only in either incoherence or an implicit but still operative philosophical vocabulary that had not been properly vetted. In this case, the postliberals seemed to teeter between incoherence and the philosophy of Wittgenstein, which stifles Barth's voice in its being unable to account for his strengths in narrative, history, and dialectic. I concluded that both Barth's theology and Ricoeur's philosophy were being less than ideally served in the North American theological conversation, but that Ricoeur's philosophy could be of great service to Barth's theology.

A hermeneuticist should be the last to claim to have accomplished something alone, and there are a great many people to thank. The Jesuits at Regis College in Toronto, particularly Ron Mercier and Ron Barnes, and the theological ethics faculty at Boston College, particularly Jim Keenan and David Hollenbach, gave a headstrong graduate student a great deal of much-appreciated support and freedom to pursue his own questions. This has continued with the encouragement and support of the late Stephen Duffy, Denis Janz, and others at Loyola University New Orleans. Also, my peers such as Sean McGrath, Jeremy Wilkins, Martin O'Malley, Brian Treanor, Grant Kaplan, and Joe Berendzen have been very helpful in conversations and in simple intellectual friendship, both of which are appreciated. A special thanks goes to Andrzej Wiercinski, who is the very definition of hospitality, both physical and intellectual, and who has for a decade helped me in developing the courage to think the necessary. And finally, thanks to Richard Kearney, who graciously agreed to direct the out-of-department dissertation that formed the nucleus of this book and who has been unstinting in his support ever since.

To my wonderful children, Gracelyn and Avery, who have already learned that if Daddy has not made eye contact he may well not be listening: you give me the joy and energy that helps me write. And to my lovely wife, Laura, who has done more to help me refine my ideas than anyone else: not only do you make it all possible, you make it all worth it.

ABBREVIATIONS

CC   Ricoeur, Paul. *Critique and Conviction: Conversations with François Azouvi and Marc De Launay.* Trans. Kathleen Blamey. New York: Columbia University Press, 1998.

FS   ———. *Figuring the Sacred: Religion, Narrative, and Imagination.* Ed. Mark I. Wallace. Minneapolis: Fortress Press, 1995.

OA   ———. *Oneself as Another.* Trans. Kathleen Blamey. Chicago: University of Chicago Press, 1992.

TA   ———. *From Text to Action: Essays in Hermeneutics 2.* Evanston, Ill.: Northwestern University Press, 1991.

TN 1   ———. *Time and Narrative.* Vol. 1. Trans. Kathleen McLaughlin and David Pellauer. Chicago: University of Chicago Press, 1985.

TN 3   ———. *Time and Narrative.* Vol. 3. Trans. Kathleen Blamey and David Pellauer. Chicago: University of Chicago Press, 1988.

BHD   Wiercinski, Andrzej, ed. *Between the Human and the Divine: Philosophical and Theological Hermeneutics.* Toronto: Hermeneutic Press, 2002.

BSS   ———. *Between Suspicion and Sympathy: Paul Ricoeur's Unstable Equilibrium.* Toronto: Hermeneutic Press, 2003.

CD   Barth, Karl. *Church Dogmatics,* ed. Geoffrey W. Bromiley and Thomas F. Torrance. Edinburgh: T & T Clark. All citations are taken from this series of volumes and will hereafter be referred to as *CD,* with volume and number.

PPR   Hahn, Lewis E., ed. *The Philosophy of Paul Ricoeur.* Chicago: Open Court, 1995.

SN   Wallace, Mark I. *The Second Naiveté: Barth, Ricoeur, and the New Yale Theology.* 2nd ed. Macon, Ga.: Mercer University Press, 1995.

Paul Ricoeur between Theology and Philosophy

INTRODUCTION

Theology in North America is in a peculiar situation. Despite the large Christian population, academic theologians make no ripples in the public discourse. Not since Reinhold Niebuhr in the middle of the twentieth century has any theologian commanded serious attention from the general public. In the academy, theology is dwindling in importance and prestige as the institutions of secular modernity look askance upon explicitly Christian discourse. Departments of theology have been overtaken by or merged with departments of religious studies, and many who consider themselves theologians work in such departments. Although modernity can rightly be said to have crumbled under the postmodern critique, there is a great deal of inertia that would need to be overcome before the institutional bias against an overtly Christian discipline in the academy is removed. It is not clear that we are even heading in that direction, despite John Milbank's optimistic assessment of "a new theological mood at the outset of the twenty-first century."[1]

The general response by theologians has gone in two directions. The first, which I call the "ostrich" approach, is to simply abandon the academy altogether and start an alternative set of institutions that are so dominated by "theology" that its position within those institutions cannot be questioned. The second, which I call the "long defeat" approach, is to maintain a foothold in a hostile academic environment by gradually ceding ground until theology itself becomes so disfigured that it is no longer recognizable. The key to any solution to the problems created by both approaches is to understand what each approach is trying to protect, so that the positive features of the approach are not lost. The ostriches are desperately trying to protect the *integrity* of theology, while the fighters of the long defeat are trying to protect its *relevance*. Both approaches are noble, but are doomed to failure if the integrity and relevance of theology are considered as separate matters.

A potential solution to this problem is found in the hermeneutic philosophy of Paul Ricoeur. This book is an engagement of the dominant pattern in his work, detour and return, with a view to its implications for the practice of a theology that maintains both its integrity and its relevance. By his own account, it is the central motif of his philosophy: "Detour/return is the rhythm of my philosophical respiration."[2] The pattern is so pervasive that it shaped the trajectory of his entire career: a philosophy of the will that *detours* through analyses of sign, symbol, metaphor, and narrative, *returning* to a richer account of personal identity in his hermeneutics of the self.[3] Although there are numerous occurrences of this pattern operative throughout Ricoeur's work, they can be organized into two general types: the critical arc and the narrative arc.

The critical arc takes place at the level of understanding texts, with the notion of "text" being construed as broadly as possible. It traces the dialectic between the *understanding* of a text and the *explanation* of a text in terms of its structure. The arc begins with a simple or naïve understanding, detours through a moment of critical distanciation, returning to a deeper involvement in the text that is to be understood. This pattern, which has been referred to as a "hermeneutic dialectic,"[4] a "critical hermeneutics,"[5] or "diacritical hermeneutics,"[6] manifests itself in numerous variations, many of which will figure in what follows.[7] Among these are detours from a hermeneutics of tradition through a critique of ideologies to a critical hermeneutics, from conviction through critique to deeper conviction, and from ethical aims through moral norms to practical wisdom. The consequence of the critical arc, as Andrzej Wiercinski has eloquently put it, is an "unstable equilibrium" between suspicion and sympathy.[8] The dialectical tension of the critical arc is between contextual participation and universalizing doubt.

The narrative arc traces the dialectic between living action and a poetic narrative. It is predicated on the conviction that text and action are closely interrelated: action can be considered in terms of text,[9] and text can be explored in terms of action.[10] This interrelation is particularly prominent in the case of history and fiction, where each borrows from the other in their production. The arc begins with a moment of *prefiguration,* in which action is preunderstood in terms of the structures and symbolic networks in which the action takes place. From this preunderstanding, there is a detour through a moment of *configuration*, in which isolated incidents are transformed into a narrative unity through the process of emplotment. Having established a "concordant discordance" by way of narrative, the arc returns in a moment of *refiguration*, where the configuration is taken back into the field of action by its readers and applied as a paradigm for both the making of decisions and the interpretation of new experiences. The dialectical tension of the narrative arc is between concordance and discordance, held together through an act of the productive imagination. The critical arc and narrative arc each follows its own path, but they are often interpenetrating, particularly in Ricoeur's hermeneutics of the self.

What has this to do with theology? As Christianity is at its core both historical and textual, the pattern of detour and return is pervasive throughout theology. From the Gospels and Epistles to the creeds and councils, theological reflection has functioned as a detour, finding its source in what God has done in the world through Jesus Christ and seeking to return to the world by orienting the lives of Christians. The Gospel writers configured the life of Christ in an attempt to communicate its importance to their readers. The creeds function according to the critical arc, detouring through a distanciating moment of critical reflection on what is essential in the Gospel story in order to help those who live by that story understand it better and live it more fully.

The narrative arc of telling and retelling is also constitutive of the ethical life. We each have a life story that we tell to ourselves and others, retelling it as new facts come to light or new avenues of interpretation are opened. We take the events that occur in our lives and narrate them into our life story, making ethical decisions in part based on how we perceive the logic of that story. We also have recourse to the critical arc when we pause to reflect on whether the story of our life and the patterns of behavior it engenders are coherent. We pass through the detour of analysis in order to re-enter our daily living with a deeper and richer involvement.

THEOLOGICAL APPROPRIATION:
THE THREE RICOEURS

Ricoeur is, by his own declaration, a philosopher and not a theologian,[11] but is a uniquely helpful interlocutor in reflecting on the person from a theological perspective. While rejecting the label of "theologian," he does admit being a "member of that community that reads and interprets

Scripture."[12] Ricoeur's impact on the discipline has been significant, particularly in North America. His philosophical work has been engaged by many notable theologians, especially those at the University of Chicago Divinity School, where he held the John Nuveen Chair of Philosophical Theology from 1967 to 1992. He has been influential enough to warrant an attack on his "hermeneutical theory" by *postliberal* theologians Hans Frei and George Lindbeck as well as those who studied with them at Yale. As a result, Ricoeur quickly became identified with the *revisionist* or *correlational* theology of the so-called Chicago School in the Chicago-Yale debate, despite the fact that it is a debate on theological method and Ricoeur claims no competence as a theologian. In the spirit of his own construal of the relationship between the author and the text, we may allow Ricoeur his self-styling as a non-theologian while nonetheless maintaining that his texts are theologically significant.[13]

In engaging Ricoeur theologically, there are three "Ricoeurs" from which to choose. The most obvious choice would be Ricoeur as biblical hermeneuticist. However, he claims no "professional" status in biblical studies, while there is no question of his status in philosophy. Indeed, his reflections on Scripture seem to be, if not a hobby, then at least a *personal* project, and one that he has approached piecemeal. To engage Ricoeur in the area of his biblical hermeneutics, although profitable, is not to engage him on his strongest ground. As Lewis Mudge reminds us, "Ricoeur's chosen task is not the exposition of the Bible within the community of faith. It is, rather, the rational clarification of human existence in the world."[14] Emmanuel Levinas once called himself a *talmudiste du dimanche,* and Ricoeur might similarly be labeled a "weekend exegete."[15]

A second Ricoeur, a philosopher of religion, attempts to bring his hermeneutics to bear on religious reflection. This is something different from being a theologian. As David Tracy aptly states, Ricoeur's influence "has always been, from Ricoeur's side, intended as a strictly philosophical contribution to theological self-understanding. Unlike some of his admirers, Ricoeur himself never allows philosophy or theology to be confused or conflated."[16] The misapprehension of Ricoeur as a theologian rather than a philosopher in dialogue with theology is for the most part a North American phenomenon. This is the case for two reasons. First, Ricoeur's primary base of operations in the United States was the Divinity School at the University of Chicago, so his reception has been skewed in the direction of theology. Second, and more important, there are two collections of Ricoeur's essays that are compiled by others, existing only in English: Mudge's collection,

Essays on Biblical Interpretation, and Mark I. Wallace's collection, *Figuring the Sacred*.[17] Moreover, the latter volume contains essays on both biblical exegesis ("On the Exegesis of Genesis 1:1–2:4a") and philosophical reflections on religion ("Naming God, Toward a Narrative Theology"), which leads to a further confusion of Ricoeur's multiple identities. While both collections, especially the latter, have performed a valuable service in bringing Ricoeur's religious reflections to the English-speaking world, they have also contributed to the misconception that Ricoeur is more of a theologian than he actually is. Ricoeur himself, prior to 1998, had never published anything longer than an essay on any religious topic, and even then it was in collaboration with a biblical scholar.[18]

Ricoeur's *professional* project, to which he has devoted the majority of his immense energy throughout his philosophical career, has concentrated on a philosophical anthropology and the hermeneutic concerns that arise from it. This is what is addressed by his "scientific works" or "serious books," as he calls them, contrasting them with his essay collections or lectures.[19] Ricoeur's early philosophy worked toward a phenomenology of the will, but it was left incomplete and (by his own admission) not successful. His middle work addressed the problems that made his early work unsuccessful, namely the hermeneutic *detours* (sign, symbol, metaphor, and narrative) that one must take in order to gain perspective on one's own identity. His mature work *returns* to the problem of personal identity with his newly developed hermeneutic tools in hand.

While Ricoeur's work has received much attention from theologians, it is the first two "Ricoeurs" that have tended to draw most of the sustained attention.[20] In some ways, this is to be expected. The most obvious place to begin a theological engagement with Ricoeur is where he makes clear theological overtures. This is also unfortunate, however, because the first two Ricoeurs are merely applications of the third Ricoeur, and not taking this into account can lead to misconstruals of Ricoeur's intentions. But as Mudge points out, "the expectations we bring to Ricoeur's work must not betray us into holding him responsible for matters outside his professional vocation."[21] Ricoeur is first and foremost a hermeneutic philosopher, and his work on biblical exegesis and philosophy of religion are but two examples of his hermeneutic engagements of a variety of disciplines. Ricoeur is no more a professional exegete or theologian than he is a structuralist or psychoanalyst.

Paul Ricoeur between Theology and Philosophy: Detour and Return is an attempt to articulate the potential of Ricoeur's pattern of detour and return by both describing and using the pattern itself. Rather than engaging him where he comes closest to theology, I encounter him where he takes the most distance from theology, at precisely the places where he acknowledges his religious convictions but, for methodological reasons, refuses to engage them explicitly. The former approach is most appropriate when there are specific theological questions under consideration that Ricoeur has addressed in his work. The latter is most appropriate when engaging not *what* he thinks about something, but *how* he thinks about everything. I engage him as a *detour*.

Since Ricoeur's work on narrative and the self is regarded by the philosophical community as his most influential work,[22] and both the narrative and critical arcs cross through narrative identity, it is a promising point of contact. Even by Ricoeur's own account, his theory of narrative identity stands as one of the most significant contributions that he has made to philosophy. He has referred to his opening of the question of narrative identity as the "principal achievement" of *Time and Narrative,* and as "the poetic resolution of the hermeneutic circle."[23] Narrative identity is the terminus of a critical arc that begins with a posited *cogito* and detours through semantics and pragmatics. It is also a mediating moment within Ricoeur's hermeneutics of the self, which is organized around a hermeneutic triad: describe, narrate, and prescribe. The accomplishment of narrative identity, being the middle moment of the narrative arc, can be understood only within the context of a broader hermeneutics of the self, which also has the advantage of containing all of the basic moves of his philosophy.

STRUCTURE AND ARGUMENT

Both the critical and narrative arcs are at play in the structure of this work, also functioning as continuing leitmotifs. The question driving the process is whether Ricoeur's entire philosophical project can function as a hermeneutic detour for theology, and if so, what kind of detour it will be. It is not merely a theological appropriation of Ricoeur's philosophy, because the question of what it means to appropriate philosophy into theology is precisely what is at issue. It is not that a method of appropriation already exists, and it remains to put Ricoeur's hermeneutics of the self through that process. Generating a structure of engagement in advance and applying it to hermeneutics would go against the fundamental grain of hermeneutics, resulting in a method of appropriation hostile to the thing appropriated.

The philosophical detour will concentrate on *Time and Narrative* and especially *Oneself as Another.* As Kathleen Blamey and David Pellauer have emerged as the "canonical" translators of Ricoeur, their translations will be used as the primary texts. The merits of quoting the English translations reside primarily in the nature of the task that has been set. Because one of the difficulties surrounding the reception of Ricoeur involves collections that exist only in the English language, it seems appropriate that English-language texts be used. And since the most careful attention will be paid to *patterns* as they emerge, and because Ricoeur exhibits a Germanic sense of organization, the nuances of individual French words have minimal impact. This is, at any rate, my own experience as a translator of Ricoeur.[24] Where they are significant, such as in the translation of the title *Soi-même comme une autre,* the French will be addressed. In the case of untranslated texts, my own translation will appear in the main text.

The first chapter, "Fundamental Loyalties," opens a discussion on theological appropriation in general, framing the issue in terms of fundamental loyalties. When theology engages other disciplines, especially philosophy, it runs a risk of itself *being* appropriated. A Christian theologian has a loyalty both to the body of Christ and to the academy, and it is important that these loyalties be ordered. The theological model of David Tracy, his "correlational" or "revisionist" theology, is taken as an exemplary case. This is done for three reasons. First, it is a very influential model that demonstrates the dangers of conflicting loyalties. Second, Tracy is the royal gate through which Ricoeur's philosophical hermeneutics has entered North American theology and thus must be taken into account.

The third reason for engaging Tracy is taken up in the second chapter, "Theology, Hermeneutics, and Ricoeur's Double Life." Tracy's argument that theology would be well served by engaging Ricoeur's hermeneutics is not negated by the flaws in his own attempt to undertake such an engagement. The antipathy that runs between the intellectual descendants of the postliberals and the revisionists has falsely dichotomized the options available for the reception of Ricoeur into theology.[25] Tracy's embrace of Ricoeur's hermeneutics is on his own revisionist terms, and Hans Frei's and George Lindbeck's rejection is in fact an unwitting rejection of Tracy's *appropriation,* not of Ricoeur's hermeneutics. Ricoeur's work, which is, as Tracy says, "beautiful in the Reformed sense,"[26] is in fact much more suited to Barth-inspired postliberalism than it is to Tracy's revisionist theology. This sets up a sort of exit ramp from the theological main road to the philosophical detour. While the general thrust of philosophical hermeneutics is covered in this chapter, understanding what it is about Ricoeur's philosophy that makes it amenable to a more Barthian framework requires a more detailed investigation.

The second part of the project leaves the main road altogether and fully engages the philosophical detour. As a whole, the detour is an attempt to articulate the structure of detour and return in both its critical and narrative forms, while progressing toward the theory of narrative identity and its ethical implications. It begins with the third chapter, "Prefiguration: The Critical Arc and Descriptive Identity," opening the question of identity and marking its role in the genesis of Ricoeur's detour and return method. It also establishes the "critical" variation of the detour and return pattern with references to Ricoeur's chief influences, Gabriel Marcel and Edmund Husserl. Marcel's own method of primary and secondary reflection is a prefiguration of Ricoeur's own pattern. Marcel's method of dynamic approximation, however, was insufficiently rigorous for the more systematically oriented Ricoeur, and he employed Husserl's phenomenology as a corrective detour. The central method of phenomenology, the "eidetic reduction," brackets out all metaphysical or empirical "common sense," putting the phenomenologist in the role of allowing the phenomenon to emerge. However, Ricoeur's philosophy is fundamentally a hermeneutics, not a phenomenology, recognizing and indeed emphasizing the impossibility of such a reduction. But the fact that the phenomenologist can never achieve the full critical distance that the method describes in no way negates the value of the attempt. The "detour," the moment of critical reflection, in Ricoeur's detour and return pattern is a re-insertion of phenomenological methods into the hermeneutic process. This can be seen in his critical hermeneutic engagement of ideology critique, structuralism, and analytic philosophy.

Having established the critical arc, the fourth chapter, "Configuration: The Narrative Arc and Narrative Identity," articulates the narrative arc and situates the question of identity within it. The key to the narrative arc is first found in metaphor, namely, that it is an act of the productive imagination rather than the critical intellect. Ricoeur's theory of emplotment is encapsulated in *threefold mimesis* as outlined in *Time and Narrative,* setting up the prefiguration-configuration-refiguration triad that is the core expression of the narrative arc. This in turn raises the question of narrative identity, which is pursued in *Oneself as Another.* Narrative identity resolves the paradoxes of identity that arise when one fails to distinguish between two types of identity. The first type is *idem* identity, or "sameness." This type of identity is characterized by empirical perseverance; it is a "substantialist or formalist identity."[27] The second is *ipse* identity, or "selfhood." It is characterized by self-constancy, reflexively implying others in its very constitution. The two types of identity are held together by narrative and overlap on the key aspect of *character.* Narrative identity is the terminus of the detour that began in the third chapter with eidetic identity and detoured through narrative, but it is also the middle moment in the new triad of description, narration, and prescription.

The fifth chapter, "Refiguration: Ricoeur's 'Little Ethics,'" addresses the *prescription* moment of the triad. It is only within the context of narrative identity that an ethics of selfhood can be pursued, but ethics is also an integral dimension of narrative identity. As Ricoeur explains, "the broadening of the practical field and the anticipation of ethical considerations are implied in the very structure of the act of narrating,"[28] and he takes this up in a three-study subset of *Oneself as Another* he calls his "little ethics."[29] At this point both patterns of detour and return, the critical and narrative arcs, are in play. The ethics is the return moment in the narrative arc that has passed from description through narration. Within the ethics itself, the ethical aim detours through the critical moment of the moral norm and returns to "critical *phronesis*," a practical wisdom that is able to cope with novel ethico-moral situations.

The third and final part begins with the sixth chapter, "Chalcedonian Hermeneutics," which returns from the philosophical detour to the theological main road. It suggests a potentially productive path for the appropriation of Ricoeur into theology based on the pattern of detour and return. Appropriation is an aggressive act, and I show that this aggression is muted by the natural affinity that exists between the projects of Ricoeur and Karl Barth. This takes its cue from Mark Wallace's comparison of Ricoeur's and Barth's biblical hermeneutics in *The Second Naïveté: Barth, Ricoeur, and the New Yale Theology*, and expands to their overall pattern of thought. Ricoeur accepts both that his philosophy is moved by sources that he does not control and that it can say no final word without transgressing the boundaries of philosophy. Since one of those uncontrollable sources is an explicitly biblical Reformed Christian faith, a theology that sees itself as grounded in such a faith can with good conscience undertake the act of appropriation. Using Barth's essay on the relationship between philosophical and theological ethics,[30] I show that the apparently stern limits that Barth places on philosophical ethics are respected and even endorsed by Ricoeur.

The seventh and final chapter, "Theological Anthropology: Removing Brackets," puts that affinity to work in the area of anthropology. It returns to the issue of the fundamental loyalties of the theologian raised in the first chapter by performatively attempting to engage a philosophical position without theology being colonized. Karl Barth's distinction between the "real" and the merely "phenomenal" human is read through the lens of Ricoeur's detour and return. Ricoeur provides, unsurprisingly, a more satisfactory account of the "phenomenal" than Barth, who exhibits a Marcellian desire to return quickly to the concrete reality of the Word. Ricoeur's distinction between sameness (*idem*) and selfhood (*ipse*) enriches Barth's account of the distinction between the real and the phenomenal, and his account of narrative identity opens up new applications for Barth's theological anthropology.

THE MAIN ROAD

It would be a mistake to view hermeneutics merely as a method. As Wiercinski has said, "hermeneutics is much more than the methodology of interpretation practiced in the human sciences."[31] To engage texts hermeneutically is to understand that we must first "fore-understand," anticipating the meaning of what is to be understood. We have expectations when we approach a given text or set of texts, but these "fore-projects" are revised in light of what is there in the text. The interpreter needs not only to engage the matter of the text, but also explicitly to engage the prejudices that made the text interesting in the first place. As Hans-Georg Gadamer puts it: "The recognition that all understanding inevitably involves some prejudice gives the hermeneutical problem its real thrust."[32] When reading hermeneutically, the goal is not to be without prejudices, which is impossible, but to be *transparent* about them. A phenomenological engagement attempts to bracket out the reasons for engaging while describing the object engaged. A *hermeneutic* phenomenology recognizes that our presuppositions cannot be bracketed out completely and thus should be made transparent. What are being bracketed out in this case are the theological concerns that brought us to the question of Ricoeur's hermeneutics. When the brackets are removed, the critical and narrative arcs that have been disclosed will serve as guides for the overall project of appropriating Ricoeur into theology.

One of the "prejudices" of my approach is toward a Barthian theological anthropology and an expectation that Ricoeur's philosophical anthropology will be compatible. At first glance, Barth may seem an odd choice for a pairing with Ricoeur. Barth's massive influence on postliberalism and Ricoeur's association with the revisionists would seem to pit the two against one another. This proves not to be the case. Ricoeur regards himself as indebted to Barth, particularly regarding the self, noting: "It was in fact Karl Barth who first taught me that the subject is not a centralizing master but rather a disciple or auditor of a language larger than itself."[33] Furthermore, Ricoeur and Barth seem to share the same desire to keep philosophy and theology distinct. This should be interpreted not as hostility, but as respect. While Barth goes to great lengths to outline a *theological* anthropology that is not dependent on a philosophical anthropology, he is not hostile to philosophical anthropology as such. As George Hunsinger summarizes:

>Nontheological anthropologies are not thereby consigned to "a night in which all cats are gray," for that is a separate question entirely. They may be judged, on the basis of theological anthropology, as being more or less compatible with the latter without ever being thought to become identical with it. . . . They might even spark insights which theology could appreciate in the mode of assimilation.[34]

I am proposing that Ricoeur offers a philosophical anthropology that is more rather than less compatible with Barth's theological anthropology, one that can spark many insights. This is partly because Ricoeur is as concerned about the infringement of philosophy on theology as Barth is. He goes so far as to say that he would rather be accused of personal inconsistency than of "confusionism," which he defines as "mixing crypto-theology on the philosophical plane and crypto-philosophy on the plane of exegesis and theology!"[35] Both Ricoeur and Barth see a place for the other's discipline, and both are concerned that each discipline be granted its autonomous mode of discourse. They are a good fit, and the reason for this is as much the *shape* of their thought as the content.

Ricoeur's detour and return pattern bears a fascinating resemblance to what Hunsinger refers to as Barth's "Chalcedonian pattern." This pattern has three characteristics—unity, differentiation, asymmetry—which are taken from the Christological doctrines of the Chalcedonian creed, and more specifically from Barth's account of the relationship between soul and body as one of "ineffaceable difference, inseparable unity, and indestructible order."[36] The two patterns are not identical, but I shall argue that both achieve similar goals and that their similarity is strong enough to suggest compatibility between the theology of Barth and the philosophy of Ricoeur. Both patterns have two poles, which are inseparable but nonetheless distinct. More notable is that both patterns are *asymmetrical*. For both, one side of the conceptual relationship has precedence, but *not* in a hierarchical fashion (which would result in confusion and change). While the respective patterns may not necessarily aim to *achieve* the same goals, they do nonetheless *protect* against the same errors: separation, confusion, and disorder. Barth accepts philosophical insights in the "spirit of assimilation." Ricoeur is offering such insights, and expects them to be assimilated. All that he asks is that philosophical hermeneutics be given the room to do its work. Furthermore, Ricoeur acknowledges that his biblical faith has an impact on his philosophical project, and accepts that there are theological moments that exist *before* his reflection on the self. He also acknowledges that such moments may come after. It is this, as he says in *Oneself as Another,* that saves philosophical hermeneutics from the "hubris" of the *cogito* philosophies to which it is heir.[37]

In engaging Ricoeur's hermeneutics hermeneutically, *Paul Ricoeur between Theology and Philosophy* seeks to establish a *mimetic* relationship to his thought. In taking his "diacritical hermeneutics" as the object of my reflection, I will follow his own guidelines on how to engage an object hermeneutically. I use his method of detour and return, a naïve understanding that detours through an objectifying, critical process of explanation before returning to an enriched, deeper understanding. This preliminary appraisal of what I take Ricoeur's significance to be, this "naïve" reading, will then go through a detailed process of *explanation,* following Ricoeur's dictum that "to explain more is to understand better what has already been preunderstood."[38] Finally, there will be an appropriation of Ricoeur into my own project, but, again following Ricoeur, I will be willing to *dis*-appropriate my own project in the act of appropriation, in much the way that the self must cease to possess itself in the act of appropriating a text. The self, or in this case the project, becomes another aspect of the interpretation.

The self-imposed limits of Ricoeur's philosophy can be taken as an overture to theology. It does not run toward theology with an enthusiastic embrace, nor does it expect or even desire that in return. Crypto-philosophy and crypto-theology are to be avoided at all costs. Maintaining a discreet distance, Ricoeur's philosophy humbly offers an intellectual friendship to a theology that is committed to the task of thinking through the consequences and possibilities of an authentic Christian faith. It is to such an overture that this work responds.

Part One   The Main Road

The premise of the first part of this book is that the debate on theological method, and particularly theology's engagement with philosophy, that was carried out by the so-called revisionists and postliberals has all the characteristics of a proxy war. Without any disrespect to the key figures in this debate, they have become the most prominent exponents of positions more significant than their own in the North American theological conversation. The task is to break through to the major powers and extricate them from the proxy war, for I will argue that if they can face each other across the table directly, a productive peace can be forged. The major powers here are the philosopher Paul Ricoeur and the theologian Karl Barth. Ricoeur's philosophical contribution has been under-serviced by Tracy's appropriation, and the postliberal theology's use of Wittgenstein for their "cultural-linguistic" model also does not do justice to Barth, though in both cases a great deal is accomplished.

The first chapter deals with David Tracy's correlational model as outlined most precisely in *The Analogical Imagination*. This model is tried and found wanting primarily on the grounds that, in its driving concern to be "public," it betrays a fundamental loyalty by construing fundamental theology as loyal first to the academy rather than to the church. The second chapter endorses Tracy's argument for the place of philosophical hermeneutics in theological reflection, defending it against the attack of Hans Frei, with the primary task of extricating Ricoeur from the whole debate. This prepares the way for extended engagement of Ricoeur's philosophy in the second part, and in the third part for an appropriation of that philosophy into a theology for which it is better suited.

1

Fundamental Loyalties

Over the course of the twentieth century, there has been a significant shift in academic theology toward an attitude that is resolutely *public*. This phenomenon gained so much moral momentum that the common antonym in theology for public is no longer *private* but *sectarian*. Those unwilling to give publicly accessible arguments are considered not so much wrong as ill-mannered. If a theologian makes an argument in academic discourse that relies explicitly on a confessional truth such as the deity of Christ or the operation of the Spirit as the third person of the Trinity, such that the argument makes no sense without it, it makes even those academics who are serious and of good will a little uneasy. Even when there is agreement, there is the sense that the argument should not be so crudely theological, and a search is made to translate the argument into less problematic, that is, more publicly accessible language. This shift of criteria raises the odd question of "good manners" in theology. There is a widely accepted etiquette to public discussion, one that demands a certain personal detachment on the part of its participants. Anyone who openly demonstrates too much personal involvement in their inquiry, implying that those who are not similarly involved are actually unable to understand the view of those who are, is guilty of a serious breach of this etiquette. Such ill-mannered behavior is too earnest and can bring public discussion to a grinding halt. It is, in a word, rude.

This chapter explores what is at stake when theologians take it upon themselves to behave as well-mannered members of the academy. If theology is to be presented as, to use David Tracy's phrase, a "fully critical modern discipline," then theology's actual role in the academy is problematic. Is theology a full-fledged member of the social sciences, with all the academic acceptance that goes with it? If so, what is it that theology has to offer? If not, how does theology relate to the academy in general, and to philosophy and the social sciences in particular?

In considering these questions, I will restrict myself to an engagement of one of the most significant attempts to provide a public model for theology in the academy: Tracy's fundamental theology. In doing this, I hope to expose one of the inherent tensions that exists in the North American scene between the word "public" and the word "theology." I will first outline what is involved in Tracy's theological model, especially the fundamental specialty, which outlines what is required for theology to be public. I will then turn to two remarkably similar criticisms that come from opposite directions. Jürgen Habermas, the German philosopher whose discourse ethics is appropriated by Tracy, criticizes Tracy from the side of the academic public that fundamental theology addresses. Stanley Hauerwas, the Duke Divinity School ethicist who often is labeled "sectarian" because of his bad manners, criticizes Tracy's approach from the "theological" perspective that is to be modeled.[1] The fact that both Habermas and Hauerwas reach the same negative conclusion from their very different perspectives suggests a crucial flaw in Tracy's model. This flaw will then be explored in terms of fundamental loyalties and good manners. The chapter will conclude by offering suggestions as to how Tracy's "functional specialties" of theology could be reconfigured to better maintain the integrity of theology in its conversations with other academic disciplines.

TRACY'S THEOLOGICAL MODEL

Tracy's correlational model divides theology into three "functional disciplines" held together by two hermeneutical constants. Any theologian will always be involved in interpreting: (1) a religious tradition and (2) the "religious dimension" of a contemporary situation. This is true regardless of whether one's functional specialty is *fundamental, systematic,* or *practical.* Each specialty, however, is quite distinct within the constraints of those two constants. Each has its own reference group, mode of argument, ethical stance, faith-understanding, and formulation of meaning/truth. (See table 1.1.)

Table 1.1. Tracy's Functional Specialties

	Fundamental	*Systematic*	*Practical*
PRIMARY REFERENCE GROUP	Academy	Church	Society
MODE OF ARGUMENT	Reasonable	Re-presentation	Praxis (Informed-Informing)
ETHICAL STANCE	Honest, Critical Inquiry	Loyalty, Creative-Critical Fidelity	Responsible Commitment To Praxis
SELF-UNDERSTANDING OF PERSONAL FAITH	Abstract from All Faith Commitments	Personal Involvement in and Commitment to:	
		Particular Religious Tradition	Praxis Movement with Religious Significance
FORMULATION OF MEANING AND TRUTH	Philosophical	Hermeneutic	Transforming
HERMENEUTIC CONSTANTS	Interpretation of a Religious Tradition		
	Interpretation of the Religious Dimension of the Contemporary Situation		

Fundamental Theology

Here we are concerned primarily with the *fundamental* specialty, whose primary reference group, its public, is the academy. The mode of discourse for fundamental theologians involves "arguments that all reasonable persons, whether 'religiously involved' or not, can recognize as reasonable." Their ethical stance is one of "honest, critical inquiry." Regarding their faith-understanding, fundamental theologians will, regardless of confessional stance:

> in principle abstract themselves from all religious "faith commitments" for the legitimate purposes of critical analysis of all religious and theological claims. They will insist upon the need to articulate the arguments for theological discourse as openly public arguments in the obvious sense of argued, reasoned positions open to all intelligent, reasonable and responsible persons.[2]

The picture Tracy paints is of the fundamental theologian as mediator. As a Christian, any theologian has a commitment to the texts and practices of

Christianity. As a modern academic, the fundamental theologian also has a commitment to rational scientific inquiry. The task of the theologian is to correlate the two; to bring the Christian tradition to bear on an analysis of the "religious dimension" of human experience, and vice versa.[3] However, Tracy suggests that the particular publicness of fundamental theology requires that it submit itself to scientific scrutiny, and when the fundamental theologian is forced to choose between the two, it is tradition that comes out on the short end:

> In principle, the fundamental loyalty of the theologian *qua* theologian is to that morality of scientific knowledge which he shares with his colleagues, the philosophers, historians, and social scientists. No more than they, can he allow his own—or his tradition's—beliefs to serve as warrants for his arguments.[4]

Theology that stubbornly refuses to engage in correlating its positions to competing positions in the context of secular modernity runs the risk of dying as a serious academic discipline, being unable to meet the crisis of cognitive claims suffered by religion in light of the demystifying demands of the Enlightenment. Essential to the project is an optimism regarding the possibility of such a correlation, the belief that Christianity *can* ultimately be fused with secular reason, and has little to fear from such a process. The grounds for this optimism is that the secularist has a faith in "the ultimate significance and final worth of our lives," which is what Tracy means by "the morality of scientific knowledge." The secularist, however, lacks the "existentially appropriate symbolic representation" by which to express his faith, and the Christian tradition can provide this.[5]

When expressing truth claims, therefore, fundamental theologians must adapt to the general conversation structure of the academic community in which they operate. This involves tailoring their message to the restrictions regarding topic, warrants, and backing that are prevalent in the community. To ascertain what impact this might have on theological truth claims, we must consider these parameters in the concrete.

Public Discourse

Tracy's description of what constitutes public discourse in the academy is an appropriation of the discourse ethics of Jürgen Habermas, the person after whom Tracy models his contribution to theology.[6] In *Moral Consciousness and Communicative Action*, Habermas presents his model for "discourse ethics," which sets out the necessary parameters for discourse to proceed in an ethical manner. In its simplest form, everyone who is part of the discussion must have a chance to speak and be listened to, and everyone who is to be affected by the outcome of the discussion must be a part of the discussion. These are universal rules for any discourse, guarding against the exclusion or silencing of those who might be negatively affected by decisions reached. Habermas presents these as the principles of universalization (U) and discourse (D):

> (U)   *All* affected can accept the consequences and the side-effects of its [U's] *general* observance can be anticipated to have for the satisfaction of *everyone's* interests (and these consequences are preferred to those of known alternative possibilities for regulation).
>
> (D)   Only those norms can claim to be valid that meet (or could meet) with the approval of all affected in their capacity *as participants in a practical discourse*.[7]

The rules of discourse are designed so that (1) no claim—which might be unpopular but have good reasons—is prematurely dismissed from the discussion, and (2) no claim, or set of claims, is allowed to "colonize" another, setting up parameters for discussion without going through the process of argumentative justification.

This model divides possible modes of discussion into two major categories: the public realm and the lifeworld. The public realm is the arena of public discussion where interlocutors can discuss issues in an egalitarian fashion according to Habermas's rules of universal discourse. There are no topics that are excluded a priori from such a discussion, though in practice many topics will not survive the criteria for discourse.[8] In this arena, the criterion for legitimate interaction is argumentation, where one must offer "good reasons" for the statements one makes. These reasons must appeal to publicly verifiable norms or scientific facts, not to traditional authorities recognized only by the speaker.

The lifeworld is where we operate for the vast majority of our time. Religion, art, culture, and family are all elements of the lifeworld. The formation of our opinions, the development of our tastes, the inculcation of our moral values—all this happens in the lifeworld. Communication in the lifeworld is characterized by conversation, and this is the more encompassing of the two styles.[9] The lifeworld gives rise to all the topics that will be discussed in the world of public discourse.

No lifeworld has authority in public discourse, however, which necessarily entails involving participants from different lifeworlds. I cannot appeal to my aesthetic preferences, you cannot appeal to your religious texts, and she cannot appeal to her family values. That would be how discussion happens in the lifeworld of friends, churches, and families. In argumentative discourse, on the other hand, "validity claims which previously remained implicit because they arose performatively are expressly thematized."[10] When one moves from the lifeworld to the world of public discourse, the sources of one's claims must be identified and excised, leaving the opinion itself available for consideration. If good reasons cannot be offered for the claim, then it too will drop out of public discourse. This does not negate the claim, but merely excludes it from the public realm. For example, Christian commands such as "thou shalt not steal" survive the process of public discussion, because good publicly accessible reasons can be offered for such a command. If challenged, however, fundamental theologians can refer neither to Scripture nor to tradition to justify their beliefs.[11]

Tracy is fundamentally in accord with Habermas on the distinction between "lifeworld" and "public realm," and presents his own definition of the public realm: "that shared rational space where all participants, whatever their other particular differences, can meet to discuss any claim that is rationally redeemable."[12] The rational space that might be shared by participants is threatened, and Tracy applauds Habermas's articulation of a communicative rationality that is derived from speech acts. This, Tracy believes, is a valuable tool in saving the public realm from the death that has already been pronounced by Rorty, Lyotard, and Hauerwas.[13] Tracy is less enthusiastic about the manner in which Habermas's model results in a *de facto* exclusion of religious claims from public discourse. Tracy allows that the "peculiar logic of religious claims" creates awkward issues for regulating argumentation, but these can be addressed: "[U]nless one assumes, rather than argues, that no religious or theological claims are argumentatively redeemable, a modern critical social theory should also account for and argue over just these claims."[14] Tracy expresses dismay over Habermas's glib dismissal of theology as acceptable public discourse. Not only does he argue that theology should be given a chance to prove itself in the public arena, but he is also quite confident that theology is equal to the challenge: "Indeed, both the discipline of philosophy of religion . . . and the discipline of modern theology . . . are, at their best, fully modern critical disciplines. Both philosophy of religion and modern theology should be acknowledged as modern critical disciplines."[15] This explicitly apologetic appeal affirms Habermas's notion that only good, publicly accessible reasons should be allowed into the public discussion, but argues that theology is up to the task of supplying them. It is crucial to note that Habermas's criteria are not being questioned by Tracy; the only objection is to Habermas's assessment of theology as failing to meet them. It is clear that Tracy believes that theologians can play Habermas's game and win, for they have the most "existentially appropriate symbolic representation" for what others in the public realm are trying to say. The possible cost of such a victory, however, can be seen when both "modern theology" and "philosophy of religion" are defended in the same breath.

ENGAGING PUBLIC THEOLOGY

Habermas Responds

There are two incisive criticisms leveled at Tracy's model, and the first comes from Habermas himself. In his only direct response to the theological appropriation of his critical theory, Habermas addresses Tracy's model specifically, and raises several concerns as to its appropriateness for theology.

Habermas sketches a brief history of how religion and reason have interacted since the early modern period. The philosophical appropriation of religious content requires a "neutral" philosopher who does not bring her own self-understanding into the matter. Philosophy must content itself with a "methodical atheism in the manner of the philosophical reference to the contents of religious experience. Philosophy cannot appropriate what is talked about in religious experience as religious experiences."[16] Habermas recognizes that this "methodical atheism" presents a crucial obstacle for philosophy. There is a point at which philosophy must simply admit that it can go no further, and this is reached when there is no publicly accessible language by which a claim from a specific tradition can be redescribed.

Turning to the theologians directly, he confronts Tracy on the issue of validity claims and investigates what theologians are committing to when they present theology as a "fully modern critical discipline." The theologians seem willing to surrender theology's right to "privilege" so that theology, like every other discipline, will have to meet the demands for academic justification. Answering such demands successfully guarantees theology's position as a serious academic discipline, since it will be able to stand on the same critical ground. Habermas, however, sees it from a different angle: "If this is the *common ground* of theology, science, and philosophy, what then still constitutes the distinctiveness of theological discourse? What separates the internal perspective of theology from the external perspective of those who enter a dialogue with theology?"[17] This is most incisive when it is recalled that Tracy consistently defends the philosophy of religion and modern theology in one breath. What does the theologian have to offer in a conversation with the philosopher of religion? What, if anything, separates their perspectives? If nothing, then what point is there in having a theologian in the conversation at all? Habermas sees this as a distinct possibility, and closes with a sobering prediction:

> The more theology opens itself in general to the discourses of the human sciences, the greater is the danger that its own status will be lost in the network of alternating takeover attempts. . . . Theology also loses its identity if it only cites religious experiences, and under the descriptions of religious discourse no longer acknowledges them as its own basis.[18]

Habermas expresses concern on behalf of the secular discourse, which will lose a valued lifeworld perspective if theologians are willing to submit themselves without reservation to his criteria of argumentation. While the public theologians are busy attempting to demonstrate the *likeness* between theology and other disciplines (argumentative justification), Habermas points out that they have abandoned their claim to *distinctiveness*. He goes on to investigate the distinctiveness of theology on their behalf: if theology is not to be subsumed by other disciplines, what characterizes it? It is not distinctive simply by its reference to religious experience, for the retrieval of "religious experience" as a phenomenon into the arena of argumentative discourse falls under the headings of anthropology, religious studies, sociology, and psychology. The distinctiveness of theology is in the manner in which it embraces religious experience. Theology, unlike philosophy and the social sciences, accepts religious experience as a basis or warrant for its discourse. Theology is not under the same constraints as public discourse. It seems to Habermas, however, that the public theologians are voluntarily constraining themselves in this manner. If they insist on doing so, they sacrifice their identity as theologians. In their eagerness to achieve full status as an "ology," they will have sacrificed the "theos," at least insofar as their method is concerned.

Postliberal Theology

While Habermas criticizes public theology from a secular position, there are also attacks from the perspective of the theologian. Postliberal theologians such as Hans Frei, George Lindbeck, and Stanley Hauerwas are deeply concerned with the integrity of theological identity, and are strongly opposed to the imposition of any external criteria on theological discourse.[19] For Lindbeck, who coined the term "postliberal" in his seminal book, *The*

Nature of Doctrine,[20] the main thrust of the postliberal argument is to present a "cultural-linguistic" model to oppose the liberal "experiential-expressivist" model that he sees as dominating theology today: "Liberals start with experience, with an account of the present, and then adjust their vision of the kingdom of God accordingly, while postliberals are in principle committed to doing the reverse."[21] This confrontational (and falsely dichotomous) statement is indicative of what many find frustrating about the postliberal position, but the claim is not made lightly. The liberal approach, from Schleiermacher to Niebuhr, has a commitment to being relevant, to being involved in the broader social issues of the day in such a way that theology has an impact. Simply muttering among ourselves (or, worse, shouting from our soapboxes) that contemporary social practices violate the standards presented to us by the Christian tradition will serve only to relegate Christianity to an increasingly powerless position on the margins of society. Rather, we must "translate" our Christian "doctrines" into a language that the secular listener can understand, so that we can meet them halfway. This serves a double purpose (as all "correlational" dialogues do), since we will better understand ourselves as well. The demanding nature of scientific inquiry enables us to examine our own tradition, helping us to shed our more naïve pre-suppositions and further develop Christian thought in a new context. We, as Christians, will ultimately rise and fall on the basis of how well we "articulate or represent and communicate that inner experience of the divine . . . which is held to be common to them all."[22]

This approach, says Lindbeck, gets it precisely backward. His *cultural-linguistic* approach describes religious faith as a comprehensive totality that forms us; it makes little sense to speak of "experience" that *precedes* it. Religion is "a kind of cultural and/or linguistic framework or medium that shapes the entirety of life and thought."[23] The crucial issue to be decided is where one is to begin, and Lindbeck points out that there is no definitively "better" place to begin than the Gospel. For every question that is directed toward Christianity, there is an analogous question that can be asked in return. Whenever one queries the Gospel in terms of rationality, modernity, personal experience, Hinduism, science, and so on, the question is: what are your "terms" precisely, and what is their claim to primacy? What do they claim that supersedes the claims of the Gospel, and what are your criteria for making this judgment? Questioning the Gospel in rational terms, as Tracy does, explicitly presents criteria (in this case "rationally redeemable") by which the Gospel should be judged, which forces a very particular reading of the text.

Stanley Hauerwas is suspicious of any tendency to look anywhere but the Christian community for validation of theological principles. In his 1985 essay "On Keeping Theological Ethics Theological," Hauerwas presents his case for a more unapologetically communitarian theological identity. He wants to know where these criteria come from, and why they should have primacy. To be sure, the manner in which Christians shape the world is not static, but the method of change is to take foreign insights and incorporate them into the Christian tradition. On the other hand, to take (for example) modern criticisms regarding the "plausibility" of the resurrection or the divinity of Jesus seriously *on their own terms,* and attempt to modify Christianity in light of these criticisms, is theologically unsound. It presents a change that is discontinuous with the tradition that it proposes to change, with a corresponding fracture of *identity.*[24] Hauerwas identifies the problem that the liberals are trying (wrongly, he thinks) to address: "Christianity is at an awkwardly intermediate stage in Western culture where having once been culturally established it is still not clearly disestablished.... The biblical heritage is just present enough in our culture to make redescription a useful means to keep many people vaguely related to the church."[25] When Western non-Christians find the underlying reasons for theological claims (which they might otherwise find acceptable) offensive or implausible, the instinct is to correlate our underlying reasons with elements from the modern Western tradition (generally Enlightenment reason), thus preventing further disestablishment.[26] Since the prevailing tradition is one of "methodical atheism," the fundamental theologians' commitment to that tradition requires them to answer questions that are not proper to Christian self-understanding, and modify their positions if they cannot answer them to the satisfaction of their academic public.

Hauerwas also answers two charges against his model of interaction: (1) it fails to respect the plurality of our society; and (2) it is a "failure of nerve," an irresponsible sectarian retreat. If we are going to engage in dialogue with our culture, no matter how diverse, Hauerwas argues that it is best to begin by articulating what is meant by "we." It is not until this question is at least provisionally resolved that "we" can enter dialogue. Are "we" like the "they" with whom we propose to dialogue? Hauerwas is not so sure. Recalling the history of apologetic theology, he notes: "The apologist of the past stood in the church and its tradition and sought relationship with those outside. Apologetic theology was a secondary endeavour because the apologist never assumed that one could let the questions of unbelief order the theological agenda."[27] The language of "inside" and "outside" casts the issue in an interesting light. Can those outside a faith tradition fully comprehend what is going on inside? Does their opinion of what constitutes a valid theological project merit consideration?

This does not mean that those of different philosophical and religious traditions will never speak to one another. There may well be conversations over the backyard fence, as it were, and these may be richly rewarding. However, these conversations require no "model," but will progress naturally according to the subject matter. If they begin at the grocery store, the discussion may well revolve around diet, while if in line at the bank, the subject might be usury. These can develop into fruitful theological discussions, but the "common ground" for the dialogue, insofar as there is one, is quite concrete. The dialogue takes place on a different level than a theological dialogue, precisely because faith is not shared. Furthermore, as Hauerwas notes, the Christian view on issues such as diet and usury will have no power if the fact that such a view *is* Christian is hidden: "Their first task is not, as has been assumed by many working in Christian ethics and still under the spell of Christendom, to write as though Christian commitments make no difference in the sense that they only underwrite what everyone in principle can already know, but rather to show the difference those commitments make."[28] What public theologians see as an inevitable source of conflict is what Hauerwas sees as making the conversation interesting in the first place. And while the importance of such conversations should not be underplayed, can it be extrapolated into the increasingly dominant view that it is *necessary* to discuss my faith with non-Christians if I am to understand what it is to be truly Christian? Such conversations will occasionally happen in any event, but it seems odd to claim that Christians *must* seek them out. With the thousands of cultural expressions of the Christian faith that we have at our disposal, why must we seek out those even *more* different?[29] Indicative of this trend is the use of the "at its best" modifier. Tracy maintains that "the discipline of [philosophy of religion and] modern theology are, *at their best,* fully modern critical disciplines," and the "at its best" modifier belies the notion that this is a neutral description of philosophy. The simultaneously descriptive-evaluative function of such claims obscures the fact that theology, as it has been practiced through history, simply does not fit such descriptions.

Engaging other religions (including secular humanism) in ethical conversations and calling them theological marks a dramatic shift from the apologists of old. This not only suggests a category error, but can render the dialogue bloodless by robbing the interlocutors of that which motivates them. Dealing effectively with a pluralist culture need not entail becoming pluralist about our own religious identity. Christians must have a coherent identity with which to engage pluralism, or they will have nothing to offer: "If theologians are going to contribute to reflection on the moral life in our particular situation, they will do so exactly to the extent they can capture the significance of the church for determining the nature and content of Christian ethical reflection."[30] If, in facing the demands of an academic environment, theologians adopt the strategy of omitting the specifics of the Christian faith due to their distressing particularity, then theologians will finally self-censor themselves right out of theology.

A Sectarian Retreat?

The question of the breakdown of civilization and the visible suffering that could accompany it (often used as a whip to drive the discussion) is at least as compelling for Hauerwas as it is for Tracy. It is, however, only tangentially related to the question of public theology. The well-being of the world is not our *primary* problem, although the well-being of the world will almost invariably be involved in living for Christ. However, if a sound strategy were proposed that would ensure the indefinite continuation of "civilization" that entailed sacrificing Christian identity, then we, as Christians, should reject the proposal because the strategy negates why we were concerned about the problem in the first place. It is one thing to have strong humanist convictions, but quite another to be a humanist before one is a Christian. Hauerwas condemns "survivalist" appeals, noting, "we do not live because we are afraid to die, but because we believe that our living is a gift that offers us opportunity for service."[31]

The contention that the pluralist model is the only one that addresses the problems of injustice that confront us depends on the assessment that the sociopolitical structures that exist need to be modified according to how they meet the criteria of emerging "global ethics." This assessment in turn rests on the assumption that there is no radical alternative to these structures. Hauerwas asserts that instead of addressing the structures of injustice in a way that proposes to repair them somehow (implying that they are good but broken), Christians should be presenting a radical alternative. Working out this alternative, and modeling it to the best of our abilities, may well be the best service we can offer to the suffering world. As Lindbeck puts it: "[R]eligious communities are likely to be practically relevant in the long run to the degree that they do not first ask what is either practical or relevant, but instead concentrate on their own intratextual outlooks and forms of life."[32] This is not advocating any kind of retreat from society. On the contrary, it is a forceful proclamation that Christians have a unique gift to offer the entire world: a place where one can encounter Christ in a community of His believers. Christians can offer a model of what is *good,* which is more fundamental than a statement of what is right. This cannot be done, however, if we attempt to distill our beliefs into principles that will be universally palatable:

> The justification of our moral principles and assertions cannot be done from the point of view of anyone, but rather requires a tradition of moral wisdom. Such a tradition is not a "deposit" of unchanging moral "truth," but is made up of the lives of men and women who are constantly testing and changing that tradition through their own struggle to live it.[33]

If there is no community of believers who are working out this tradition "intratextually," then Christians have nothing at all to offer the contemporary conversation. Hauerwas, by demonstrating the inextricable link between Christian ethics and the community that espouses them, shows that any proposal to universalize discourse based on a purely "ethical" impulse (justice) is ineffective because the very motivation for espousing it is removed. If, on the other hand, this same call for social justice is both espoused and modeled by Christians as a Christian alternative in light of a particularly Christian notion of the grace of God and the sacrificial love of Christ, then there is indeed a powerful approach that Christians can take toward injustice.

Hauerwas takes particular aim at any theologian who "tries to locate the 'essence,' or at least what is essential to religion, in a manner that frees religion from its most embarrassing particularistic aspects."[34] Not only is this not an appropriate way for Christians to engage non-Christians, it is also inherently self-defeating: "[I]f what is said theologically is but a confirmation of what we can know on other grounds . . . then why bother saying it theologically at all?"[35] Notice that this is almost precisely what Habermas said to the revisionist theologians in Chicago: "If this is the *common ground* of theology, science, and philosophy, what then still constitutes the distinctiveness of theological discourse? What separates the internal perspective of theology from the external perspective of those who enter a dialogue with theology?"[36] Taken together, the criticisms of Habermas and the postliberals constitute a compelling indictment of Tracy's correlational model for fundamental theology. Seeking to please both sides, it pleases neither because it voluntarily surrenders its distinctive identity. Hauerwas denies the very possibility of translating Christian insights into the framework of the public discourse in the academy, and Habermas is for the most part in agreement. But the issue can be framed even more concisely: the extent to which theologians are successful in such a translation is precisely the extent to which theologians have nothing to say.

As theologians, we must have a coherent, distinctive identity (integrity) in our engagement of the academy, or we will have nothing to offer (relevance). To refuse to bring our own specific Christian tradition into the discussion is to refuse to bring anything worthwhile. This is *not* advocating any kind of retreat from academic discussion. But neither does it allow the theological agenda to be set by external sources, which will invariably happen if Tracy's fundamental theology is practiced as a specialty. Central Christian doctrines (e.g., the Trinity, the deity of Jesus) that cannot be conceptually redescribed in neutral language will be not so much abandoned as simply neglected. They will not be rejected, but will gradually fade from view.[37]

FUNDAMENTAL LOYALTIES

In this engagement of Tracy's approach to public theology we have begun to see the inherent tension that exists between "public" and "theology." It can be seen largely as a question of manners. If theology is to be successful in the academy, theologians must display good academic manners. So, how should we train our theologians to behave out in public? It is clear that we should respect that our discussion partners may not share our beliefs, but what does this respect entail? Moreover, is there a time and place when we must reach the reasoned judgment that the discussion is not worth having?

Answers to these questions require a clear identification of our loyalties, and this is where Tracy errs. The "fundamental loyalty" (Tracy's term) of the fundamental theologian is to a conversation that is methodologically atheistic in its form. It is *fides quaerens intellectum* without the *fides,* which is why Tracy can consistently use the terms "modern theology" and "philosophy of religion" interchangeably. He somehow manages to stay the course amidst these conflicting tensions in his own work, but only at the cost of ambiguity that borders on confusion. That he manages to hold the tensions at all is, I think, an act of theological and hermeneutic virtuosity. Lesser theologians have failed. For example, Paul Knitter explicitly appeals to Tracy's fundamental theology to support a scientifically generated "cosmological faith" that serves as a "basic criterion for religion in general."[38] The finality of the Christ event is to be dropped because it is not a rationally redeemable position, and as such is a kind of arrogance. "How," wonders Knitter, "can we have a genuine dialogue if we walk in convinced that Jesus is the final word?"

He even goes so far as to call it "idolatrous."[39] While this is a position that Tracy himself would never hold, the structure of fundamental theology is such that it will prescind from its own faith position in order to adapt to the demands of the discussion, so there is nothing *technically* wrong with Knitter's application.[40]

Any correction to public theology must involve a re-assessment of both *theology* and *public,* and it is here that we find the genuine confusion in Tracy's presentation. Commenting favorably on the development in Catholic social ethics, he states: "the appeals to inner-Christian resources have now rendered Catholic social ethics a fully theological enterprise. This is evident in appeals to biblical symbols in Catholic ethics."[41] "Fully theological" in what sense? The systematic sense, whose primary "public" is the church; the practical sense, whose primary "public" is the wider society; or the "fundamental" sense, whose primary "public" is the academy? Only the systematic "public" presently accepts explicitly Christian symbols as warrants for arguments. There are many (even most) reasonable and intelligent people in the academy and wider society who will not accept such warrants.

The confusion deepens when we seek to determine the meaning of "public." Tracy asserts that the nature and reality of God "logically" demands publicness,[42] but as Owen C. Thomas notes, Tracy vacillates between two uses of the word public, "without indicating the shift in meaning": "1) the nature of a claim, namely to universality or universal significance, and 2) the nature of the grounds offered for a claim, namely, evidence, warrants, and backing."[43] Even the "sectarian" Hauerwas is significantly public in the first sense; he certainly claims that the Christian witness has universal significance. He will converse with anyone who wants to listen, and many who do not.[44] This is indeed logically demanded by Christian faith. What is *not* logically demanded is Tracy's Lonerganian criterion, which demands that we speak in a certain manner, "that any attentive, intelligent, reasonable and responsible person can understand and judge in keeping with fully public criteria for argumentation."[45] If the latter is to be the definition of "public," then Tracy's systematic specialty (the only of the three specialties whose "public" is the church) is not public at all, but rather takes place in the *privacy* of the Christian community. In taking the scriptures and creeds as articles of faith, systematic theology explicitly rejects the "fully public criteria" to which Tracy refers.

If we are to keep the "functional specialties" framework at all, then a configuration that widens the scope and importance of systematic theology is required. The relationship between fundamental and systematic theology needs to be ordered, with fundamental theology accountable to systematic theology. *Every* Christian theologian, regardless of specialty, needs to have a "fundamental loyalty" to the body of Christ, which will in turn order other loyalties. This would, of course, entail that fundamental theology is no longer fundamental, re-opening a space for a Christian *philosophy*, a discipline that does not figure in Tracy's model. A truly fundamental theology, as we will see in the final chapter, is the living theology that takes place in the prayer and worship, the concrete practices of Christians.

Tracy is right to insist that any theologian should be willing to discuss her position with anyone, that theology is directed outward by its very nature. But if an academic interlocutor is simply not willing to listen to what is said because it is explicitly theological, the last thing to do is compromise the content of the message to improve its presentation. Theologians, when speaking *as* theologians, will inevitably speak in theological language. An interlocutor who resolutely objects to the use of theological language is someone who does not want to talk to a theologian. And since the general plausibility structures are presently set by an academy that often reacts with confusion, indifference, or even hostility when faced with explicitly theological language, this will happen all too often.[46]

In order to keep their names on the invitation lists for future academy parties (i.e., continue to have a positive impact in the academic world), theologians must behave with the good manners appropriate to the occasion. The question is: How badly does theology want to be at this party? When is it time to leave? Tracy's position requires him to answer the second question "never"; it would betray a fundamental loyalty. This is not to say that the appropriate answer is "now." But the fact is that theologians *are* radically different from other academics, in that theology is differentiated not merely by its subject matter, but also by the lived commitments of theologians to Christ and church. This will inevitably be unsettling in the present secular academic environment, where personally invested truth claims are often looked upon with a polite disdain. Theologians will assuredly be reproved for lacking the proper critical distance, or some variation on that theme, and perhaps not invited to the next gathering. But perhaps these quirky theologians will be invited regardless, with a chance to make a genuine contribution. For not all parties are the same, and there are some in the academy more amenable to the eccentricities of theological discourse than others.

Theologians who prescind from this personal investment in their theology, however, become weak substitutes for philosophers or sociologists of religion. Milbank derisively dismisses the well-mannered culture of "correlationist" theologians, "which to most young scholars today appears now like a bizarre academic twilight zone inhabited by the intellectually craven and impotent."[47] Such theologians are still invited to the party, but at best only as those tiresome *poseurs* who have good manners but nothing interesting to say. At worst, they blend in beautifully, having ceased to be theologians at all.

2

Theology, Hermeneutics, and Ricoeur's Double Life

The relationship between theology and hermeneutics now has its own *Wirkungsgeschichte,* and as is the case with many relationships, the lines of communication are strained. New questions arise faster than they can be answered, and the original questions get lost along the way. One original question that remains unanswered is: can philosophical hermeneutics be productively appropriated into theology? Responses to this question when it was first raised in North America can be divided into two dominant types, enthusiastic affirmation and equally charged rejection. These two responses represent twin pitfalls that theology ought to avoid when engaging hermeneutics: an enthusiastic *embrace* of philosophical hermeneutics by theology, which allows the former to colonize the latter; or an outright *rejection* of the claims of hermeneutics, which results in an impoverished theological discourse.[1] Rather, I will argue that theology *must* engage hermeneutics, but must do so cautiously, for both disciplines have a "foundational ambition,"[2] to use Ricoeur's term, and each will tend to disfigure the other in the struggle for primacy. By remaining at arm's length, however, theology can benefit from everything that hermeneutics has to offer, with neither discipline in danger of being subsumed by the other.

Ricoeur's original framing of the hermeneutics/theology question has been largely overlooked despite his being greatly influential as both a "professional of philosophy" and a member of what he calls "a community that listens to and interprets biblical Scripture."³ It is the task of this chapter to recover this contribution, placing Ricoeur in his proper context in North American theological discourse. The first part summarizes Ricoeur's account of philosophical hermeneutics from Friedrich Schleiermacher to Hans-Georg Gadamer, culminating in Ricoeur's critical supplementation to Gadamer's hermeneutics of tradition. The second part examines the "embrace" and "reject" pitfalls of theological appropriation. David Tracy's influential endorsement of Ricoeur's hermeneutics is undermined by his more fundamental commitments to academic relevance, which lead to a loss of theological identity. Hans Frei's equally influential attack on Ricoeur's philosophical hermeneutics in defense of the theological tradition of the *sensus literalis* turns out to be for the most part an attack on Tracy's *appropriation* of philosophical hermeneutics, and very little of the attack actually reaches Ricoeur. Frei opposes the conflation of philosophy and theology, but is guilty of conflating a philosopher and a theologian.⁴ With Ricoeur extricated from the debate, the final part shows how he explicitly offers his philosophical hermeneutics to be appropriated by theology, and how his emphasis on textuality provides a means of keeping the two disciplines at arm's length. Moreover, his "double life" of publication embodies the arm's-length approach with which theology can productively engage hermeneutics. Ricoeur's approach will prove to be more compatible with Frei's position than with Tracy's because Ricoeur and Frei (both under the influence of Barth) agree that the confusion of the embrace is a more serious danger than the poverty of the rejection. The overall emphasis of the chapter will therefore be more on the enriching of Frei rather than the clarification of Tracy.

PHILOSOPHICAL HERMENEUTICS

Ricoeur defines hermeneutics as "the theory of the operations of understanding in their relation to the interpretation of texts."⁵ He characterizes his own contribution as a "critical supplementation" to Hans-Georg Gadamer's "hermeneutics of tradition,"⁶ and Gadamer's own contribution is characterized in turn as the synthesis of two major movements in the recent history of hermeneutics. Ricoeur's account is oriented around these two movements—from the *regional* to the *general*, and from the *epistemological* to the *fundamental*—and his task is to enter into discussion with the textual sciences (e.g., semiotics, exegesis) without sacrificing the gains of a general and fundamental hermeneutics. This section will proceed chronologically. First, the two movements will be outlined as they proceed from Schleiermacher to Heidegger. Second, Gadamer's crucial contribution, his "hermeneutics of tradition," will be presented, which will in turn lead to Ricoeur's "critical supplementation." The term "critical supplementation" is important because it affirms the *validity* of Gadamer's hermeneutics while identifying a crucial *deficiency*: the perceived lack of a positive role for critical distance. This lack will find a parallel in the theological hermeneutics of Frei. Both Gadamer and Frei are intent on protecting the integrity of particular *traditions,* which can lead to a hypersensitivity to the *critical methods* that threaten to colonize the tradition. Ricoeur shares Gadamer's (and Frei's) concern, but argues that *distanciation* need not be opposed to *belonging,* and that a place can and must be made for a "critical instance" in the hermeneutics of tradition. Ricoeur's critical supplementation to Gadamer accomplishes this by emphasizing *textuality,* and this emphasis can be appropriated by a theological hermeneutics.

Toward a General and Fundamental Hermeneutics

Ricoeur's account of modern hermeneutics begins with Friedrich Schleiermacher's movement to incorporate all regional hermeneutics into a general hermeneutics.[7] At the time, there were two separate branches of hermeneutics: the philology of classical texts and the exegesis of sacred texts.[8] Hermeneutics arose in the attempt to become a *science,* to give a unified account of these two branches by bringing them under the general rubric of *understanding,* subjecting all texts to the same rules of interpretation. Ricoeur sees this as an epistemological move entirely compatible with Kantianism: "the capacity for knowing must be measured before we confront the nature of being."[9] Apprehending the meaning of a text cannot surpass our ability to interpret it. But this attempt to universalize the process of interpretation by the appeal to impersonal criteria of validity is counterbalanced by Schleiermacher's other major influence: the Romantic attachment to the creativity of the gifted individual. This "divinatory" moment of interpretation seeks to "understand the text at first as well as and then even better than its author."[10] It is finally central to Schleiermacher's hermeneutics, and cannot be fully reconciled with the quest for universal validity.[11] Ricoeur suggests that this paradox is deeply embedded in the hermeneutic process, that "hermeneutics is forever marked by this double filiation—Romantic and critical, critical and Romantic."[12]

The second major figure of the story is Wilhelm Dilthey, who also brought exegesis and philology into a single arena, but foregrounded the

question of *history*.[13] The great texts to be interpreted are historically separated from the interpreter, which raises the question of the *Zusammenhang*
(interconnection) of history before the meaning of any given text can even be
addressed. This expands Schleiermacher's concerns from the understanding
of particular authors to the interpretation of history itself, and thus expands
the scope of hermeneutics from textual interpretation to the entire range of
the human sciences. But while this advances the quest for a *general* hermeneutics, there still remains a psychological grounding to Dilthey's hermeneutics that seeks to access the mental life of the author. As Ricoeur frames
it, "the object of hermeneutics is constantly shifted away from the text, from
its sense and reference, toward the lived experience that is expressed there-
in."[14] The interpreted text necessarily remains an epiphenomenon, and the
tension between the generality of texts and the particularity of an author
remains. It is an unavoidable tension, because the problem "is still posed in
terms of the epistemological debate characteristic of the whole neo-Kantian
period."[15] While Dilthey's attention to history unites all human texts in their
historical situatedness, where one part of history grasps another via the interpretation of texts, the conceptual vocabulary of epistemology prevented a
full exploration of the implications.

With Heidegger the focus of hermeneutics moved from epistemological
concerns to ontological preoccupations, where "*understanding* ceases to appear as a simple *mode of knowing* in order to become a *way of being* and a way
of relating to beings and to being."[16] Through Schleiermacher and Dilthey
hermeneutics became *general* discipline, but remained secondary to epistemology and psychology. In Heidegger, hermeneutics becomes *fundamental*.
The central claim of *Being and Time* from the perspective of Ricoeur's project
is that hermeneutics "contains the roots of what can be called 'hermeneutic'
only in a derivative sense: the methodology of the human sciences."[17] This is
first done by *situating* Dasein within Being. Dasein breaks out of the subject/
object dichotomy to become a being within Being. Analyzing Dasein first
as being-in-the-world rather than as an isolated subject or as a being-with-
another de-psychologizes the investigation. Dasein is not simply situated in
the static sense, but has the structure of a *thrown* project. Understanding
one's possibilities as a thrown project necessarily involves dynamic concepts
such as "fore-having, fore-sight, and fore-conception," terms that have the
"pejorative connotation of prejudice." But this is pejorative *only* if one is considering Dasein from the perspective of epistemology. Ricoeur counters with
a different perspective: "For a fundamental ontology, however, prejudice can
be understood only in terms of the anticipatory structure of understanding.

The famous hermeneutical circle is henceforth only the shadow, on the methodological plane, of this structure of anticipation."[18] Heidegger succeeded in digging beneath epistemology to the question of fundamental ontology, defusing the part-whole tension by incorporating both into the anticipatory structure. But Ricoeur, while impressed with this accomplishment, also notes that Heidegger leaves us no path of return to methodological deliberation: having resolved the epistemological problem by moving to the plane of ontology, how do we get *back* to the plane of epistemology? Ricoeur contends that Heidegger's fundamental ontology is structurally incapable of answering this question, and so to find the beginning of an answer, he moves on to the work of Gadamer.[19]

Gadamer's Hermeneutics of Tradition

In Ricoeur's account, Gadamer's entire contribution is organized around a central problematic: the *alienating distanciation* (*Verfremdung*), that is, "the ontological presupposition which sustains the objective conduct of the human sciences."[20] Gadamer focuses on questioning the methodological account of the human sciences, especially in the philosophies of aesthetics, history, and language. The ideally dispassionate scientist of the Enlightenment—who deliberately maintains a critical distance from what is being studied in order to be "unprejudiced" and "objective"—is taken as the target of Gadamer's investigation. Upon examination, it turns out that the desire to be unprejudiced is itself a prejudice. Furthermore, this "prejudice against prejudice" is not incidental, but a manifestation of a deeper prejudice against authority. Obedience to authority is characterized as an intellectual subordination to another that abdicates one's responsibility as a rational, autonomous being. This is shunned in favor of a distrust for authority, which is warranted not only to minimize domination and violence, but also to foster the intellectual maturity of the individual. But, as Gadamer argues:

> this is not the essence of authority. It is true that it is primarily persons who have authority; but the authority of persons is based ultimately, not on the subjection of and abdication of reason, but on recognition and knowledge . . . and hence on an act of reason itself which, aware of its own limitations, accepts that others have a better understanding.[21]

It is in fact quite *reasonable* to recognize limitations and accept authoritative statements, and the refusal ever to do so would be more arrogant than mature. And not only is it reasonable to recognize something authoritative, it is impossible to avoid doing so. The "consciousness of historical efficacy" (*wirkungsgeschichtliches Bewusstsein*) refers to the fact that we are already shaped by the history that we propose to study. This has obvious repercussions for historiography, since we cannot study a history of which we are not also a part. Gadamer argues that "modern historical research itself is not only research, but the transmission of tradition,"[22] which situates the historian *inside* the history being studied. As Ricoeur puts it: "History precedes me and outstrips my reflection; I belong to history before belonging to myself."[23] The emphasis that runs through Gadamer's hermeneutics is on this "belonging-to" (*Zugehörigkeit*) and "dependence-on" (*Abhängigkeit*) that is fundamental to all experience.

This sense of belonging to and being dependent on history finds its primary expression in language. The *Sprachlichkeit* (linguality) of all experience is an indispensable expression of the primordiality of belonging and dependence. The claim to universality of Gadamer's philosophical hermeneutics is anchored in its struggle against the alienating distanciation that does not acknowledge this linguality, and thus our belonging and dependence.[24] Dialogue is not just something that we engage in, but is something *that we are*. The supposedly impartial interpreter is almost laughable in his pretension to objectivity because he cuts himself off from the very source of interpretation: "To try to eliminate one's own concepts in interpretation is not only impossible, but manifestly absurd. To interpret means precisely to use one's own preconceptions so that the meaning of the text can really be made to speak for us."[25] The absurdity arises from the fact that if there were no preconceptions, there would be no engagement of texts in the first place. Not only would we not be *able* to understand a text without "prejudices," we would not even be inclined to try. Unprejudiced objectivity emerges not as a good to be achieved, but rather as an alienation to be overcome. Ricoeur summarizes Gadamer's hermeneutics as "the discourse which tells how *belonging-to* language provides the universal medium of *belonging-to* being."[26]

Ricoeur's "Critical Supplementation"

On the whole, Ricoeur is in accord with Gadamer's hermeneutics of tradition; he sees the main problem as being one of overemphasis. Gadamer's zealous renouncing of alienating distanciation is a product of his extended rehearsal of the conflicts between Enlightenment and Romanticism as they played out down to Heidegger's struggle against neo-Kantianism. But Ricoeur contends that Gadamer has given so much to the refutation of *Verfremdung* in the name of protecting *Abhängigkeit* and *Zugehörigkeit* he is in danger of creating a new dichotomy. Ricoeur wonders, "to what extent the work deserves to be called *Truth AND Method,* and whether it ought not be entitled instead *Truth OR Method.*"[27] The disjunctive/conjunctive problem is one not of structure, but of emphasis, and is what Ricoeur's account has been pointing toward: "*how is it possible to introduce a critical instance into a consciousness of belonging that is expressly defined by the rejection of distanciation?*"[28] In other words, to overcome Gadamer's seeming *rejection* of distanciation, Ricoeur must determine how hermeneutics can *engage* objective scientific methodology without *embracing* the methodology and becoming subordinated to it. The task is then to find a positive, non-alienating role for distanciation *within* philosophical hermeneutics. Ricoeur's offers a critical supplementation of the hermeneutics of tradition that is *critical* because it introduces an explanatory moment into the process of understanding, but is only a *supplementation* because it draws from concepts of understanding that already exist in Gadamer's hermeneutics of tradition.

Ricoeur addresses the problem by moving from discourse to text, assigning a positive role for distanciation. Rather than concentrating on *linguality (Sprachlichkeit),* which is acknowledged as the more "primordial,"[29] he shifts the analysis to *textuality (Schriftlichkeit).* One must begin the analysis from somewhere, and as Gadamer began with art as a way of challenging the priority of distanciation over belonging, Ricoeur begins with text as a way of challenging the Diltheyan dichotomy between explanation and understanding. Ricoeur is not offering a "hermeneutics *of* the text," but rather a "hermeneutics *based on* the problematics of the text."[30] There are four characteristics of textuality: the relationship of speaking and writing, structure, the "world of the text," and mediated self-understanding.

The transition from speech to writing presupposes discourse, and the belonging of discourse is acknowledged as more primordial than the distance of text. However, the added distance that is part of a text's "persona" is a clear extension of the *said* (as opposed to the *saying*), which disconnects the meaning of the text from whatever the author may have meant to say. A text is decontextualized from its original author, intended reader, and situation, and is available to be recontextualized by anyone who reads it. In this way, distanciation now belongs to the textual mediation itself, and is a *positive* aspect rather than a negative one. The distanciation that constitutes the textuality of the text is the very thing that has allowed human discourse to span historical distances.

Secondly, a text is not merely the freezing of a moment of discourse, it is also a deliberate composition with a unifying *structure.* An interlocutor can be questioned in the free play of discourse in a way that an author of a text cannot, so the author must compose the text according to certain formal guidelines if it is to be understood. The author plays the role of both artisan and speaker, and one must engage the artisan to reach the speaker. Hermeneutics has not strayed from its primary task of "identifying the discourse within the work," but Ricoeur argues that "this discourse is given nowhere else than *in* and *by* the structure of the work."[31] As writing opened up a place for *distanciation*, structure opens up a place for *objectification*, as evidenced by the flourishing linguistic sciences of semiotics and structural analysis. The explanatory moment of discerning the structure of a text, of clearly articulating the codification of patterns in textual "artifacts," is a necessary (although never primary) moment in the process of understanding a text.

It is in the explication of the "world of the text" that Ricoeur's hermeneutics finds its primary task. Just as a propositional sentence has a reference, that is, its claim to reach reality, so too does a text as a whole. The notion of reference when applied to a text in its entirety is what Ricoeur means by the world of the text. This applies to fictional and poetic texts as well, which address reality in a way that is unavailable to more direct reference. One can refer directly to something in the world, but to refer to being-in-the-world, where "in" no longer implies the locative, requires indirect reference. To interpret a text is "to explicate the being-in-the-world displayed before the text."[32] It is not the psychological intention of an author residing *behind* the text that is sought, but rather the projection of a world *before* the text that is mediated *through* the "matter" of the text itself. Ricoeur says: "The *matter* of the text is not what a naïve reading of the text reveals, but what the formal arrangement of the text mediates."[33] There is no bypassing the distanciating and objectifying moments of interpretation in the quest to understand the discourse within the work.

Finally, the text not only discloses variations of my world, but also discloses variations of my *self*. In contrast to the *cogito* philosophies that present the subject as immediate and self-transparent, Ricoeur argues that self-understanding must pass through "the detour of the signs of humanity sedimented in the works of culture." All self-appropriation occurs via a moment of dispossession, a distanciation from ourselves that is mediated by the text. Again, distanciation and appropriation are related in a productive dialectic. Ricoeur is adamant that this not be taken as a cover for subjectivism, stressing how the Gadamerian notion of play and the psychoanalytic notion of illusion combine to dispel any sense of the subject as master of the process. On the contrary, "it would be more correct to say that the *self* is constituted by the 'matter' of the text."[34] The detour through texts (broadly construed) is the only way to achieve enough distance from oneself to critique illusions and realize new possibilities, an idea Ricoeur goes on to develop more fully in *Oneself as Another*.

These four aspects taken together illuminate the hermeneutic function of distanciation. Gadamer stresses the priority of participation, almost to the point of rejecting distanciation altogether. Ricoeur also objects to the modern embrace of distanciation, and certainly recognizes the participatory mode as primordial, but in the interests of protecting distance from being completely negated, he adds his "critical supplementation." The epistemological mode of explanation is in a subordinate role, but is nonetheless a necessary detour in the ontological event of understanding. This productively incorporates a critical moment into the hermeneutics of tradition by keeping them *at arm's length* through an increased attentiveness to textuality.

THE THEOLOGICAL RECEPTION OF HERMENEUTICS

Two theologians, David Tracy and Hans Frei, have dominated the reception of Ricoeur in North American theology, and characterize the initial positive and negative responses to Ricoeur's hermeneutics. Tracy is the most prominent proponent of hermeneutics in the conversation. He co-taught many seminars with Ricoeur at the University of Chicago, and has been deeply influenced by Ricoeur's thought. Frei, along with Lindbeck, stands at the head of an opposing tradition that is now commonly referred to by Lindbeck's term "postliberal." Along with several colleagues at Yale, he objected to the application of philosophical hermeneutics to theology as part of what George Schner once called "an allergy to German Idealism." The intellectual antipathy between Frei and Tracy grew into a long-running (and now dormant) debate between the so-called postliberal and revisionist schools. It is important to understand how this debate originated because Ricoeur became deeply enmeshed in it despite his lack of participation, and its polarization has led to falsely dichotomized options when considering his hermeneutics. Those who find fault with the theological methods of the revisionist theologians (e.g., Tracy, James Gustafson, William Schweiker, Francis Schüssler Fiorenza) tend to project those methods onto Ricoeur as well. Both Frei and Lindbeck label Ricoeur an "experiential-expressive" theologian, and accuse him of betraying the "literal sense" of the Gospel narratives by subsuming them into his general account of meaning.[35] This rejection turns out to be a view of Ricoeur through the partially distorting lens of Tracy's *embrace*, and if this lens can be removed, Ricoeur's hermeneutics can be considered afresh.

David Tracy's Embrace of Hermeneutics

Tracy argues that the successful engagement of existing philosophical categories has been characteristic of Christianity throughout the entire tradition. The most prominent example is the ease with which early Christians appropriated the forms of Platonism. Platonic philosophy was a natural ally for early Christianity because of its "sheer sense of wonder at the engifted gracious possibilities within which we live and move and have our being."[36] Tracy suggests that as Platonism is now in its "twilight," hermeneutical philosophy should be the new ally because it "provides the kind of contemporary philosophy needed by a revelational theology."[37] There are several key aspects of hermeneutics that inform Tracy's endorsement. Hermeneutics reorganizes the metaphysical concept of truth, moving away from notions of *correspondence* or *coherence* toward those of *disclosure* and *manifestation*. It also takes history with a seriousness unprecedented in philosophy, and prioritizes *possibility* over *actuality*. Furthermore, hermeneutics is characterized by its concentration on texts, and Ricoeur in particular concentrates on the structuring of texts in terms of genre and style.

These aspects of hermeneutics are particularly relevant for Christianity, which has an authoritative *text* comprising multiple genres (e.g., historical, prophetic, hymnic). Of central importance are the *historical* texts (the Gospels), which make concrete claims about God's self-*manifestation* in the person of Jesus Christ. Hermeneutic philosophy can articulate the form in which this revelation has been historically structured, and supply categories that "genuinely clarify and develop the meaning of revelation itself,"[38] with reference to the primary "Form" of Christ. Hermeneutic analysis of the texts themselves can supply "an understanding of the text disclosing in and through form (*Dar-stellung*) a *possible* mode of being in the world."[39] Tracy goes on to accord hermeneutics an even more important task: "to clarify, and, when necessary, challenge and correct theology's own self-understanding of revelation as manifestation of *reasonable*, even if formerly unimagined, possibility."[40] Tracy's emphases are important to the understanding of the ensuing debate. The "*possible* mode of being in the world" will raise warning flags for Frei, as it seems to reduce Jesus to a mere exemplar. But it is Tracy's concern with being "*reasonable*" that is the more serious problem, and represents the intrusion of Tracy's fundamental specialty into his discussion of hermeneutics.

As we saw in the previous chapter, Tracy's model for theology includes a fundamental and a systematic discipline, each defined by their "publics": the church and the academy, respectively.[41] Each discipline has its own mode of argument, ethical stance, faith-understanding, and formulation of meaning or truth. Which discipline controls the relationship to philosophical hermeneutics is not immediately obvious because Tracy characterizes the fundamental specialty as "philosophical" and the systematic specialty as "hermeneutical." A closer reading, however, finds that the systematic specialty cannot control the relationship because it is entirely subservient to the fundamental specialty, and as such is ultimately too weak to control any relationship. Tracy's argument above is an example of a fundamental theologian who, upon careful consideration of the merits of philosophical hermeneutics, is advising those of the systematic specialty that they need it. In fact, if one of Tracy's primary hermeneutic theses—that the classic texts of theology can also function as broader cultural classics—turns out to be wrong, "then systematic theology should be eliminated."[42] It is unquestionably the fundamental specialty that holds all the power in Tracy's model.

It is important to note is that fundamental theology is a *general* model for the theological engagement of other academic disciplines, and there is no direct link between this model and philosophical hermeneutics. In fact, there are several other more prominent theological and philosophical influences at work. The language of "intelligent, reasonable, responsible persons" is that of Bernard Lonergan, the "abstraction from all religious faith commitments" alludes to Schubert Ogden, and the category of "common human experience" has its roots in the thought of Paul Tillich. Most significantly, the casting of theology as a "fully modern critical discipline" is addressed directly to Habermas, the philosopher after whom Tracy modeled his contribution to fundamental theology. It is not clear that all of these diverse influences can peacefully co-exist in a single theological model.[43] Tracy's embrace of philosophical hermeneutics is but one example of his embrace of the academy in general. Because the fundamental specialty is the gate through which philosophical concepts enter Tracy's theology, when the claims of philosophy and the claims of theology come into conflict, he is forced to come down on the side of philosophy. Far from theology appropriating philosophical insights, theology ends up *being appropriated* by philosophy. But this is a result of the method of engagement, not the thing engaged. One can go along with Tracy in recognizing what philosophical hermeneutics has to offer theology without also sharing his other commitments that force him into an enthusiastic embrace of philosophical hermeneutics.

Hans Frei's Rejection: Protecting the Literal Sense

Hans Frei's account of hermeneutics (much like Gadamer's) aims to preserve the authority of a tradition, and has harsh words for those who pretend to have some more objective means of passing judgment on the validity of Scripture. Frei maintains that prior to what he calls the "eclipse of biblical narrative" in the eighteenth century, a *sensus literalis* approach to Scripture had dominated throughout the Christian tradition.[44] There were variances, but the tradition had consistently read the "central" portions of Scripture (i.e., the Gospels) literally. One could argue for a spiritual or allegorical reading of some parts, but not of the central parts, and certainly not of the entire sacred text.

Frei identifies three distinct versions of *sensus literalis* that have persisted throughout the tradition. The first version of *sensus literalis* describes the text as enacting the "author's intention." The texts quite literally mean what they say. Frei notes the pitfalls of such a procedure: the text can be taken as the simply realized intention of the author and given a life of its own, which leads to "bibliolatry" or "fundamentalist biblical literalism."[45] Conversely, it can lead to an overly historicized approach that concentrates only on what the text might have meant in the first century. The second version of *sensus literalis* deals with the signifier and the signified of the text, alternatively called the "sense" and "reference," or the *verbum* and *res*. This version maintains that the text actually gives a true accounting of the reality it is describing. That the Gospels are in narrative form is not a deficiency, for there is no other adequate description. The final version of *sensus literalis,* and the one most preferred by Frei, is "the way the text has generally been used in the community."[46] Rather than a *literary* investigation into the "author's intention," or an *metaphysical* investigation into "true description," we have here a *sociological* investigation into the use of the text in the tradition.

Whatever the precise status of *sensus literalis*, be it literary, metaphysical, or sociological, its *function* is to safeguard the integrity of Scripture: "[W]hat we have in the *sensus literalis* is a reading about which one needs to say first that it governs and bends to its own ends whatever general categories it shares—as indeed it must share—with other kinds of reading."[47] Frei is intent on protecting the primacy of the Gospel accounts. The problem, according to Frei, began with the "mediating theologians" of the eighteenth century (e.g., Schleiermacher) who reversed the traditional order of priority when reading Scripture. They prioritized their own philosophical or ethical categories ahead of the *sensus literalis*. In this way, interpretation of Scripture became "a matter of fitting the biblical story into another world with another story rather than incorporating that world into the biblical story."[48] Frei finds this process disturbing, in that the biblical narrative is "eclipsed" by these second-order questions. If the Gospel is to have primacy, then why must it jump through some external hoop in order to establish its meaningfulness? Frei insists that we must let the Gospel set its own terms, else it will be distorted by attempts to make it "fit" into some foreign system of meaning. It is not that external tools cannot be used, but rather that no *single* system be permitted to judge the Gospel message. Frei argues that Ricoeur's philosophical hermeneutics is just this kind of system, and that when it is applied to the reading of biblical texts, "the literal reading will break apart under its ministrations."[49] It seems to Frei that Ricoeur will inevitably turn the Gospel into a mere "regional instance of the universally valid pattern of interpretation."[50] The litmus test will be whether the biblical text is allowed to say anything that was not already accounted for by philosophical hermeneutics.

Frei launches a three-pronged attack against Ricoeur under the rubric of discussing the "consequences" of philosophical hermeneutics when applied to the biblical texts. First, Frei explores the impact of philosophical hermeneutics on the story of Jesus. His primary objection is that such an approach robs Jesus of his definitive uniqueness. Rather than allowing the stories of Jesus to be "about a specific fictional or historical person by that name, and therefore about his identification through narrative descriptions," it turns Jesus into a mere exemplar. Hermeneutics, as Frei sees it, is constrained to view Jesus as the instance of a general form of being-in-the-world, "the verbal expressor of a certain preconceptual consciousness which he then, in a logically derivative or secondary sense, exhibits in action."[51] Thus, the crucifixion of Christ need not have been a historical event, as it was merely one option for Jesus's expression of self-sacrificial righteousness. Frei's second line of attack focuses on the role of "meaning" in hermeneutics. He objects to the shift in fulcrum from the thing understood to the reader doing the understanding, the interpreter. He then curiously shifts his attack to Tracy and his "precise regional application" of Ricoeur's general hermeneutics.[52] This approach, which views religious language as disclosive of "the religious element of common human experience," robs the subject of the Gospel narratives, Jesus himself, of any personal density. Though hermeneutics tries to make Jesus the "irreducible ascriptive subject" of the Gospel accounts, this is stretched to the point of breaking if general religious experience is the primary referent of these same accounts.[53] Frei's final move is a direct assault on philosophical hermeneutics, since the viability of employing philosophical hermeneutics in Scripture is obviously dependent on the viability of the theory itself. Frei forges an alliance of convenience with the deconstructionists, the intent being to undermine the credibility of philosophical hermeneutics to the point where one would be hesitant to apply it anywhere. While certainly no friend of the deconstructionists, Frei uses the notion of *différance* and the critique of signifier/signified relationships to undercut the stability of hermeneutics, going so far as to suggest that we are in a "post-hermeneutical" situation.[54] This leaves us with no general theory at all, once again freeing up Scripture to be read with a "more modest" hermeneutics, employing various literary theories in an ad hoc manner.

Frei's assault on the viability of philosophical hermeneutics itself proves to be ill-advised. He finds himself in the dangerous position of critically engaging Ricoeur in a purely philosophical discussion, and Frei is clearly out of his element.[55] His haphazard use of Derrida and Foucault seems designed only to muddy the waters, and despite its length—at ten pages, an essay in itself—he shows little appreciation for the philosophical issues at play.[56] As Tracy noted in his criticism of Lindbeck's even more bizarre claim that not only Ricoeur but Derrida (!) is an experiential-expressivist: "Lindbeck's long footnote on the Yale deconstructionists leads me to believe that he has not reflected very much on the rhetorical (hermeneutical and/or deconstructive) aspects of the question of interpretation of texts."[57] There is, on the whole, a lack of seriousness on the part of Frei and Lindbeck in particular when it comes to the engagement of continental philosophy, a point I will return to at the end of this chapter.

However, Frei's primary fear—that philosophical hermeneutics would overwhelm theological discourse with its foreign rules and concepts, leaving theology as a mere "regional application"—is a legitimate one. To reduce Jesus to a mere exemplar, a mere instance of "meaning" that is projected from the reader, would surely constitute a break with the traditional reception of the biblical witness. Similarly, Frei's concern that Jesus might become "the verbal expressor of a certain preconceptual experience" would indeed be a case of judging a sacred text by externally generated rules. These challenges, however, seem to be aimed directly at Tracy, and do not directly address the viability of appropriating Ricoeur's hermeneutics. Theological hermeneutics would certainly become a regional application of philosophical hermeneutics under the rules of Tracy's fundamental theology. When Tracy proposes that hermeneutics "challenge and correct" theological self-understanding in the interest of making theology "reasonable," this is a perfect example of the mediating theology that so concerns Frei. Frei is justified in objecting to this particular engagement of philosophical hermeneutics, but again this has to do with the method of engagement, not the thing engaged.

There is another relevant problem in Frei's account. He argues that the *sensus literalis* breaks under the ministrations of Ricoeur's hermeneutics, but what is it that is breaking? Frei advances three definitions of *sensus literalis:* literary (author's intention), metaphysical (true description), and sociolinguistic (traditional use). First, these are three quite different uses of the same term, which calls into question the assertion that this is a *single* approach at all.[58] It is important for Frei's argument that *sensus literalis* be "the closest one can come to a consensus reading of the Bible as the sacred text in the Christian church."[59] If there are plural "traditions" (and thus no virtual consensus), then he must give reasons for preferring his own over others, a task that cannot but appeal to categories external to theology. That it is more accurate to refer to three traditions rather than one is supported by Frei's having a favorite amongst the three, which necessarily entails treating them as distinct. But even if we allow Frei to maneuver here (by either allowing *sensus literalis* to function as a genus with three species or allowing the sociological version to stand as the "consensus"), there is a disconcerting recursiveness to this third use of *sensus literalis.* Frei maintains that the consensus has been to look to how Scripture has been read throughout the tradition, but the term itself refers (in its sociological sense) to how Scripture has been read throughout the tradition. This is just to say that the way we have always done it is *to look at the way we have always done it.* Even if this were the case (which it is clearly not, since this would involve both a denial of any innovation in the tradition and an infinite regress),[60] it hardly functions as a compelling argument that we should continue to engage Scripture in this way. Far from being "more modest," Frei's hermeneutics is as controlling as any theory of understanding to which he objects.[61]

It is notable that in his pointed criticism of Ricoeur's philosophical hermeneutics and its application to theology, he did not address Ricoeur's own essay on that very topic. It is possible that Frei had never seriously engaged Ricoeur's work, but took Tracy as a reliable representative of philosophical hermeneutics.[62] Unfortunately for everyone, those who tend to side with Frei against Tracy seem to follow Frei's lead in projecting the structure of Tracy's fundamental theology onto Ricoeur, and Ricoeur's contribution to the relationship between theology and hermeneutics becomes a casualty of the conversation. This is unfortunate, because Frei could have enhanced his already robust theological hermeneutics with a more serious engagement of Ricoeur's philosophical hermeneutics, and his followers would not seem so hermeneutically naïve when discussing their readings of the very sacred text they hope to protect.

AT ARM'S LENGTH

If theology cannot embrace hermeneutics without being over-whelmed, but cannot afford to reject it, what remains? It is Ricoeur himself who provides clues to how this relationship might be productive for both theology and hermeneutics. Furthermore, it is a method of engagement that would seem to satisfy Frei's concern for the integrity of theological discourse while addressing Tracy's case for hermeneutics as a natural ally for theology. Frei's attack on Ricoeur's hermeneutics was in *defense* of theological integrity, but this is not to be equated with a hostility toward philosophy in general. He was a *proponent* of the "thorough-minded, disciplined probing" of philosophy in seminary education.[63] Conversely, Tracy is obviously not eager to see theology become overwhelmed by its engagement with hermeneutics. It is Tracy himself who praises Ricoeur for keeping theology and hermeneutics distinct, noting that Ricoeur's influence "has always been, from Ricoeur's side, intended as a strictly philosophical contribution to theological self-understanding. Unlike some of his admirers, Ricoeur himself never allows philosophy or theology to be confused or conflated."[64] It is ironic that Tracy would have to number himself as one of those admirers, but it is nonetheless a keen observation.

How, then, does Ricoeur envision the relationship between hermeneutics and theology? What is most remarkable about the question is that there is a clear and detailed answer that predates the entire discussion. It is a matter of resetting the clock to 1976, where he outlines with great care his plan for how the two disciplines would interact:

> At first glance theological hermeneutics will appear as a mere *application* of this general problematics of the text. But a more complex relationship will emerge as we go along, a relationship which can be expressed in terms of a mutual inclusion . . . my thesis is that only the treatment of theological hermeneutics as *regional,* as applied to a certain category of texts—in our case biblical texts—can prepare a reversal in the relation between both hermeneutics. Only the specificity of the task of interpreting these specific texts will require that theological hermeneutics ultimately encompass philosophical hermeneutics and transform it into its own *organon.* . . . Nothing is more able to reveal the "ex-centric" character of theology than the attempt to "apply" to it the general categories of hermeneutics.[65]

This is as clear an articulation of the proposed relationship as one could hope to find. It reproduces the dialectics of mutual inclusion between truth and method on a different plane, with the concentration on textuality acting as a buffer between the universal claims of philosophical hermeneutics and the universal claims of theology. Of course Ricoeur, first and foremost a philosopher, will begin with what is most familiar, which is to use his hermeneutics as a method. Yet before he even begins to deploy it, he is already making space for the inevitable "ex-centricity" of theology. Frei insists that theology must bend philosophical concepts to its own ends, and this is precisely what Ricoeur's project articulates. Biblical narrative for Ricoeur is not simply "a regional instance of the universally valid pattern of interpretation," as Frei portrays it, and the very attempt to make it such an instance serves mainly to prove that point. Ricoeur argues that theological hermeneutics "presents features that are so original that the relation is gradually inverted."[66] He is keenly aware that while Scripture is an instance of a text for the perusal of philosophical hermeneutics, so too philosophical hermeneutics is itself a theory of understanding at the disposal of theology. Philosophical hermeneutics has neither the first nor the last word in the process, but is nonetheless a necessary moment in understanding the biblical text. These sacred texts must pass through the philosophical detour of being read and engaged as the texts that they are before the entire project can be appropriated theologically.

It was noted above that Ricoeur's critical supplementation of Gadamer emphasizes four aspects of textuality. First, the passage from *speech* to *writing* incorporates distanciation into the very constitution of a text, allowing the discourse to span history and come to us. Second, there is a *structure* to texts that is different from the free play of discourse, and requires an explanatory moment within the process of understanding. Third, allowing the "world of the text" (the reference of the entire text) to unfold shifts the focus away from the psychological intention of the author *behind* the text to the projection of a world *in front of* the text. Finally, the text mediates the reader's self-understanding by subordinating the self to the "matter of the text," allowing the very reader to become one more element of the interpretation. Since both Gadamer and Frei share the same desire to protect tradition from being overwhelmed by critical methods, let us see if Ricoeur's attention to textuality can provide the same critical supplementation to Frei's theology of *sensus literalis* that it did for Gadamer's hermeneutics of tradition.

If theology is to be centered around the *sensus literalis* of Scripture, as Frei suggests, then it must be acknowledged that what is being dealt with is a *text*. It may be a unique text that bends categories to it own ends, but those categories must be articulated before they can be appropriated. Ricoeur's philosophical hermeneutics enables theology to recognize how text differs in form from verbal discourse, and provides us with "a warning not to be too quick to construct a theology of the Word which does not include, from the outset and as its very principle, the passage from speech to writing."[67] A vast array of symbols and signs have carried the Christian tradition down to the present day, and these are constantly undergoing a process of interpretation. Moreover, textual interpretation is at the very core of the Christian message, in that a hermeneutic of the Old Testament "is implied by the proclamation that Jesus is the Christ."[68] But is this not to treat sacred Scripture as just one more instance of writing among many? Ricoeur concedes this point, but argues that whatever it is that makes Scripture unique, "it is nothing that belongs to the relation between speech and writing as such."[69] It is as true for Scripture as for any other text that it is the distanciation of writing that allows Scripture to be passed down through history to us. This is not an external constraint on what Scripture is allowed to *say,* but rather a close analysis of how it is *said,* and more importantly, *written.*

The canon of Scripture presents an unparalleled example of the necessity of the explanatory moment in discerning the *structure* of a text. Because the Scripture is simultaneously a single text, a pair of texts (the Old and New Testaments), and a collection of dozens of texts, it is already a unique case. Ricoeur's primary point here is that "[t]he 'confession of' faith' which is expressed in the biblical documents is inseparable from the forms of discourse there."[70] The multiplicity of texts yields a multiplicity of forms, that is, prophetic, mythic, historical, hymnic, narrative, a point that Tracy aptly made in his argument for the necessity of engaging hermeneutics. Readings that acknowledge the interplay and tensions between the various forms of Scripture will perhaps constitute a fourth version of *sensus literalis.* To Frei's list of metaphysical, literary, and sociological versions, we might now add hermeneutic. The hermeneutic version would take the biblical texts as seriously as the other versions, not subordinating them to "foreign" theories of meaning, but would be characterized by its increased attention to the forms of discourse that constitute the sacred text. Frei wants the special "character" of the biblical texts to shape our understanding of them, but Ricoeur would insist that we cannot do that until we determine what that character *is,* and this can be achieved only by passing through the detour of the objectifying, distanciating moments of textual hermeneutics.

Whether the hermeneutic version of *sensus literalis* represents a stretching or a breaking of the term depends largely on how the third and fourth aspects of textuality are understood. Frei accuses Ricoeur of reducing Jesus to a mere exemplar, a general form of being-in-the-world that discloses possibilities for us. But this is not implied by Ricoeur's hermeneutics: "the first task of hermeneutics is not to proceed immediately to a decision on the part of the reader, but to allow the world or being which is the 'issue' of the biblical text to unfold."[71] The biblical text *as a whole* discloses possibilities for living in a world that has been created by God and redeemed by a living Christ. The testimony of the Gospels, the theological reflections of Paul, the praises and lamentations of the psalmist, all work together to disclose possible worlds. The theological implications are enormous. One no longer searches for the inspired intention of the author, but rather sees revelation as "a trait of the biblical *world*."[72] It is at this point that theological hermeneutics reverses its relationship to philosophical hermeneutics. Scripture opens up a world in which God is active as Creator and Redeemer, and Ricoeur emphasizes that "'God' does not function as a philosophical concept." The God that is disclosed in Scripture, and given a special *density* in the person of Christ, escapes the grasp of philosophy, literature, or history, "at once the coordinator of these varied discourses and the index of their incompleteness."[73] All partial discourses, of which philosophical hermeneutics with its claims of "belonging" and "dependence" is one, are now *appropriated* by theological hermeneutics and positioned within the biblical world. But the text must be read *as a text* before this world can be disclosed.

Finally, there is the question of the subject. Frei lumps Ricoeur in with those mediating theologians who subordinate Scripture to their own philosophical or ethical convictions. But Ricoeur is mystified by such accusations, since the hermeneutic notion of *play* and the psychological notion of "*illusions of subjectivity*" necessarily imply that the subject is *not* the master of the interpretive process, but is in fact one of the things interpreted. In engaging the matter of the biblical text, "a *critique* of the illusions of the subject must be included in the very act of 'self-understanding' in the face of the text."[74] To simply project one's own preconceptions onto the text would be to deny the self-dispossession that is part of textual distanciation, and as such would not engage the matter of the text at all. For Ricoeur the "hermeneutics of suspicion" is not something used to discredit the biblical text, but is instead turned against the reader, whose illusions and prejudgments can "impede our letting the world of the text to be."[75] A mastering subject is not only bad theology, it's bad hermeneutics.

Ricoeur's sensitivity to the integrity of theology is no mere stylistic move—although his appreciation of genre has no doubt sensitized him to the dangers of confusion—but comes from a genuine appreciation for the limits of philosophy. He explains, "faith is indeed the limit of all hermeneutics, while at the same time standing as the nonhermeneutical origin of all interpretation. . . . The thematic of faith eludes hermeneutics and attests to the fact that the latter has neither the first nor the last word."[76] Hermeneutics is not a self-founding project that can encompass all of human existence. Indeed, Ricoeur argues that an engagement of theology by hermeneutics can protect hermeneutics from precisely this kind of "hubris" that was characteristic of the *cogito* philosophies.[77] This protection is reciprocal. Hermeneutics, while acknowledging faith as its "non-hermeneutical origin," nonetheless insists that "biblical faith cannot be separated from the movement of interpretation that raises it to the level of language."[78] This protects theology from any triumphalist temptation. Having stood apart from the battle between modernity and postmodernity, the theologian could declare all foundational claimants to be pretenders and proceed to reassert theology's claim to primacy, "assigning to biblical faith a cryptophilosophical function."[79] Hermeneutic awareness of the fragility of a faith that is transmitted through history via a network of symbols restores a humility appropriate to recipients of a freely given gift.

RICOEUR'S DOUBLE LIFE

Ricoeur's respect for the distinction between philosophy and theology manifests itself most clearly in how he organizes his publications. He has led a "double life" in his published work, having been inspired by Karl Barth not to mix philosophical and theological reflection.[80] His contributions to scriptural exegesis and biblical studies are never published in the same volume as his philosophical work.[81] He makes every effort not to colonize theology, and is equally committed to avoiding the opposite error. The clearest example of this double life can be seen in his editing choices for *Oneself as Another*. The book is based on his Gifford Lectures, and it is a rule of these lectures that there be two given on "natural theology." Ricoeur eliminated these two studies from the final publication and published them elsewhere, "in order to keep the promise I have made to myself not to mix the philosophical and the theological."[82] Ricoeur is aware that some have found this practice "regrettable,"[83] and that this double life opens him to accusations of inconsistency, but he prefers that to "confusionism."[84]

The most important advantage of Ricoeur's double life is that his *own* attempts at biblical interpretation need not be taken as the paradigm for the appropriation of hermeneutics by theology. He makes no claim to professional expertise in this area, referring to himself as "an amateur of enlightened exegesis." As Levinas once called himself a *talmudiste du dimanche*, so too might Ricoeur take on the label of "weekend exegete." His exegetical efforts are but one of many ways that philosophical hermeneutics might be appropriated by a biblical faith, and as Ricoeur is a philosopher by profession, they are not even an example of a truly *theological* appropriation. But these works are entirely separate because of his double life. Frei may well be correct that Ricoeur's various essays on biblical interpretation are well intentioned but theologically unsound. Even if one were to extend this further (which would be unwise) and declare all of Ricoeur's work on biblical exegesis worthless, it would still not address Ricoeur's more substantial contribution in hermeneutics precisely because Ricoeur has so carefully kept the two separate.

I would suggest that productive appropriation of Ricoeur's hermeneutics into theology is in the hands of those whose theological sympathies lay with Frei and Lindbeck. Both Ricoeur and the postliberals, unlike Tracy, operate in the theological shadow of Karl Barth, and thus tend to concentrate more on the *integrity* of theological discourse rather than on its perceived *relevance* to the wider public. The sticking point at present is the curious fact that the postliberals have chosen to operate in the *philosophical* shadow of Ludwig Wittgenstein, who seems a poor choice as a partner for working out Barth's richly dialectical and historically grounded theology. Wittgenstein, who expressed great hostility for the "arrogance" of Barth's verbal "gesticulating"[85] and whose logico-grammatical approach to the philosophy of language, valuable though it is, is almost entirely lacking in appreciation for the importance of tradition and narrative, concepts dear not only to Barth's theology, but also to Frei's. The postliberals can certainly appropriate Wittgenstein's "language game" as a model to protect the tradition of *sensus literalis* in their cultural linguistic approach to theology, but only at the cost of sealing off theological discourse. It is indeed hard to imagine a more dialectical theologian being interpreted through the lens of a less dialectical philosopher. And indeed, everything about the language of ad hoc and the overt suspicion with which Frei confronts hermeneutics indicates that this sealing off is a feature of the postliberal program rather than a bug.

In concluding part 1, I should note that my talk of a "postliberal program" is heuristic at best, and not meant to caricaturize a complex group of theologians for whom I have a great deal of not only respect but affinity. Paul DeHart's *The Trial of the Witnesses* gives a clear and penetrating narrative of the development of what came to be called postliberalism, as well as its *Wirkungsgeschichte* in recent years, noting, "So those theologians active today who can be conceived in one way or another as sympathetic to the world of ideas of Frei and Linbeck . . . simply cannot be grouped together as developing a common methodological agenda." DeHart invokes the analogy of a river delta that has many less distinct streams running off from the main river of Frei and Lindbeck.[86]

The role of postliberalism in these first two chapters has been twofold: (1) it has been postliberals such as Frei, Lindbeck, Placher, and Hauerwas who have offered the most trenchant criticisms of the revisionist theology that has become associated not only with Tracy but with Ricoeur; (2) Frei's combative engagement with and ultimate dismissal of Ricoeur's hermeneutics has led to all the many streams of the postliberal delta ignoring Ricoeur's philosophy together. It is indeed ironic that Frei's followers, who are closely identified with the role of narrative in theology, follow him in rejecting the very philosopher who not only shares their Christian convictions, but will also go on to develop a rigorous philosophy of narrative and its role in constituting human identity.

Theology has always needed and still needs philosophical partners in its attempt to express its conceptual content in any coherent way, but these partners must be chosen with care. The Anglo-Analytic tradition of philosophy as a whole is unlikely to produce suitable partners because it is steeped in the Cartesian method of radical doubt.[87] If theology adopts a conceptual vocabulary that greatly privileges doubt over belief—a system that is strongly biased toward the notion that disbelieving any given truth claim is more rational that believing it—then theology will operate in a perpetual defensive crouch, always defending why any Christian belief is warranted. Nor is postmodern philosophy likely to be a better partner, *pace* the Radical Orthodoxy movement. While it is a suitable ally of convenience in exposing the inconsistencies of modernity, on the issue of doubt it is better called *hypermodern* philosophy, consistent enough to turn the critical modern gaze on modernity itself.

Interpreters of Barth might find it more productive to engage a philosophy that is not biased against tradition, but still manages to incorporate the critical moment that is the legacy of modernity. In Ricoeur, we find a philosopher who shares not only Barth's Christian *faith,* but also his background in the Reformed tradition, dialectical method, appreciation of narrative, and concern for the integrity of both philosophy and theology. With a "critical supplementation" to Frei's theology of *sensus literalis,* a supplementation that enables theology to keep the claims of philosophical hermeneutics at arm's length without rejecting them, the way is open for such engagements.

Part Two   Detour

The second part of this book comprises three chapters that follow the pattern of Ricoeur's narrative arc: prefiguration, configuration, refiguration. But the three chapters as a whole are a critical detour through Ricoeur's philosophical hermeneutics, which will return in the third part to an enriched theological discourse. Chapter three establishes the structure of the critical arc by following Ricoeur through a series of detours: from existentialism through phenomenology to hermeneutics, from Gadamer's hermeneutics through Habermas's critical theory to Ricoeur's own "critical" hermeneutics, from a hermeneutics of symbols through semiotics and structuralism to a hermeneutics of metaphor and narrative, and a detour through analytic philosophy to the hermeneutics of the self. These four critical arcs combine to form the detour in a much larger arc that originates in Ricoeur's project on the philosophy of the will and ends in the mature reflection on identity in *Oneself as Another*.

The fourth and fifth chapters pick up the thread from the analytic detour, inscribing it into yet another arc. Ricoeur's detour through analysis is also a means of establishing a *descriptive* approach to the self in the first four studies of *Oneself as Another*. The middle moment (the detour) in this arc is *narration*, and the fourth chapter both presents Ricoeur's "threefold mimesis" model of the narrative arc and itself acts as the *narrative* detour that leads from *description* to *prescription*. The fifth chapter is the return, an overview of Ricoeur's little ethics, which is itself organized by the critical arc: a detour from the *ethical aim* through the *moral norm* to *practical wisdom*. There are thus two threads of a single pattern that wind their way through this part. Ricoeur's pattern of detour and return will be explained by engaging the mechanics of the critical and narrative arcs, and demonstrated by engaging the application of those arcs to his hermeneutics of the self.

This Detour will find its Return in the third part as Ricoeur himself becomes a detour for the theology, and particularly the theological anthropology, of Karl Barth. Among the concepts that will be deployed are the critical and narrative arcs, the theory of narrative identity, the distinction of sameness and selfhood, and the mutual solicitude of Self and Other that is part of the ethical aim.

3

Prefiguration:
The Critical Arc and Descriptive Identity

THE PHENOMENOLOGICAL DETOUR

Perhaps the best known of all the many metaphors surrounding Ricoeur's work is that of the "graft," in the sense that hermeneutics is grafted onto phenomenology.[1] This is a metaphor rich in resonance, harkening back to the apostle Paul's characterization of the Gentiles as being "grafted" onto the tree of Israel.[2] I would like to explore the extent to which Ricoeur's characterization of his hermeneutics is accurate. Jean Greisch has pointed out that Ricoeur also claims that hermeneutics subverts phenomenology, and wonders whether we can speak of both a graft and a subversion and still be referring to the same relationship.[3]

We can begin with Ricoeur's own description of his philosophy in terms of its three major lines of influence: "it stands in the line of a *reflexive* philosophy; it remains within the sphere of a Husserlian *phenomenology*; it strives to be a hermeneutical version of this phenomenology."[4] At first glance, this would seem to reinforce the metaphor of the graft, at least insofar as Husserl is the only influence that is mentioned by name; Ricoeur's phenomenology is first and foremost Husserlian, and hermeneutics enters only in an adjectival form, modifying phenomenology. However, the influence that is given pride of place, the line of *reflexive* philosophy that goes from Descartes through to

Jean Nabert, seems to imply that phenomenology, in whatever form, is first related to reflexive philosophy. One need not stop there; Ricoeur's list of productive conversation partners outside these three lines (e.g., Freud, Hegel, Schelling, Spinoza, Aristotle) is too long to list exhaustively. But there is another figure, less a conversation partner than a deep influence, who might enable us to account better for Ricoeur's itinerant movement among the reflexive, phenomenological, and hermeneutic versions of philosophy. That figure is Ricoeur's great mentor, Gabriel Marcel, with whom he has maintained a relationship of *creative fidelity*.

Gabriel Marcel

Ricoeur's relationship with Marcel spanned forty years, from the time of Ricoeur's *agrégation* at the Sorbonne in 1934 to Marcel's death in 1973, and Ricoeur was in regular contact with Marcel throughout that entire time. He attended the famous "Friday evenings," a very popular informal discussion group in Marcel's home, which were for Ricoeur "a kind of discussion that was entirely lacking at the Sorbonne."[5] Ricoeur felt that it was this exposure to open, vibrant debate that gave him "the courage to try to do philosophy and to do it in a situation assumed polemically,"[6] and inspired him to host his own discussion group when he took up his position in Strasbourg. Marcel was Ricoeur's personal friend as well as intellectual mentor, and helped shape Ricoeur's intellectual disposition in a way that emphasized participation and the embodiment of the human person. By nature, Ricoeur always "needed order," and it was Marcel who continually strove to temper Ricoeur's "systematic spirit," fearing that Ricoeur himself would fall victim to what Marcel called the "spirit of abstraction."[7] I would like to focus on the spirit of abstraction and the related practice of *réflexion seconde*, for it is this philosophical mode that most strongly links Marcel and Ricoeur.

THE SPIRIT OF ABSTRACTION

The feature of Marcel's philosophy that best encapsulates his intellectual sensibilities is his battle against the spirit of abstraction. For Marcel, the spirit of abstraction is in play whenever the conceptual structures of a person's thought begin to dominate the person who is doing the thinking. As he expresses it: "As soon as we accord to any category, isolated from all other categories, an arbitrary primacy, we are victims of the spirit of abstraction."[8] The primacy of concrete existence of the embodied person is so strong in Marcel that he characterized the "dynamic element" that runs through his entire philosophy as "an obstinate and untiring battle against the spirit of abstraction."[9]

The process of abstraction, which Marcel also refers to as *primary reflection*, "is, roughly speaking, purely analytical and which consists, as it were, in dissolving the concrete into its elements."[10] It is important to note that Marcel is not against abstraction as such, because to be so would be to embrace the romantic notion that we begin in some pristine state of concrete existence, completely uncluttered by abstractions. Marcel argues that "nothing could be more false" than the notion that abstractions are not embedded in our experience of the concrete. This process is necessary to achieve any coherence in our apprehension of the world; it is "a mental operation to which we must have recourse if we are to achieve a determinate purpose of any sort."[11] In other words, we need to abstract in order to think at all. There are dangers in this, however, for the process of abstraction can quickly overwhelm the concrete, embodied existence from which it is abstracting, detaching itself and becoming an independent system. As Marcel describes it: "it can happen that the mind, yielding to a sort of fascination, ceases to be aware of these prior conditions that justify abstraction and deceives itself about the nature of what is, in itself, nothing more than a method."[12] It is necessary to abstract, but equally necessary to acknowledge both that one is abstracting and that the abstraction is not the point of the exercise. To confuse the two is to initiate "a violent attack directed against a sort of integrity of the real,"[13] which results in a willful ignorance of the concrete reality before us.

One of the chief motivations for Marcel's "untiring battle" is the tendency of the spirit of abstraction to lead to violence on a large scale. In the face of such ossified abstractions, the most significant casualty is the human person, who loses her concrete reality and thus her dignity, making it easier to account for violence against her in terms of an overall conceptual "system." A person becomes *nothing more than* a communist, a Muslim, or, as is more common and pervasive, an "agglomeration of functions," be they psychological, physical, social, or economic.[14] Nor is this merely an intellectualist problem. On the contrary, Marcel argues that the spirit of abstraction operates at the level of the passions, and that "it is passion, not intelligence, which forges the most dangerous abstractions."[15] Having lived and worked in France through both world wars, Marcel had experienced the full range of the effects of the spirit of abstraction and the violence that tended to accompany it. This remains a salient issue today, when otherwise laudable terms such as "democracy" and "rights" slide toward a level of abstraction that robs human beings of their dignity.

Two pairs of dialectically related terms are operative throughout Marcel's work on abstraction, and indeed Marcel's work as a whole: Being and Having, and Mystery and Problem. Primary reflection belongs to the side of *having* and *problem,* and the spirit of abstraction is in play when one refuses to go beyond that point. For Marcel, a problem is a puzzle, an issue in which the person who addresses it is not directly implicated in the issue itself. A problem can be laid out in front of me to be examined at my leisure. A mystery, on the other hand, is something in which I am unavoidably implicated; it is not laid down in front of me, but rather encompasses me in such a way that I find myself *inside* it.[16] Philosophy concerns itself with mysteries and not problems, for philosophy addresses the issues that bother us or make us uneasy. It does so by problematizing the issue, treating it at an abstract level, which deepens our understanding of the issue and even its relationship to other similar issues. It attempts to identify the core elements of the issue and isolate particular facets for more detailed study. If philosophy remains at this level, however, it succumbs to the spirit of abstraction. Primary reflection, as important as it is, seeks to reduce reality to the level of concepts. It demands a coherent unity, and will seek to generate a system, that is, a technical solution for the issue at hand. The relationship between the person and the problem is one of *having;* the "answer" to the problem is something that is possessed, which is possible only if the person doing the possessing was not implicated in the problem. One does not *participate* in a problem.

RÉFLEXION SECONDE

To combat the tendency to succumb to the spirit of abstraction, Marcel proposes a constant push from the abstract back to the concrete, the "resolutely concrete mode of thinking" that he refers to as "secondary reflection" (*réflexion seconde*).[17] Secondary reflection is a doubling back, a re-collection of the original situation in which the problem arose. Primary reflection works at the level of the abstract, but secondary reflection acts as a *reflection on* the act of primary reflection, and reaffirms that the abstract "problem" arose in the context of an existential mystery. A so-called intellectual problem is not merely intellectual and thus is not merely a problem; to treat an existential question in the abstract without going back to the concrete is to succumb to the spirit of abstraction. Secondary reflection identifies primary reflection as the useful tool that it is, but does not allow it to "universalize its own limited horizon."[18] The moment of abstraction is not negated in this process, but rather is affirmed as a necessary moment in the quest for the concrete. "It is only by going through and beyond the process of scientific abstraction that the concrete can be regrasped and reconquered."[19] The concrete makes no sense without abstraction, but abstraction itself is not real, so the only way to proceed is in a constant reflective dialectic that is employed "for the sake of the concrete."[20] This activity of primary and secondary reflection requires that the philosopher be in a dynamic mode of exploration, for the ground underneath is neither level nor solid enough upon which to erect a structure. This is one of the reasons that Marcel consistently resisted the label "existentialist" to characterize his philosophical work: "I suspect that the idea of existentialism implies a contradiction, for I do not see how a philosophy of existence worthy of the name could be an 'ism'."[21] The "ism" suffix is an indicator that one has succumbed to the spirit of abstraction. To the extent that Marcel would accept a label, he found "neo-Socratism" to be the "least misleading" because it preserved the dynamic process of interrogation that characterized his thought.[22]

This mode of primary and secondary reflection is the single most important dynamic that Ricoeur absorbed from his mentor, and it proceeded to shape the way he pursued his own philosophical research. It would not be quite accurate to call Ricoeur a "Marcellian" philosopher, but it would be more accurate than ascribing a greater influence to anyone else. This is not meant to diminish the impact that Kant or Husserl or Nabert[23] have had on Ricoeur, but rather to emphasize that Ricoeur appropriates their thought within a Marcellian pattern. The pattern of primary and secondary reflection manifests itself in Ricoeur's pattern of detour and return, although Ricoeur has taken Marcel's rather sketchy approach and given it more conceptual clarity and rigor.[24] Marcel's philosophy was always more polemical in nature; he judged that the spirit of abstraction was such a rampant problem that he devoted the majority of his energy to attacking it in all its manifestations. This led inevitably to an underplaying of the value of primary reflection, which Ricoeur felt impelled to protect. Regarding his relationship to Marcel's project, he remarks: "If I have moved away from his philosophy, it is not because of his deep convictions, but because of a certain lack, in him, of a conceptual structure."[25] From the beginning, Ricoeur felt that Marcel exaggerated the faults of the abstracting intellect, which led to a somewhat caricaturized version of primary reflection. Ricoeur thus sought out ways to achieve greater clarity and structure from the very beginning, and without abandoning the fundamental values of Marcel's philosophy.

There are four major "detours" that further this quest—phenomenology, ideology critique, structural linguistics, and analytic philosophy—and the effect of these detours is cumulative, so that the phenomenological detour has such an impact on the later detours that it is confused with the main road. This has led to an increased attention to those who "assist" Ricoeur in his detours, with a correspondingly decreased attention to why those detours are taken at all. The list of Ricoeur's partners in detour is very long, and there is no need to minimize the impact that each has had on his thought. And yet it is important to note the *pervasiveness* of Marcel's influence: no matter which philosopher or group of philosophers is in the foreground of any given detour, Marcel is invariably present in the background. Let us now turn to the first, and by far the most important, detour: the eidetic method of Edmund Husserl. Husserl was not merely the first detour, but also served to articulate what a detour ought to accomplish, and thus deserves a primacy that goes beyond merely being first in an ordinal sense.

The Detour: Husserl's Phenomenology

In the mid 1930s, at the same time that Ricoeur was coming under the influence of Marcel, he also discovered the work of Edmund Husserl. In fact, his first exposure to Marcel's work (*Metaphysical Journal*)[26] and Husserl's work (*Ideen I*)[27] happened in the same year (1934), and he refers to this as a "twofold debt" that he never ceases to repay and reassess.[28] By the autumn of 1939, however, Ricoeur was no longer either a student or a teacher, but an officer in the French army. In the spring of 1940, Ricoeur's unit was separated from the rest of its regiment: all were captured by the Germans, and he spent the next five years of his life in a prison camp for officers in Pomerania. The captives made every attempt to simulate a working society inside the camp, and through this Ricoeur was able to continue the intellectual life he had left behind. He read and studied the great German writers, Goethe, Schiller, Jaspers, and Husserl, and this intimate knowledge of German philosophy and literature played a large part in his becoming regarded as one of France's leading phenomenologists. By the time he was liberated, in 1945, he had translated Husserl's *Ideen I* in the margins of the book itself (there being no other paper on which to write), as well as begun his own extension of Husserl's analysis, which later became the first volume of his phenomenology of the will.

In his first published monograph, a comparison of Marcel and Jaspers, we find a clue to Ricoeur's agenda. In the section dedicated to *réflexion seconde*, under the sub-heading "*L'intuition réflexive*," Ricoeur criticizes Marcel's somewhat caricaturized view of epistemology, and suggests the following solution: "The works of Husserl could be of great help in fleshing out the rather narrow conception of intelligence that Marcel vigorously criticizes."[29] In other words, Marcel, in his criticism of the spirit of abstraction, which chastised those who did not leave the sphere of primary reflection, was himself guilty of not remaining in the sphere of primary reflection long enough. Any attempt to shorten the detour through the analytical mode of primary reflection ultimately weakens second reflection as well, and thus Ricoeur turns to the work of Husserl. But when it came to the actual publication of *Freedom and Nature,* his "eidetics of the will," he points out that "meditation on Gabriel Marcel's work lies at the basis of the analyses in this book,"[30] and he dedicates the book to him.

The central thrust of Husserlian phenomenology is a return "to the things themselves," a positive agenda that "bids us to turn toward phenomena which had been blocked from sight by the theoretical patterns in front of them."[31] The central method that Ricoeur takes from Husserlian phenomenology is the eidetic reduction, the suspension of all presuppositions so that the phenomena under investigation might be studied in their essences.[32] This process of reduction brackets out all metaphysical or empirical common sense, which allows the phenomena to emerge. This is a moment not of doubt, but of deliberate non-participation, which follows from the subject's understanding of her role in the constitution of her world, and her interest in how the constitution takes place.

However, while Ricoeur was in accord with the *methods* of Husserl's phenomenology, he was also keenly aware of the *limits* of those methods. He follows Maurice Merleau-Ponty's famous assessment of Husserl's phenomenological reduction: "The most important lesson which the reduction teaches is the impossibility of a complete reduction."[33] Just as Marcel approached abstraction by treating it as an indispensable method, but for all that only a method, so too Ricoeur is intent on maintaining that the phenomenological method (primary abstraction *par excellence*) is an indispensable method, but for all that only a method. This distinction between phenomenology as a method and phenomenology as an extension of Idealism is a core distinction that is operative throughout Ricoeur's assessment:

> To Husserl I owed the methodology designated by the term "eidetic analysis"; to Gabriel Marcel I owed the problematic of a subject at once embodied and capable of placing desires and powers at distance, in short a subject who was master of himself and the servant of necessity in the figure of character, the unconscious, and life.[34]

It is important to note that having such a twofold problematic is more Marcel than Husserl; a design that contrasts existence and objectivity is "completely foreign to Husserl," who instead seeks "the progressive determination of objectivity."[35]

It is not clear whether Ricoeur's bifurcation of Husserl into its "idealist" foundations and its "eidetic" method is fair to Husserl, or even possible on Husserlian grounds.[36] Ricoeur's tendency to downplay the transcendental reduction in favor of the eidetic seems to indicate that he is unwilling to take up the stand of subjectivity that is central to Husserl's phenomenology. In fact, he goes further and explicitly rejects this approach, arguing, "all our considerations drive us away from the famous and obscure transcendental reduction which, we believe, is an obstacle to genuine understanding of personal body [corps propre]."[37] No one could accuse Ricoeur of not having treated Husserl with sufficient rigor, but Husserl, like Marcel, often used a "seeker" approach to his investigations, which makes generalization difficult. Husserl's general tendency to deal in "small change" often goes against his more programmatic statements in the Ideen or the Meditations, statements on which Ricoeur relies to make his case against "Husserlian Idealism."[38] And yet Ricoeur is not indulging in selective reading. Unlike some who wish to divide Husserl's work into chronological phases, Ricoeur maintains that it is the same Husserl all the way along. He nevertheless divides up Husserl, though along different lines. Herbert Spiegelberg notes that Ricoeur's phenomenology was "emphatically a descriptive and even an eidetic phenomenology of essential structures."[39] The phenomenological reduction and the phenomenological constitution were appropriated by Ricoeur only in limited forms, while phenomenological idealism was rejected altogether. Spiegelberg's reading is supported by Ricoeur's own characterization of phenomenology as "first of all an art of bringing the description of experience to the level of eidetic distinctions."[40]

What is important for us here is that Ricoeur wished to make such a sharp distinction in the first place. From the very beginning, Husserl's phenomenology was being judged in terms other than Husserl's; the criticism was not merely internal but external, and this is at least partly because Ricoeur was working toward a phenomenology of human action (Merleau-Ponty having covered human perception),[41] and the reflexivity of the project ultimately (although not immediately) displaced it from the plane of problem to the plane of mystery. Since, according to Ricoeur's rendering of phenomenology's thesis of intentionality, "consciousness constitutes itself by the type of object to which it projects itself," and in this case the object is the human will, the problem becomes "singularly delicate."[42] The eidetic method, insofar as it is addressing the person, will ultimately need to be supplemented by a return movement, which is a movement not toward the constituting subject, but toward re-integration with the embodied, suffering subject.

The eidetic method of phenomenology is permanently integrated into Ricoeur's pattern of thought as a way of extending primary reflection to its limit, and thus acts as a corrective to Marcel's premature return to second reflection. This dialectical interplay between these two great influences on Ricoeur, with the methods of Husserl at the service of the project of Marcel, serves to shape each successive detour. As Ricoeur puts it: "it is precisely the questions suggested to me by a long association with Marcel's work that make me ceaselessly return to the work of Husserl."[43] Husserl's method does not generate the *questions*, although it is an indispensable tool for answering them.

In light of this, when Ricoeur argues that "phenomenology and hermeneutics presuppose one another only if the idealism of Husserlian phenomenology succumbs to the critique of hermeneutics,"[44] it is difficult to see how hermeneutics is being grafted on to phenomenology. The ease with which he separates out the "method" of phenomenology from the "idealism" implies that it is phenomenology rather than hermeneutics that is undergoing the process of grafting. In this sense, Ricoeur's phenomenology was not a "pure" phenomenology onto which hermeneutics was later grafted; rather it was an existential phenomenology that developed into a hermeneutic phenomenology. Or, to be more precise, if less elegant, it was a phenomenological existentialism (in Marcel's sense of existentialism, which stresses the embodied, participating subject) that developed into a phenomenological hermeneutics.[45] On this reading, hermeneutics was not grafted onto phenomenology, but rather the phenomenological method was *transplanted* from existentialism to hermeneutics. To cast it in terms of detour and return, Marcel's reflexive philosophy of existence was the original moment of belonging, Husserl's eidetic method was the distanciating detour, and the return to belonging was the enriched sense of belonging-to (*Zugehörigkeit*) and dependence-on (*Abhängigkeit*) characteristic of Gadamer's hermeneutics. In Ricoeur, the three moments are held together in the pattern of detour and return that was derived from Marcel's practice of secondary reflection.

ESTABLISHING IDENTITY

Phenomenology of the Will

Ricoeur's own work on an eidetic analysis of the human will was, by his own admission, an ill-conceived project from the start, but it achieved a great deal in spite of its failure to measure up to its promise. It also achieved a great deal *because* of this failure, which turned Ricoeur toward the issue of mediating signs, and finally to the reflections on time that made a coherent theory of narrative identity possible. The first part of the projected trilogy was *Freedom and Nature: The Voluntary and Involuntary*, with the second volume, *Finitude and Guilt*, being broken into two parts: *Fallible Man* and *The Symbolism of Evil*. The projected third volume, a poetics of the will, was never written, although some argue that the goal of such a work "has been achieved in subsequent works," most notably in *Oneself as Another*.[46]

To receive his doctorate, Ricoeur had to submit two theses: a smaller, technical work and a longer, more constructive "grand thesis." For the smaller thesis, Ricoeur submitted his translation of and introduction to Husserl's *Ideen I*.[47] In his introduction, Ricoeur set about separating out the "descriptive core of phenomenology from the idealist interpretation in which this core was wrapped." We can see the influence of Marcel here: Ricoeur's attraction to the system and order of Husserl's phenomenological method only goes to a certain point; beyond this point, that is, in Husserl's own idealist interpretation of what phenomenology could accomplish, Ricoeur could readily identify the spirit of abstraction at work. For the larger thesis, Ricoeur submitted what became the first volume of his projected three-volume *Phenomenology of the Will*, entitled *Le volontaire et l'involontaire*.[48] This first volume appropriated Husserl's eidetic analysis and extended it to the phenomena of affection and volition, but this was done within the context of Marcel's dialectic of problem and mystery.[49]

The second installment of Ricoeur's *Philosophy of the Will* was entitled *Finitude and Guilt*, which was in turn divided into two parts: *Fallible Man* (finitude) and *The Symbolism of Evil* (guilt). The first volume examined the ontological consequences of the dialectic between the voluntary and the involuntary that had been explored in *Freedom and Nature*. The constitution of personal identity is raised as an anthropological problem in terms of *fallibity*, prefiguring the discussion that will take place in *Oneself as Another* in terms of *capability*. Ricoeur demonstrates that the finitude of the human will accounted for human frailty but not human evil: "The phenomenology of the voluntary and the involuntary appeared to me to be capable of accounting only for the weakness of a being exposed to evil and capable of doing wrong, but not of actually being evil."[50] Ricoeur here continues to operate in a pure phenomenological mode, "bracketing" the actual performance of evil in the world of lived history. This topic was taken up in the second volume, and it was there that Ricoeur began what came to be known as his "hermeneutic turn."[51] The "evil will" presents a problem for the methods of eidetic analysis since the phenomenon of evil will always appears as represented through symbols, signs, and myths, and his decision to address this problem "contained the seed of what I would later call the graft of hermeneutics onto phenomenology."[52] This decision spelled the end of the *Philosophy of the Will* as originally conceived, namely as an eidetics, empirics, and poetics of the will, for it confirmed the suspicion that Ricoeur voiced in his "small thesis" on Husserl, that the "opacity of the *Cogito* did not in principle concern only the experience of bad will, but the entire intentional life of the subject."[53] It is in the *Symbolism of Evil* that he coins the famous phrase "*la symbole donne à penser*," and the symbol, which contains "a surplus of meaning," must ultimately be *interpreted* and not simply analyzed. This puts Ricoeur into the hermeneutic circle:

> "We must understand to believe, but we must believe to understand." The circle is not a vicious circle, still less a mortal one; it is a living and stimulating circle. We must believe to understand: never, in fact, does the interpreter get near to what his text says unless he lives in the *aura* of the meaning he is inquiring after.[54]

It is through his own work on symbol that Ricoeur comes into contact with Gadamer's hermeneutics, which gives him new and better tools with which to pursue his project.[55]

The Pattern at Work

As we saw in the previous chapter, Ricoeur fully endorses the Gadamerian emphasis on the *Zugehörigkeit* and *Abhängigkeit* of Being. But Ricoeur's unique contribution, his "critical supplementation," is to pursue the process of phenomenological bracketing to the extent that it is possible. The fact that the phenomenologist can never in fact achieve the full critical distance that the method requires in no way negates the value of the attempt; that the reduction is never complete does not imply that the reduction ought not to be as complete as possible. The "detour," the moment of critical reflection, in Ricoeur's detour and return pattern is a re-insertion of pure phenomenological methods into the hermeneutic process.

FREUD AND THE UNCONSCIOUS

Ricoeur's frank acknowledgement that the subject could not be transparent to itself led naturally to an engagement of Freud.[56] Ricoeur views psychoanalytic theory as the "other" of phenomenology, a falsifying instance of a place where phenomenology could not go. He read Freud as a philosopher of culture, bringing psychoanalysis into conversation with phenomenology and reflexive philosophy. Psychoanalysis is a regressive movement toward the *arche* of conciousness, while phenomenology progressed toward a *telos* of fulfillment. Neither was reducible to the other, and both were indispensable, and a "'conflict of interpretations' thus took shape in the form of an archaeology of consciousness opposed to a teleology of meaning, the right of each being fully recognized and respected."[57]

This "conflict of interpretations" became the cornerstone of Ricoeur's approach to his now hermeneutical phenomenology, his *hermeneutics,* because the ground upon which this conflict of interpretations takes place is that of language. Gadamer's hermeneutics stressed the linguality (*Sprachlichkeit*) of human experience, and Ricoeur points out that a reading of Freud leads to a complementary conclusion: "there is no emotional experience so deeply buried, so concealed or distorted that it cannot be brought up to the clarity of language."[58] Freud, whom Ricoeur labels a "master of suspicion" alongside Marx and Nietzsche, brought this hermeneutic of suspicion to his treatment of the human subject.[59] Were this hermeneutics given full sway, the acting subject would be obliterated by the competing desires that drive it. But while Ricoeur wants to emphasize the indispensability of such suspicion, it remains a detour through which any reflexive philosophy must travel. The suspicions raised by psychoanalysis strike so deeply that certainty is abandoned altogether. The most that can be achieved is *attestation.*

THE CRITIQUE OF IDEOLOGY

The paradigm case for the critical arc is the dialectic between the hermeneutics of tradition and the critique of ideology. What Ricoeur's detour-and-return pattern gains from Gadamer's hermeneutics is a consciousness of what the main road looked like before the detour began. Marcel's point of departure was our incarnate being, which resulted in a laudable emphasis on concrete participation, but which also resulted in an emphasis on the concrete *present.* In Gadamer's hermeneutics of tradition, the primacy of participation is deepened to include historical participation. The appreciation of "belonging to" and "dependence on" that is central to Gadamer's "fundamental gesture," to use Ricoeur's term, signals an affinity between philosophical hermeneutics and Marcel's resistance to the spirit of abstraction. This affinity is enhanced by what Ricoeur calls Gadamer's "critique of critique," which closely parallels Marcel's secondary reflection, which could be called a "reflection on reflection." However, Ricoeur's dissatisfaction with Marcel's downplaying of *abstraction,* which necessitated the detour through

Husserl's eidetics, also finds its counterpart in Gadamer's downplaying of the importance of *critique,* which necessitates a detour through Habermas's critique of ideology.

In his mediation of the dispute between hermeneutics and the critique of ideology,[60] Ricoeur presents the protagonists, Habermas and Gadamer, as esteemed colleagues and worthy dialogue partners who can converse as equals. He adopts a conciliatory stance, "to show that each can recognize the other's claim to universality in a way which marks the place of one in the structure of the other."[61] He continues this presentation right to the very end, where the final sentence calls for the two camps to remain dialogically linked, lest both become ideologies. This mode of presentation becomes more and more strained as the essay progresses, for he addresses the *work* of Gadamer and Habermas in very different ways. Ricoeur questions the *completeness* of Gadamer's hermeneutics,[62] but goes beyond that to question the *very possibility* of a critique of ideology that isn't simply a part of hermeneutics.[63] Gadamer's hermeneutics is addressed with the respect due to an esteemed colleague to whom Ricoeur is deeply indebted, even if there are some issues that need clarification—something Ricoeur can provide. Habermas is treated more like a talented but somewhat reckless graduate student who has overstepped his bounds. Ricoeur is constantly correcting Habermas's assumptions, pointing out where he has not thought the matter through sufficiently. He repeatedly implies (and sometimes explicitly states) that critical theory cannot stand on its own without hermeneutics, which is in complete agreement with Gadamer's assessment.[64] Yet whenever he emerges from analysis to a more general reference to the two sides, he is again extolling the importance, universality, and unique place of the critique of ideology.

Ricoeur critically engages three of Habermas's main arguments. In the first section of his criticism (interests) he immediately launches into a rather curt demand for the authorization of virtually *all* of Habermas's theses (there are seven listed in the one paragraph). After considering and rejecting potential empirical and theoretical justifications, Ricoeur points out that any analysis will ultimately involve hermeneutics. In the second section (critical social sciences), Ricoeur explicitly rejects Habermas's delineation of emancipation as a distinct interest that warrants special treatment.[65] He then proceeds to reject critique as a starting point at all, instead pointing to the necessity of a hermeneutics of tradition: "It seems to me that critique can be neither the first instance nor the last. . . . He who is unable to reinterpret his past may also be incapable of projecting concretely his interest in emancipation."[66] This sentiment is even stronger in the third section (distortion). Ricoeur, having raised problems for the transposition of Freud into ideology, now raises similar problems for transposing Marx into the present. Habermas's emancipatory call is for the restoration of the practical sphere of communicative action. And, as Ricoeur asks, "upon what will you concretely support the awakening of communicative action, if not upon the creative renewal of cultural heritage?"[67] This leads to a trap that Habermas cannot avoid. No matter which path he selects as his primary motivator, be it emancipatory interest, unconstrained communication, or an eschatology of nonviolence, hermeneutics is waiting patiently at the other end, asking: "Where did you come by this idea, and why does it motivate you?" Such answers can be found only in an appeal, no matter how oblique, to a tradition. This is a problem that "imperiously returns the theory of ideology to the hermeneutic field,"[68] a startling comment, given Ricoeur's repeated emphasis on Habermas's distinct claim to universality.[69] Finally, Ricoeur points out that both critique and emancipation are themselves traditions, which situates them firmly within the field of hermeneutics.

By placing critique as "neither the first instance nor the last," Ricoeur locates it as a detour within his detour-and-return method. Gadamer's hermeneutics requires a "critical supplementation" that can be supplied by an appropriation of Habermas's critique of ideology, but this does not work in reverse. The critique of ideology does not detour through hermeneutics, which would imply that it could appropriate hermeneutics into its own project, but rather *is appropriated* by hermeneutics, and is thus at the service of the hermeneutic project. Habermas's critique of ideology does for Gadamer's hermeneutics of tradition what Husserl's eidetics did for Marcel's philosophy of existence.

STRUCTURALISM

The centerpiece of Ricoeur's "critical supplementation" to Gadamer's hermeneutics of tradition is the move from linguality (*Sprachlichkeit*) to textuality (*Schriftlichkeit*), which emphasizes the positive role for distanciation. This eventually led to a thorough engagement of the various structuralist schools that followed the work of Ferdinand de Saussure, most notably his distinction between language (*langue*) and discourse (*parole*). Ricoeur points to five common features that appear throughout the structuralist debate.[70] The first is that language is an empirical object that can be observed and quantified. Second, the state of a linguistic system at any given moment is logically prior to changes within the system, with the latter always understood in terms of the former. Third, language is coherentist; there are no Archimedean points upon which language rests, and all terms depend on other terms for their meaning and cannot exist independently. Fourth, the linguistic system, composed of these mutually referential signs, must be treated as a closed system. Finally, this means that the signs do not "refer" to some extra-linguistic reality, but to other signs within the system itself.[71]

The consequence of such a semiological approach is that both the author and the intended audience completely disappear from the analysis of texts. The very notion of "intention," which reaches beyond the system, necessarily disappears. Ricoeur finds this move unwarranted, because "it was not as a hermeneutics of suspicion that structuralism appeared to me to question the notion of the subject, but as an objectifying abstraction, through which language was reduced to the functioning of a system of signs without any anchor in a subject."[72] Here we can once again see the Marcellian language of "objectifying abstraction" used in the pejorative sense. Nor is the subject the only loss resulting from this accession to the spirit of abstraction; also lost is a person who is addressed by the discourse, as well as the world of reference.

While the structuralist works with the smallest possible unit (the sign) positioned within the largest possible field (language itself), Ricoeur's Marcellian drive for a more concrete embodied experience leads to an investigation of language as it is actually used. Calling on Émile Beneviste's linguistic theory, Ricoeur seeks to move beyond a deadened view of language as a "taxonomy" of phonological, lexical, and syntactical elements to a living view of language in the "instance of discourse." With the move from language to the "utterance," the primary unit of language is no longer the word but rather the sentence.

Ricoeur proposes five points of his own that characterize this move from language to discourse: event, choice, innovation, reference, and subjectivity.[73] First, the "instance of discourse" is an actual *instance;* it takes place as an act in time, which counters the atemporality of the structuralist system. The second is a theme of freedom, of "choices by which certain meanings are selected and others excluded," which counters the constraint of system. Third is the "virtually infinite number" of new combinations available through these choices, as opposed to the "finite and closed collection of signs." The fourth point recalls the Fregean distinction between "sense" and "reference"; discourse "refers" to the world, although not always directly, and the move from the "(ideal) meaning toward the (real) reference is the very soul of language." Finally, in contrast to the anonymous system, there is a subject who actualizes the language, who chooses these new meanings to refer to the world. Hence the famous "4S" definition of discourse: *someone* says *something* to *someone* about *something*. What semiotics addresses is only the first "something" that is said, without considering the speaker, the addressee or the reference of the discourse.

Much as he did with Husserl, Ricoeur goes to great lengths to distinguish between the structuralist method and structuralists' own interpretation of that method:

> On the one hand, I was always very careful to dissociate structuralism as a universal model of explanation from the legitimate and fruitful structural analyses as they were applied in specific cases to a well-defined field of experience. On the other hand, I strove to eliminate from my own conception of the thinking, acting, and feeling subject everything that would make it impossible to include a phase of structural analysis within the reflexive operation.[74]

Here again, Ricoeur finds himself *between* disciplines, in this case structural linguistics and reflexive philosophy.[75] He maintains that neither can be reduced to the other, but this does not imply that he places the two on an equal footing. Structural analysis is a "fruitful" and "legitimate" application within a circumscribed area, but it is no more than a "phase" within the operations of reflexive philosophy. This detour and return begins and ends with Ricoeur; there is no longer any need to refer to Marcel or Gadamer as the origin points. The Ricoeur who was a hermeneut of symbols took an extensive detour through structuralism and emerged as the Ricoeur of the productive imagination as it is used in metaphor and narrative.

PREFIGURING THE SELF: THE ANALYTIC DETOUR

Having established the critical arc of detour and return, we are now in a position to understand its application to the hermeneutics of the self. In *Oneself as Another*, Ricoeur reconfigures the problem of identity, arguing for the reflective mediation of the self, and proposing a three step configuration: description, narration, and prescription. The first moment, description, necessitates yet another detour, and just as Ricoeur turned to Husserl's phenomenology for his detour through primary reflection in his philosophy of the will, now he turns to analytic philosophy for his detour through primary reflection in his hermeneutics of the self.

One of the key characteristics that sets Ricoeur apart from both his French contemporaries and his fellow hermeneuticists is his deep appreciation of Anglo-American philosophy, or, more simply, *analytic philosophy*. He began teaching on the works of Bertrand Russell in the 1950s, his linguistic detour was deeply influenced by the works of J. L. Austin and J. Searle, and his hermeneutics of the self is indebted to the work in semantics and pragmatics of G. E. M. Anscombe, P. Strawson, D. Davidson, and D. Parfit, just to name a few. Philosophers outside the analytic tradition are often frustrated by its "poverty" or "thinness" of examples, which seems to remove it from the concrete ethical and political fields of action, in turn leading to a sense that the work, while certainly interesting and impressive, is not quite relevant to the world that philosophy purports to address. Ricoeur, however, has always found that the "asceticism" of the analytic approach allowed for both a clarity and rigor that so-called continental philosophy often lacks.[76] To be sure, Ricoeur is no analytic philosopher, but neither is he a structuralist or a psychoanalyst. This does not prevent these fields from being productive detours:

> The detour through analytic philosophy is one more detour in a method which rests on detours. . . . I have always been very sensitive to the force of argumentation in analytic philosophy, which seems to me to accord completely with the great conceptual concerns that Husserl had and which phenomenologists after him did not always share.[77]

The detour through analytic philosophy is not cast as an attempt to heal some mythical analytic/continental rift, but takes place merely because analytic philosophy is the "richest in promises and results." It addresses the "great conceptual concerns" of Husserl, who was the original detour for Ricoeur, and is thus a natural choice. Once again, however, this detour is placed within the overall context of a reflexive philosophy: "*The recourse to analysis,* in the sense given to this term by analytic philosophy, *is price to pay for a hermeneutics characterized by the indirect manner of positing the self.*"[78] Just as the understanding of texts necessitated a long detour that came in the form of a thorough engagement of structural linguistics, so too the understanding of the reflectively mediated self necessitates a long detour that comes in the form of a thorough engagement of the analytical philosophies of language and action.

As this is the "descriptive" section of the "describe, narrate, prescribe" triad, and the aim of the description is to address a person's life, the first four studies are organized according to how we speak about persons and actions. Each study has "main characters," the primary dialogue partners that Ricoeur engages in his quest for a hermeneutics of the self. In the first, it is P. F. Strawson, whose exploration of "basic particulars" allows the "who?"

question to be answered in the accusative terms, specifying of whom we are speaking when we speak about persons. In the second study, the characters are J. L. Austin and J. Searle, whose "speech act" theory enables Ricoeur to explore the "who?" question in terms of who is doing the designating. In the third study, it is G. E. M. Anscombe and D. Davidson who are engaged for their theories of intention and action, respectively, which offer an "ascetic" description of action that makes no reference to a particular agent. The fourth study seeks to return to the agent, and as this is not a strength of analytic philosophy, Ricoeur returns to his more reliable partners, Kant and Aristotle, to show that the entire detour has been very productive in terms of the "what?" and even the "why?" of human action, but that ultimately it lacks the resources to return to the "who?" that is central to the investigation.

Studies one and two form a pair that revolve around the nominative (who?) and accusative (whom?) forms of the overall question of personal designation, with the latter taken first. Strawson's great work, *Individuals*, sets up the question by bringing persons into the basic categories of identifying reference. This is situated within the broad analytical trend of seeking precise, impersonal descriptions of all objects, including persons. The three categories of individualization—definite descriptions (the forty-third president of the United States), personal names (George W. Bush), and indicators (him, that one there)—can ultimately be compressed into the first category, with the latter two merely serving as convenient shorthand terms. Strawson builds on this with his primary thesis that there are only two "basic particulars" that cannot be avoided in the act of reference: persons and physical objects. This is radicalized in his second thesis, that physical objects are the most basic because a person is also a physical object and can thus be located within that class. Ricoeur's interest in this theory is grounded in its almost complete privileging of "sameness" at the expense of "selfhood": "I would readily say that, in *Individuals*, the question of the self is concealed, on principle, by that of the same in the sense of *idem*. . . . Identity is described as sameness (*mêmeté*) and not as selfhood (*ipséité*)."[79] We can see already in this first study how the triad of description, narration, and prescription is going to map onto the narrative triad of prefiguration, configuration, and refiguration. Description provides a prefiguration of selfhood, already looking to be configured by narrative.

The second study, still in the field of speech that designates, moves from the accusative "whom" to the nominative "who." Ricoeur characterizes this as "a move from a semantics, in the referential sense of the term, to a *pragmatics*, that is, to a theory of language as it is used in specific contexts of interlocution."[80] The analytic "partners" in this endeavor are J. L. Austin and J. Searle, whose theory of speech acts provides Ricoeur with a key ingredient for the constitution of selfhood.[81] There are two sets of distinctions that work in this respect: the distinction between *performatives* and *constatives*, and the distinction between *locutionary* and *illocutionary* speech acts.[82] Regarding the first distinction, it is the performatives that particularly interest Ricoeur, in that they "are remarkable in that the simple fact of uttering them amounts to accomplishing the very thing that is stated."[83] The clearest example of a performative is the making of a promise; the very act of speaking to make a promise accomplishes the act of having the promise made. This breaks down the common sense distinction between words and actions; in the case of performatives, words *are* actions. This paves the way for Searle's complication of the theory into a three-level hierarchy that comprises the second set of distinctions. The first act, locution, is simply "the predicative operation itself, namely saying something about something."[84] The second, illocutionary act goes beyond the categories of speech and reference to include the speaker of the speech act. Statements (locutionary acts) do not speak or refer, it is speakers who do this, so the illocutionary act "consists in what the speaker *does* in speaking."[85] For any locutionary statement, even one as simple as "this is a carrot," carries with it the implicit "I affirm that" which precedes it, which translates the simple constative into a performative. The two sentences, with or without the explicit affirmation, carry the same truth value. What is important for Ricoeur's purposes is that the "I" has been introduced, and indeed embedded, into the theory of speech acts, and moreover that the performative aspect of the speech act *necessarily* implies a listener. Whatever the type of interlocution, be it promise, affirmation, imperative, and so on, "utterance equals interlocution."[86] Once again we find in this a prefiguration. Just as Strawson's semantics pointed toward the sameness/selfhood distinction that is the second task of the overall project, so to Austin's and Searle's pragmatics prefigures the self/other relation that is the third task.

The third study moves from the philosophy of language to the philosophy of action. The ultimate question driving this detour is what a theory of action can teach us about the agent who acts. The answer, at least during these studies, is minimal, as indicated by the study's title, "An Agentless Semantics of Action." Because of the manner in which action theory ascribes action to its agent, that is to say, impersonally, it ultimately prevents any *self-*designation in the reflexive sense. Furthermore, because action theory limits itself to the narrow field of first-order actions, which isolates them from the "action-chains" that we call "practices," it prevents the higher-order categories of "good" and "just" to be predicated of actions.[87] Using the paradigm of basic action questions (who, what, where, when, why), Ricoeur describes the lack in terms of the capture of the "what?" by the "why?" which leads to a concealment of the question "who?" In other words, action theory address the what of an action in terms of its *cause,* that is, why the action occurred, which reduces the action to the level of a mere event. It is not even quite accurate to refer to action *as* action in this sense since it is isolated from the symbolic networks that would give it meaning.

Ricoeur refigures the discussion into two universes of discourse: the analysis of cause based on an impersonal ontology of event and the analysis of motive based on a hermeneutics of action. In the first universe, to ask "what" action occurred is to ask "why" it happened. This is particularly problematic when the prejudice in favor of third-person description is manifested in the practice of modeling internal observations (of desires, feelings) on the pattern of impersonal observations. This mode of addressing the "who" of the action in terms designed to indicate a "what" in terms of a "why" leads to the disappearance of the "who" from the theory of action. What was the "who" becomes but one more cause within a network of causes. The second universe of discourse is absorbed into the first. Because "relating an action to a set of motives is like interpreting a text or part of a text in accordance with its context," and the ontology of impersonal events depends on precise description, "the language game of action and of the reasons for acting is swallowed up by that of events and causality."[88] Ricoeur identifies this as a systemic problem: "It is perhaps due to the very style of analytic philosophy and to its almost exclusive preoccupation with description, as well as with the truth claims appropriate to description, that it ignores problems pertaining to attestation."[89] Ricoeur takes particular aim at the two figures he feels to be the strongest in this respect: Anscombe and Davidson. Both orient their studies of action around the notion of "intention," but Ricoeur notes that both privilege the *adverbial* form "intentionally," and treat the noun as a derivative of the adverb. The adverbial form lends itself to treating action as a "subclass of impersonal events," while the phenomenological usage of "intention-to" treats action with respect to its agent. He recalls the example of Augustine "intending" the entire poem while reciting each line, the very example that oriented his theory of time, to demonstrate the difference between the two. This "disappointing" lack of flexibility in the analytic approach to intentionality points to the need for a different ontology, "one in harmony with the phenomenology of intention,"[90] in order to move back to the agent.[91]

The fourth study concerns itself with the phenomenon of *ascription,* and the aporias that arise from ascribing an action to an agent. It is here that the "who" emerges from the "what" and "why" that had eclipsed it to this point. Revisiting Strawson's "basic particulars," Ricoeur builds upon them to elucidate what he means by ascription. This is key to Ricoeur's eventual development of his ethics, since the self that is the subject of ethics undergoes a shift in meaning, and the manner in which that self is referred to does not remain unaffected. Ascription is for Ricoeur a function of attribution. The two basic particulars of Strawson's theory, bodies and persons, are basic precisely because they are irreducible to one another, and Ricoeur is particularly concerned to emphasize the irreducibility of predication as it moves from bodies to persons: "The attribution of certain predicates to persons cannot be translated in terms of attribution to bodies."[92] But persons are *embodied* persons, and thus are unique in that both kinds of predicates, psychological and physical, can be attributed to them. It is also important to note that both types of attribution are to the *person,* not one to a mind and the other to a body. Finally, the attribution of predicates such as "intentions" and "motives" remains the same whether one attributes them to oneself or to an other. The interplay of the various facets of attribution is what Ricoeur means by the ascription of action to an agent, and he argues that it is such a "peculiar type of attribution that it calls into question the apophantic logic of attribution."[93] Ascription is not simply description. This once again necessitates a move from the semantics to the pragmatics of discourse, "centered on the utterance and open to the self-designation of the utterer."[94] It is "the agent's power to designate herself" that is inaccessible to "a simple attribution of a predicate to a logical subject."[95] Attribution is sufficient for referring to the *cogito,* but the hermeneutic self requires a more complex form of ascription. The analytic detour is nonetheless indispensable if we are to avoid conflating the anthropological and phenomenological aspects of the self: "the detour by way of objectification is the shortest route from the self to the self."[96]

CREATIVE FIDELITY

The critical arc is now in place. Throughout these detours we have seen numerous pairings of dialectically related concepts: existentialism and phenomenology, belonging and distanciation, conviction and critique, utterance and language, the self and the other. This corresponds strongly to Marcel's pairing of similar concepts: mystery and problem, being and having, primary and secondary reflection, concrete and abstract. This is not a surface similarity; indeed, it is precisely on the surface level that the two thinkers appear so different. But on the deeper level of ontology, the similarities are striking. Ricoeur posed the question to Marcel as to whether his relentless attack on the spirit of abstraction was an attempt to oppose "every attempt to 'problematize' the question of existence or being." Marcel replied that he was remiss in not having emphasized the "positive foundation" of his attack: "it is precisely on the basis of ontology, of a reflection on being, that this denunciation of the spirit of abstraction becomes not only possible but necessary."[97] Ricoeur, in his treatment of phenomenology, structuralism, critique, and analysis, is for the most part in agreement, but takes a more moderate approach. Rather than denouncing the spirit of abstraction operative in these disciplines, he separates out the legitimate use of abstraction from the ideological "spirit" and uses the abstraction for his own hermeneutic purposes. Ricoeur actually seems to *prefer* engaging those fields that most clearly succumb to the spirit of abstraction because they, in having pushed abstraction beyond its limits, give him the perspective required to know where to draw the line. In going too far, they provide assurance that he has not stopped short. Moreover, he emphasizes the productive aspect of abstraction: his dictum "to explain more is to understand better" emphasizes that the more thorough the primary reflection, the richer the secondary reflection.

The most striking convergence with respect to ontology is the role that "attestation" plays in Ricoeur's hermeneutics of the self. Personal identity, from *Freedom and Nature* through to *Oneself as Another* (and beyond), has always been central to Ricoeur's thought. Marcel similarly argues, "when I ask myself who I am and, more deeply still, when I probe into my meaning in asking myself that question," I have approached "the question on which, really, all other questions hang."[98] This question is taken up in terms of the gap between "objective identity" and the "felt quality of identity." This gap leads Marcel to reflect on the "manifoldness within the self," and the sense of "my past which, in a sense, I still am," themes that are later taken up by Ricoeur in his hermeneutics of the self. Selfhood is a theme that is dominant for both Marcel and Ricoeur, although it would seem that Marcel places greater emphasis on its participatory nature. But when Marcel contrasts the "witness" and the "onlooker" precisely in terms of participation,[99] and Ricoeur places selfhood, attestation, and ontology in an interpenetrating relationship in the closing study of *Oneself as Another,* we can see that at the "deep level of conviction," to recall Ricoeur's description, he has remained creatively faithful to Marcel all along.[100] And since Marcel himself argued that fidelity is real "only when it is truly creative,"[101] this is just the kind of fidelity he would have wanted.

Any treatment of Marcel's influence on Ricoeur would be incomplete if it failed to note that both men were not only philosophers, but Christians deeply motivated by their faith. In the published conversations between Marcel and Ricoeur, there is a fascinating moment when Ricoeur questions Marcel about the role of Christianity in his philosophy:

> Doesn't the expression "ontological mystery" really say too much for the philosopher, and not enough for the believer or at least for the theologian, inasmuch as you make no specific reference to the person of Christ as such? What do you think . . . When you take up the themes of hope and fidelity, aren't you exploring theological dimensions? . . . if the bond between "I believe" and "I exist" is constitutive of your philosophy, if it contains the principle for every refutation of despair, don't you have to accept the term "Christian philosophy?"[102]

Marcel accepts "Christian philosophy," only with the reservations one would expect: namely that what makes it Christian is the fact that the lived experience upon which the philosopher reflects is in fact a Christian experience. What is so fascinating, however, is not Marcel's response but Ricoeur's questions. These are the very questions that have been posed to Ricoeur himself over and over, both before and since these conversations.[103] It is as though Ricoeur is consulting his mentor one last time on how he might respond to such questions, or perhaps allowing him to answer Ricoeur's own critics indirectly. Both Marcel and Ricoeur are intent on protecting the autonomy of philosophy, but not to the extent that philosophy prescinds from reflection on the most important existential questions. Ricoeur goes on to suggest that it is precisely Marcel's "relationship to the Judaeo-Christian tradition" that separates him from Heidegger, who preferred the Hellenic tradition, and I would suggest that it is at this level, although in a different way, that Ricoeur finds himself in a curious relationship of proximity and distance to both Derrida and Levinas. Fundamental religious convictions, especially insofar as they are *lived* convictions, cannot but reverberate all through a philosopher's work, even if the effect is largely subterranean.

It is regrettable but all too common that great teachers do not live to see their students' greatest accomplishments, and this is particularly poignant in the case of Marcel and Ricoeur. The difference in their philosophical dispositions could be characterized in terms of *patience*. Marcel was impatient with the detour through primary reflection, mainly due to his fear that it would become a Siren's call that would prevent a completion of the philosophical journey, and he constantly urged a return to the concrete. Ricoeur is a much more patient and rigorous philosopher, and has always insisted on exploring the detours to the very last step possible. This patience is what allowed Ricoeur to make his series of consecutive detours, but unfortunately, Marcel passed away while he was in the middle of this series, and was never to see the return. His concerns about Ricoeur's engagement of psychoanalysis and structuralism indicate that he was worried that Ricoeur had finally succumbed to the spirit of abstraction.[104] However, we can now see what Marcel could not: Ricoeur's patience in moving from symbols through psychoanalysis to the structures of sentences and texts has resulted in the acquisition, and even the forging, of new tools with which to approach the problem of the concrete embodied self. This is a "return" in a double sense: first in terms of the detours taken, but more importantly as a return on the investment of a quarter century. From the introduction of "refiguration" into the narrative arc, through narrative identity and the "little ethics," to the concrete political reflections of *The Just,* of *Memory, History, Forgetting,* and of *The Course of Recognition,* Ricoeur has engaged in secondary reflection at a level of intensity that was inaccessible to Marcel because of his impatience with the detours. Ricoeur's "creative fidelity" to Marcel's project has thus resulted in a level of success that Marcel could not have envisioned thirty years ago, but it is nonetheless largely Marcel's project that has come to fruition. One could with some confidence affirm that he is very pleased with the results.

4

Configuration:
The Narrative Arc and Narrative Identity

In the preceding chapter, we established the dynamic of detour and return as central to Ricoeur's thought. The critical arc passed from a mode of *participation* (conviction, naïveté) through a mode of *distanciation* (critique, suspicion) to a mode of *critical participation* (considered conviction, second naïveté). We also established the notion of personal identity, stressing the embodied, active (and suffering) person, as a motivating force in Ricoeur's overall project. The work of linguistic analysis, psychological investigation, and other hermeneutic detours find their source in the aporias encountered by Ricoeur in his philosophy of the will, but these detours are designed to return to a richer account of personal identity: "It is a text, with its universal power of world disclosure, which gives a self to the ego."[1] This statement from the sixties is true of any text, but as Ricoeur increasingly realized, there is something unique about *poetic* texts in their power to mediate the self.

In this chapter, the task is first to establish another type of detour and return dynamic: the narrative arc. Ricoeur's theory of narrative is an extension of his theory of metaphor as an act of the productive imagination, with the added complication of temporality. The process of "threefold mimesis," with its triad of prefiguration, configuration, and refiguration, is set up by Ricoeur as a way of addressing the *aporias* generated by the phenomenology of time as it has existed from Augustine through to Heidegger. Our goal is to understand fully the resources of narrative, rather than resolve the problems of time or even evaluate Ricoeur's proposed resolution. This will lead to the second part of the chapter, where the resources of narrative are deployed in the *return* movement of the problem of personal identity. *Within* personal identity, however, there is another expression of the narrative arc: description, narration, and prescription. The second part of this chapter will address only the descriptive and narrative moments, leaving the prescriptive moment to the following chapter.

NARRATIVE PRECURSORS

Productive Imagination: From Metaphor to Narrative

While the structuralists work with the smallest possible unit (the sign) positioned within the largest possible field (language itself), Ricoeur's Marcellian drive for a more concrete embodied experience of language leads to an investigation of language as it is actually used. Recall that Ricoeur's critical supplementation to Gadamer's hermeneutics was organized around the movement from *Sprachlichkeit* to *Schriftlichkeit,* a move designed to provide the objectivizing distance of structural analysis and thus to inscribe a critical moment *within* the broader project of the hermeneutics of tradition. When engaging structural analysis, the movement is in the other direction, *beyond* the analysis of individual units of language (words) to the context of those words in the act of discourse. Or rather, the basic unit is no longer the word but the *sentence,* the field is no longer structures of language but *semantics of discourse,* and the primary action is no longer denomination but *predication.*

The move to metaphor was a natural phase in Ricoeur's progression, in that the structural analysis of signs (phonemes, morphemes, etc.) and the interaction of those signs provided tools that "worked" when applied to metaphor, but only to a certain extent. Metaphor pushes semiotics to its limits, and ultimately pushes *beyond* those limits, and thus provides the paradigm for how semiotics is to be used, that is, as a detour. *La métaphore vive* was the result of this investigation, and the translation of this title as *The Rule of Metaphor* is less than ideal; the reduction of the "living" aspect of metaphor to a "rule" goes against the grain of what the work tries to accomplish. Ricoeur later points out that despite the eight years that separated their publication, *The Rule of Metaphor* was "conceived together" with *Time and Narrative* and thus functions as a sort of prequel to his *magnum opus.*[2]

The key idea linking the two together is the "productive imagination," and it is the development of this idea that reveals that we are on our way back from the level of explanation to the level of understanding, from an emphasis on analysis to an emphasis on synthesis.

Ricoeur argues that the categorization of metaphor has been a puzzle for philosophers at least since the time of Aristotle. The Greek philosopher broke his theory of *Rhetoric* down into three parts: the logic of argumentation, the style of expression, and the composition of discourse. He attempted to strike a balance between the sophistic ability to persuade and maintenance of a direct reference to truth, emphasizing the "verisimilitude" provided by the role of logic. This left metaphor in an awkward situation, cast as a technique of emotional persuasion. As long as language is perceived primarily as an instrument of *denomination,* then metaphor cannot find its proper place. It is reduced to a mere trope that—by deviating from "literal" meaning, substituting in a word that is used "figuratively"—points to a resemblance between two literal expressions *without* expanding the meaning of either expression. There is no new denomination, so there is no semantic innovation, which leaves metaphor as a sort of linguistic shorthand, condensing the indication of resemblance into a single expression without remainder. Lacking any denominative function, metaphor cannot but be a merely stylistic device of persuasion.

But metaphor was also a part of Aristotle's *Poetics,* and there the simple denominative function of metaphor is assigned to a subset of metaphor: the simile. Here the emphasis is on the act of predication, and the "impertinent attribution" of a metaphorical utterance opens up possibilities for semantic *innovation.* It acts as a "miniature poem" that does not abandon the referential dimension of discourse, but only suspends *direct* descriptive reference. On this account, direct reference, in accomplishing its act of denomination, simultaneously conceals a deeper level of reference.[3] Suspending direct reference allows the poem, or the metaphor, to access "a reality inaccessible to direct description,"[4] and thus to produce "new logical species by predicative assimilation."[5] Ricoeur labels the faculty responsible for this ability to assimilate differences the "productive imagination."

This move from "deviant naming" to "peculiar predication," from the nominative to the predicative, sets the stage for narrative, which shares many qualities with metaphor as a work of the productive imagination. The basic unit is no longer the sentence but the *text,* the field is no longer semantics of discourse but *hermeneutics of texts,* and the primary action is no longer predication but *emplotment.*

We have noted how metaphor accomplishes its task through the process of impertinent attribution, which suspends the ordinary process of direct reference so that "metaphorical reference" can be liberated. In the case of narrative, "the semantic innovation lies in the inventing of another work of synthesis—a plot. . . . It is this synthesis of the heterogeneous that brings narrative close to metaphor."[6] The similarity is furthered by the fact that both metaphor and narrative accomplish their tasks according to rules. The innovation can be recognized as an innovation only if it occurs within the context of a recognizable structure (for metaphor, the sentence; for narrative, the plot). Metaphor brings a resemblance to the forefront through an "odd predication," while narrative synthesizes logically disparate events into a unified whole by way of emplotment, and it is the "change of distance in logical space that is the work of the productive imagination."[7]

Steven Clark contends the central premise of *Time and Narrative* is that "narrative may be analyzed in terms other than those proposed by structural narratology."[8] In other words, much as the reduction of metaphor to mere trope failed to do justice to the metaphor's capacity to semantically innovate, so too the analysis of narrative in terms of "structure" and "genre" fails to account for the semantic innovation of narrative. However, just as one must pursue tropology to the very end before one can emerge into the field of semantic innovation in metaphor, so too one must go through the stages of structural narratology before the disclosive power of narrative can be understood. But also central to *Time and Narrative* is the premise that time can be analyzed in terms other than chronology. As Ricoeur argues, "time becomes human time to the extent that it is organized after the manner of a narrative; narrative, in turn, is meaningful to the extent that it portrays the features of temporal existence."[9] We are still very much in the detour and return mode that has characterized Ricoeur's philosophy all along, but the detour through narrative takes the process one step further by entrenching the pattern within the theory of narrative itself.

Confessions and *Poetics:* From Time to Narrative

The critical arc moves from participation through critical distanciation to critical participation. As we saw in the previous chapter, it has many applications. What all these applications share, however, is a *receptivity*, a mode of understanding texts that have already been created. The narrative arc, on the other hand, is a *productive* arc, a mode of generating texts that others will receive. In the mimetic triad of *prefiguration, configuration,* and *refiguration,* the dialectic is now between living action (in time) and emplotment (narrative):

> [T]o resolve the problem of the relation between time and narrative I must establish the mediating role of emplotment between a stage of practical experience that precedes it and a stage that succeeds it. . . . We are following therefore the destiny of a prefigured time [m₁] that becomes a refigured time [m₃] through the mediation of a configured time [m₂].[10]

While metaphor and narrative both employ the productive imagination, the two most significant differences between them in this context are that the latter is *temporal* and refers to a *field of action*. Ricoeur takes as his starting point two of the most influential reflections on each topic: Augustine's attempt to "think time" in Book 11 of the *Confessions,* and Aristotle's analysis of *mimesis* and *muthos* in his *Poetics*. Here again there is a detour-return dialectic, and it is Augustine who stands as the main road. It is a detour through Aristotle's poetics that will help us think time with Augustine. It is not a hindrance that Augustine never broaches the question of narrative in his reflection on time and that Aristotle never broaches the question of time in his *Poetics*. Rather, it creates a "favorable distance for an investigation into the mediating operations between lived experience and discourse."[11] The final goal of the process is to demonstrate that the time-narrative relation, as expressed in the universal response of the poetics of narrativity to the aporetics of temporality, "presents a transcultural form of necessity."

The central theme of Augustine's reflection on time is the *distentio animi*. Augustine expresses great frustration in trying to describe the experience and measurement of time, lamenting, "I am in a sorry state, for I do not even know what I do not know!"[12] It is this sense of *aporia* that Ricoeur argues is part of the originality of Augustine. But the aporias exist within the more fundamental accomplishment of the *distentio animi*: to think time without any specific reference to "cosmological time," the space-time that is utterly indifferent to humanity. Ricoeur contends that phenomenological philosophy, for all its significant advances, "cannot be definitively removed from the aporetic realm that so strongly characterizes the Augustinian theory of time."[13] Augustine's accomplishment was in his struggle with the paradoxes, and this struggle has not ceased. It is Ricoeur's contention that the advances made by Kant, Husserl, and Heidegger have not done away with the aporias of time because these aporias *cannot* be resolved speculatively, but only poetically. It is in this sense that Ricoeur finds the philosophy of time, despite its advances, substantially unchanged since Augustine.

Augustine articulates a threefold sense of time, with the three "tenses" (past, present, future) organized in terms of the present: the past is made present through *memory*, the present is made present through *attention*, and the future is made present through *expectation*. In his reflection on his experience of reciting a psalm, Augustine notes how he is simultaneously expecting the upcoming lines and remembering the lines just recited even while he is attending to the line he is reciting. His explanation is that his action is divided (*distendur*), and that "man's attentive mind, which is present, is relegating the future to the past."[14] The soul is distended in the very moment of its intentional action. The linking of distention to the threefold present is a "stroke of genius,"[15] according to Ricoeur, who characterizes the achievement as follows:

> Augustine's inestimable discovery is, by reducing the extension of time to the distention of the soul, to have tied this distention to the slippage that never ceases to find its way into the heart of the threefold present. . . . In this way he sees discordance emerge again and again out of the very concordance of the intentions of expectation, attention and memory.[16]

It is the continual emergence of discordance from concordance that interests Ricoeur, because he finds precisely the opposite move in Aristotle, "an eminently verbal experience where concordance mends discordance."[17] The paradoxes that so frustrated Augustine open a gateway for the introduction of Aristotle.

Aristotle's *Poetics,* which already made its appearance in Ricoeur's examination of metaphor, figures even more prominently in his discussion of narrative. Two central terms are considered: *mimesis* and *muthos* (emplotment).[18] There are two points stressed from the start, a difference and a similarity. The first is that both terms must be construed "as operations, not as structures."[19] We are discussing the rules for constructing poetic art, not for analyzing it. Poetics is defined as the art of "composing plots," not understanding them after the fact. Ricoeur goes out of his way to stress this dynamic aspect because he will argue that the *act* of producing plots takes precedence over any kind of structural analysis. Secondly, mimesis and emplotment are related but still distinct, with mimesis being broader than emplotment. Mimesis is an "all-encompassing concept" in the *Poetics,* while emplotment is more narrowly defined as the "organization of the events," the imitation or representation of *action* in particular. There is a sense in which the imitation of action is accomplished precisely by the organization of the events; "the imitation of action is the Plot."[20] Thus Ricoeur, in his theory of mimesis, leaves a privileged spot for emplotment, but broadens the meaning of mimesis beyond mere emplotment.

THE NARRATIVE ARC

Mimesis$_1$: The Preunderstanding of Action

To consider mimesis solely as the province of emplotment would be to reduce it to its most obvious part. But emplotment, or the act of giving a plot, is an act that occurs not in isolation, but within a pre-existing world. Ricoeur identifies three areas where there is a practical ability, a "preunderstanding" in which emplotment can take root: structural, symbolic, and temporal.

MEANINGFUL STRUCTURES

To the extent that emplotment is in fact a form of imitation, it must be understood first in terms of the action that it imitates, which means that we must look for discernible structures in the realm of action. Ricoeur argues that the poetic act of emplotting requires a proficiency in using "the conceptual network that structurally distinguishes the domain of action from that of physical movement."[21] In other words, to raise our analysis from the simple descriptive level of sheer physical motion to the meaningfully descriptive level of *action*, we must avail ourselves of the concepts that allow such a transition: concepts such as goals, motives, and agents. The concepts enable us to address the "who," "what," "why," and "how" questions that make for meaningful description. Furthermore, all action takes place within a network of other actions, which opens up to the concepts of cooperation, struggle, circumstances, and so on. For any narrative to function, there must be some "preunderstanding" on the part of both the author/narrator and the audience that the concepts will be at play in the narrative. Thus any analysis or narrative must find its roots in the semantics of action, or, as Ricoeur puts it: "there is no structural analysis of narrative that does not borrow from an explicit or an implicit phenomenology of 'doing something.'"[22]

SYMBOLIC MEDIATION

Understanding the basic structures required to describe particular actions is insufficient if these actions are not placed within a cultural context, and it is this context that is mediated by means of symbolic conventions. Holding up two fingers might indicate a wish for peace, a proclamation of victory, a request for a table in a restaurant, or an attempt to purchase stock. Without symbolic convention, these actions remain unintelligible; it "confers an initial *readability* on action." He goes on: "If we may nevertheless speak of action as a quasi-text, it is insofar as the symbols . . . provide the rules of meaning as a function of which this or that behavior can be interpreted. . . . If, in fact, human action can be narrated, it is because it is always already articulated by signs, rules, and norms."[23] It is precisely these signs, rules, and norms that allow us to make *ethical* judgments with regard to action. We can get our ethical bearings from situating the action within a rule-governed network of symbols within which it can be described and interpreted. This network can in turn be expanded into a set of norms by which the action can be evaluated.[24]

TEMPORAL CHARACTER

Building on the first two categories, a conceptual network and symbolic mediation, Ricoeur advances a third category for the understanding of action: temporality. Recalling Augustine's reflection on the *distentio animi* and his privileging of the present, Ricoeur counters with Heidegger's reflections on within-time-ness (*Innerzeitigkeit*) and his privileging of the future.[25] Although a full engagement of Ricoeur's use of Heidegger goes beyond the scope of this project, we can still address the main thrust of the argument by considering how *Innerzeitigkeit* is expressed in terms of the "now" and the "day." In Ricoeur's reading, to be "within" time is to consider the *human* aspects of time prior to any *linear* representation of time. In our finitude, especially insofar as our being-toward-death (*Sein zum Tode*) orients us to the future, we are forced to "reckon with" time, to take time into account when projecting our ownmost possibilities.[26] When we consider the "day," we are not first and foremost speaking about numbered squares on a calendar or revolutions of the Earth, but rather a way of organizing our action, "a length that corresponds to our Care and the world in which it is 'time to' do something."[27] Similarly, the indexical "now" is always situated within the past- and future-oriented categories of "retaining" and "awaiting," and is thus something quite different from the "now" considered as an abstract instant in linear time.[28] Our preoccupation with the "now" can mislead us into considering it primarily, or even solely in terms of the readout on a clock, but that is to reverse the order of our Care (*Sorge*). As Ricoeur says, "It is because we do reckon with time and do make calculations that we must have recourse to measuring, not vice versa."[29] Our concern with time derives from the problems we encounter when considering whether we "have time" for something, or if we can make up for "lost time." What is important to note is first that temporality has made its appearance here as a concern for *human action*, not as a function of cosmological motion, and second that temporality is an indispensable category for describing action. Time is no longer prefigured as a linear succession of "nows" but as a necessary concern for our Care. This opens the door to the properly *narrative* accounting of time, not as an artificial arrangement of discrete moments, but as an order of configuration that "share[s] the same foundation of within-time-ness."[30]

Mimesis$_2$: The Configuration of Action by Emplotment

Configuration by emplotment is the key moment in the mimetic arc, mediating between prefiguration (m_1) and refiguration (m_3). Returning once again to Aristotle and Augustine, Ricoeur seeks to find in emplotment an activity that "makes productive the paradoxes that disquieted Augustine to the point of reducing him to silence."[31] To do this, Ricoeur goes not only beyond Augustine's reflections on time, but also beyond Aristotle's analysis of emplotment; at once introducing the narrative resolution to Augustine and the temporal problem to Aristotle. He maintains that Aristotle's model of emplotment is not "radically altered" by these "amplifications and corrections," although it is notable that he makes no similar claim regarding Augustine.[32]

There are three ways in which the act of emplotment mediates between the "preunderstanding" and the "postunderstanding of the field of action and its temporal features."[33] The first is its capacity to take individual episodes and transform them into a story. Ricoeur points to the prepositions *from* (isolated incidents) and *into* (a meaningful story) to emphasize the mediating function of a plot (*via* the act of emplotment). The second function of emplotment is to take the fundamentally "heterogeneous" categories *from* the conceptual network of action (and its symbolic mediations) that was outlined in mimesis$_1$ and to configure them *into a concordant discordance*. To put it more technically: "a narrative makes appear within a syntagmatic order all the components capable of figuring in the paradigmatic tableau established by the semantics of action. This passage from the paradigmatic to the syntagmatic constitutes the transition from mimesis$_1$ to mimesis$_2$."[34] Narrative takes from the semantics of action, which gives structure in terms of agents, goals, motives, circumstances, and so on (interpreted through cultural signs, rules, and norms), and synthesizes them into a unified syntagmatic order. The third function of emplotment, mapping onto the third area of prefiguration, is its mediation of the temporal characteristics of action, and this is where Ricoeur's analysis both "reflects" and "resolves" the Augustinian paradox of time. Emplotment reflects the paradox insofar as there is an episodic dimension to a narrative, a succession of events that follow on each other, as indicated by the tendency to recount it in linear form: "this happened, then this, then this, etc." This episodic succession, much like the interpretation of "day" or "now" in terms of chronology rather than of human care, draws narrative time toward linear non-"human" time.

Opposed to the episodic is the configurational dimension of narrative, which mediates between the events and the story in its entirety. It is configuration that makes the story "followable." The plot of a narrative "can be translated into one 'thought,' which we refer to as a 'theme.'" Themes, in this sense, are not atemporal, but are rather instances of narrative time. Configuration also gives an end point from which the story can be "seen as a whole, " a phenomenon especially relevant in the cases of "retelling," that is, in cases where the stories are already well known. Seeing both the surprises and the expected from the point of view of the end enables the apprehension of a "new quality of time," an inverted reading of temporality that goes against the linear representation of time as "flowing" from past to future. Configuration thus allows us to "grasp together" heterogeneous events to the degree that we can refer to them as "a story" that we can follow, which addresses the paradox of time that so frustrated Augustine. As Ricoeur puts it: "It is this 'followability' of a story that constitutes the poetic solution to the paradox of distention and intention. The fact that the story can be followed converts the paradox into a living dialectic."[35]

The dialectic of singular episodes and unified story is also played out at the level of *genre*. Configuring a plot is, as was the case with metaphor, an act of the productive imagination. Just as the impertinent attribution of a metaphor occurs within the grammatical rules of language, so too the particular innovations of a newly told story take place within a narrative schematic. These paradigms of emplotment come to us through a tradition of narrative configuration, and Ricoeur hastens to clarify that this is "not the inert transmission of some already dead deposit of material but the living transmission of an innovation always capable of being reactivated."[36] Any narrative paradigm that is referred to today—for example, epic, tragedy, comedy, novel, and so on—was originally generated through the innovative construction of plots that referred to earlier paradigms; the success of these stories, such as, for example, Sophocles' *Oedipus Rex,* ensured their persisting through time long enough to go through a process of sedimentation, the end point of which is the establishment of a narrative paradigm. We are thus the recipients of myriad narrative paradigms, which, "themselves issuing from a previous innovation, furnish the rules for a subsequent experimentation within the narrative field."[37] Narrative innovation, in the form of the production of a story, necessarily occurs within the tradition of narrative paradigms, but since this tradition is itself one of innovation, a story that creatively deviates from the paradigm displays an equally strong fidelity to the tradition on another plane.

Mimesis$_3$: The Hermeneutic "Application" of Emplotment

Mimesis$_3$, or refiguration, "marks the intersection of the world of the text and that of the hearer or reader."[38] Having analyzed emplotment from the perspective of the author of the narrative, Ricoeur moves to the question of the reader's role in emplotment. From there, he takes up the question of reference from where he left it in *The Rule of Metaphor*. Finally, he responds to the objections of "circularity" that might be leveled against the theory of threefold mimesis.[39]

THE ACT OF READING

To the extent that emplotment is the act of configuring narratives, it is an act of writing. But this creative act, this act of the productive imagination, needs a *reader* in order to come to fruition. It is in the interaction between the reader and the text that the "interplay of innovation and sedimentation" achieves its goal. The text is organized according to certain narrative rules, schematized within certain traditions, and the reader brings her knowledge of these rules and traditions to bear on the reading of the story. They act as guidelines for the reader, an instruction booklet embedded within the text itself that the reader must be aware of in order to enter into the play of the text. The breaks in the story, the innovations, the twists, are all absorbed into the reader's attempt to make sense of the work. The reader thus participates in the act of emplotment, and in the case of such disorienting works as James Joyce's *Ulysses*, "it is the reader, almost abandoned by the work, who carries the burden of emplotment."[40] The critical arc of interpretation is inscribed within the narrative arc at this point, as the reader goes through the critical work of *explaining* what is going on so that the narrative can be *understood*. To label *Ulysses* as disorienting is to say that the explanatory work is more difficult because the book is a creative variation on the genre "novel." The symbolic network is called into question, leaving readers embroiled in a conflict of interpretations within their own readings. The difficulty in *under-standing* what the text means is directly correlative to the difficulty encountered in *explaining* what is going on.

COMMUNICATION AND REFERENCE

We saw in the second chapter how Ricoeur's retrieval of Gadamer's "fusion of horizons" allowed him to develop his theory of indirect reference, and his very definition of refiguration relies on the Gadamerian language of the "world." Here he extends that theory beyond literary works in general to narratives in particular. Reestablishing the primacy of Beneviste's "instance of discourse," which takes the sentence as the primary unit of language, Ricoeur reiterates, "language does not constitute a world for itself," but rather refers to its "Other," the world.[41] Metaphorical reference suspends, by way of impertinent predication, the *direct* reference of discourse to the world, which opens up the possibility of indirect or metaphorical reference. When discourse becomes text, the complex of references is referred to as the "world of the text," where the world is "the whole set of references opened by every sort of descriptive or poetic text I have read, interpreted, and loved."[42] This, of course, flies in the face of the methods and practices of structural analysis, and modern literary criticism in general, where reference to the world is methodologically excluded. But Ricoeur argues that this is done by fiat, and finally ignores "the question of the impact of literature on everyday experience," which threatens to shackle the discipline in a restrictive positivism. Once again, the suspension of reference as a *method,* a detour that can more fully explain the structure of the text, is not the target of the objection; it is the expansion of that method into a totalizing textual theory that tends toward positivism.

Having established the transition from narrative to text, Ricoeur addresses the specification of *narrative* texts in particular, especially as they relate to poetics in general. A particular problem that is raised by the concept of "narrative reference" is the interplay between narrative fiction and narrative history. The entire second part of *Time and Narrative I* is taken up with the exploration of the links between fiction and history. Only history aims at having an "empirical reference" in the attempt to recount actual events, even if that reference necessarily involves the assembly of "traces," the documents and testimonies that the historian consults. Fiction makes no such claim. But Ricoeur argues that history's configuration of traces into a narrative format "borrows from the metaphorical reference common to every poetic work, inasmuch as the past can only be reconstructed by the imagination."[43]

Furthermore, fiction also borrows from history for its mode of configuration. Stories are told in the *indicative* mood, not the subjunctive; they are presented as a world that is or was, not a world that could be or might have been. It is central to the overall argument of *Time and Narrative* that there be an "*interweaving* reference between history and narrative fiction," and further that this interweaving take place within the context of temporality and human action.

Circularity: Vicious or Productive?

At this point Ricoeur launches a sort of preemptive strike, facing head-on the two most obvious potential objections to his mimetic theory: that it is either violent or tautological. The first objection accuses the narrative theory of forcing the form of concordance on an unformed discordance. The narrative configuration can fool us by offering some modicum of "sense" to the discordant episodes of life, but it does so at the expense of honesty and truth. Far from resolving the paradoxes of time, it merely paints over them with a coat of emplotment, rendering the discordance more palatable by hiding it from view. Ricoeur counters that this objection assumes that narrative is pure concordance and that human time is pure discordance. But Augustine's reflection on time involved a paradox that sprang from the confrontation of *intentio* and *distentio*. It is the conflict of concordance and discordance, not the absence of concordance, that produces the paradox. Conversely, emplotment, insofar as it is concordant discordance, "is never the simple triumph of 'order'."[44] To be sure, there are varying levels of privilege given to order in different paradigms, and the objection of violence stands as a useful, and even necessary, warning sign against unwarranted, false concordance in a given narrative. But concordance is not the sole quality of emplotment; dissonance, surprise, reversal, and so on are integral parts of narrative configuration.

The second objection claims that the narrative structure of configuration is already present in the first moment of prefiguration, that our experience as mediated through symbolic structures (of which narratives themselves are one) already contains this narrative quality. The configurative move is thus redundant since everything that was gained in the third moment of supposed refiguration was already present in the first moment of prefiguration. Ricoeur responds by pointing to the practice of psychoanalysis, where the analyst assists the analysand in unearthing repressed, conflictual, and otherwise problematic episodes in order to "draw from these bits and pieces a narrative that will be both more supportable and more intelligible." It is at this point that narrative identity begins to emerge as a concept, for Ricoeur goes on to remark:

> This narrative interpretation implies that a life story proceeds from untold and repressed stories in the direction of actual stories the subject can take up and hold as constitutive of his personal identity. It is the quest for this personal identity that assures the continuity between the potential or inchoate story and the actual story we assume responsibility for.[45]

How we go about narrating ourselves to ourselves is not contained within the episodes that are to be narrated. There is a pre-narrative quality to these episodes that enables them to be told, but the manner of the telling, which is a profoundly *ethical* act, cannot be predetermined by the content.

THE HERMENEUTICS OF THE SELF

Ten years after its publication in English, *Oneself as Another* has already become Ricoeur's most influential and well-regarded book. He has referred to it as "the summing-up of my philosophical career,"[46] while Charles Reagan praises it as "Ricoeur's most elegantly written, clearly organized, and closely argued book."[47] The title itself is carefully chosen, designating the convergence of "three major philosophical intentions": (1) "the primacy of reflective mediation over the immediate positing of the subject"; (2) the distinction between the two significant options for the construal of identity; and (3) "the dialectic of *self* and the *other than self*."[48] These resonances are not as apparent in the English *Oneself as Another* as they are in the original French *Soi-meme comme une autre*. A point-for-point translation, which would capture the meaning of each term rather than the meaning of the title as a whole, would read "Self-Same as an Other." While the accepted translation is superior for a number of reasons, it does give up the aspect of *sameness* that addresses the stability of an identity construed in narrative, as well as the starkness of "Other" as a word on its own. Here we will work with the first two intentions, leaving the dialectic of self with the other for the next chapter, which deals with Ricoeur's ethics.

The Primacy of Reflective Mediation

Ricoeur illustrates the first point, the *Soi* of the title, by pointing out that it is a commonality of natural languages to allow the "opposition between 'self' and 'I'."[49] The majority of the introduction is taken up with the proving of this point, and interestingly enough it is carried out in terms of a narrative. As would be expected from Ricoeur, the narrative takes on the form of detour and return.

Because the work as a whole stands in the tradition of reflexive philosophy, of philosophies of the subject, it is necessary to trace the development of that tradition. Ricoeur locates the beginning of the "philosophies of the subject" in the posting of the *cogito* by Descartes, with the detour being the shattering of the *cogito* by Nietzsche, with his own contribution being the recovery of a "wounded" *cogito*.

The tradition begins with Descartes, and while Ricoeur traces the line of development through Kant, Fichte, and Husserl, it is Descartes who stands as the paradigmatic figure. It is important to note that the "I think" becomes the very foundation, for it is the extremity of Descartes's claim that accounts for the "amazing oscillations" that the philosophies have undergone since then, ranging from its exaltation as the absolute foundation of all truth to its humiliation as an utterly illusory fiction. Descartes's personal experiment with hyperbolic doubt in the *Meditations*—carried to the point of imagining an evil genius who is actively deceiving him about everything—eliminates all that could possibly fall under the category of mere opinion. All that survives this radical process is the *cogito,* since even in these extreme conditions something must be doing the doubting, and this becomes the centerpiece of reflexive philosophy. However, the "I" is "a free-floating subjectivity,"[50] and if a pure subjectivist idealism is to be avoided, "the 'I think' must be divested of any psychological resonance, all the more so of any autobiographical reference."[51] There may be a thing that is doing the thinking, but it in no way resembles anything that we might call a "who."

While several figures have attacked the *cogito* throughout the history of the philosophies of the subject, none did so with more vigor, and ultimately more success, than Nietzsche. Ricoeur sums up his approach in terms of a single claim: "*I doubt better than Descartes.*"[52] Nietzsche actually succeeds in extending doubt beyond where Descartes was able to go, namely to the *cogito* itself. He hypothesizes that the subject may well be "multiplicity," that the ascription of a unified identity to the "thinking thing" is twice mistaken, that "*both the action* [of thinking] *and the agent are fanciful.*"[53] Ricoeur's particular contribution to this well-known critique is to locate it in language. Nietzsche was first and foremost a philologist, and his attack on the *cogito* is based on a "critique of language in which philosophy expresses itself."[54] Locating the "who" will involve a detour through linguistic mediation.

Ricoeur takes up this dialectic—posited and shattered, exalted and humiliated, *cogito* and anti-*cogito*—by pointing out that "it seems that it is always through a complete reversal of this sort that one approaches the subject; one could thus conclude that the 'I' of the philosophies of the subject is *atopos* without any assured place in discourse."[55] The indeterminacy of the "I," which can be located anywhere from world-grounding foundation to pernicious illusion, is precisely because it aims so high, "its positing is invested with the ambition of establishing a final ultimate foundation."[56] Ricoeur seeks to approach question of the subject from some other direction, without such lofty ambitions, and this provides the opening for the introduction of a hermeneutics of the "self." Having gone through the process of being posited and shattered, the *cogito* emerges "wounded," giving way to a selfhood that can only be the object of attestation.

The notion of attestation, and the etymologically related "testimony," proves to be a running theme throughout the work. Attestation is a form of belief, but it is an *active,* lived belief; as opposed to "doxic" belief, which is merely a lesser form of knowledge. "Whereas doxic belief is implied in the grammar of 'I believe-that,' attestation belongs to the grammar of 'I believe-in'."[57] Attestation can provide no guarantee of any other belief, which decisively separates the hermeneutics of the self from the foundationalism characteristic of the *cogito* philosophies. But it also separates itself from the merely verificationist criteria of identity that lead to a humiliated, shattered subject. Attestation can respond to suspicion only by offering a more reliable attestation; there are no external criteria that can be appealed to in judging between competing testimonies. What brings attestation into the center of Ricoeur's hermeneutics of the self is his thesis that "attestation is fundamentally attestation *of* self."[58] This more modest approach of reflective mediation does not offer the certainty of the *cogito,* but neither does it risk a spectacular failure under the attack of anti-*cogito* philosophies: "As credence without any guarantee, but also as trust greater than any suspicion, the hermeneutics of the self can claim to hold itself at an equal distance from the cogito exalted by Descartes and from the cogito that Nietzsche proclaimed forfeit."[59]

What is interesting about this mode of configuring the narrative of the *cogito* is that the mediating moment is one not of configuration but of *disfiguration.* The sense of *certain* unity must pass through the mediating moment of disfiguration before a humbler *attestation* of unity can emerge. As with metaphor, the literal, expected reference must be broken apart if metaphorical reference is to emerge. This is where Ricoeur comes into contact with Jacques Derrida and the field of deconstruction.[60] The personal narrative of an exalted *cogito,* of a self whose identity is stable because it is grounded in its rational capacities, was once a refiguration, having emerged from Descartes's configuration of identity. But this refiguration needed to go through a process of deconstruction, of *disfiguration,* before the "wounded" *cogito,* the attesting self, could emerge as a new refiguration. The circle continues with the wounded, attesting self in the role of a prefiguration of the weakly unified identity that is necessary to have any ethics at all. This wounded cogito goes through a new process of configuration in *Oneself as Another,* and it is to this process that we now turn.

Narrative Identity

In the last chapter, we traversed the analytic detour that worked as prefigurative moment in the hermeneutics of identity. From this series of detours is gained the tools to answer the questions: who designates persons, and who is designated? Who is the cause of an event? The self appears only in the answers to these questions, unlike the *cogito* that would be immediately posited. What could not be answered precisely in these detours was: who is the agent of action? Analytic theories of pragmatics could describe the what and the why but not the who, which paves the way for narrative identity. Again it should be noted that in one sense we are returning from a detour while in another sense we are embarking upon one. As a detour, the objective analytical sciences of semantics and pragmatics have functioned as a middle moment between the exalted *cogito* and the wounded one. In this way they are the culmination of the critical arc. But looking ahead, those sciences have functioned as *descriptive* moments that will eventually issue into *prescriptive* moments by way of the detour through *narrative.* Thus while it is the case that narrative identity is the "poetic resolution to the hermeneutic circle,"[61] it is also the case that "narrativity serves as a propadeutic to ethics."[62]

The appearance of narrative identity also signals the transition from detour to return in Ricoeur's overall project. Threefold mimesis is thus the culmination of the narrative arc and the crossover point of the Ricoeurian dialectic between lived conviction and reflective critique. His first essay collection, *The Conflict of Interpretations,* could retroactively be subtitled *From Action to Text* since it finds its natural partner in the second collection, *From Text to Action.* These two collections explore the detour and return, respectively, that characterizes Ricoeur's philosophy, but do not synthesize it into a single hermeneutical arc. It is only with the mimetic triad of prefiguration-configuration-refiguration, where the first and last terms are embedded in action while the middle term is embedded in textuality, that Ricoeur synthesizes the two movements: a *detour* from prefiguration to configuration and a *return* from configuration to refiguration.

In the conclusions to *Time and Narrative III*, Ricoeur faces the aporias that still exist in his study of the relation between temporality and narrativity. These are not typical conclusions, in that they were written at the request of François Wahl, Ricoeur's editor, who asked Ricoeur to reread his entire trilogy and reflect on what he felt he had accomplished. They are not a mere summary of the results, but also "have the further aim of exploring the limits our enterprise runs into."[63] While he reaffirms his original hypothesis, that "temporality cannot be spoken of in the direct discourse of phenomenology, but rather requires the mediation of the indirect discourse of narration,"[64] he allows that the response to the aporetics of phenomenology by the poetics of narrativity opens further questions, and even creates further aporias. In yet another nod to Marcel, Ricoeur allows that he has moved as far along the path of primary reflection as possible, and that beyond this limit, "temporality, escaping from the grid-work of narrativity, moves once again from being a problem to being a mystery."[65] Ricoeur does not succumb to the spirit of abstraction, but still manages to push reflection as far as it will go. The first aporia of temporality that is faced, and the one that concerns us here, is "narrative identity," and he has since referred to his opening of this question as the "principal achievement" of *Time and Narrative*.[66]

There are three places where Ricoeur elucidates the meaning and implications of this term. He raises it in the conclusions to *Time and Narrative*, he develops it in an essay devoted to the concept (aptly entitled "Narrative Identity"),[67] and finally he situates it within his hermeneutics of the self in *Oneself as Another*. He first assigns it a provisional definition: "The fragile offshoot issuing from the union of history and fiction is the assignment to an individual or a community of a specific identity that we can call their narrative identity."[68] This definition builds on the above-mentioned interplay of history and fiction, the "criss-crossing processes of a fictionalization of history and a historicization of fiction."[69] When the question "Who?" is asked, whether it be of a person or of a community, the answer will inevitably and necessarily draw on narrative resources. Following Hannah Arendt, we can say that the answer to this question "Who?" is the *story of a life*, and further that this story "continues to be refigured by all the truthful or fictive stories a subject tells about himself or herself."[70] Ricoeur argues that we have an "intuitive precomprehension" of this, that "human lives become more readily intelligible when interpreted in the light of the stories that people tell about them," and even more so when the narrative categories of history and fiction, that is, plot and character, are utilized. Thus the following argument can be made:

> [S]elf-knowledge is an interpretation; self-interpretation, in its turn, finds in narrative, among other signs and symbols, a privileged mediation; this mediation draws on history as much as it does on fiction, turning the story of a life into a fictional story or a historical fiction, comparable to those biographies of great men in which history and fiction are intertwined.[71]

Ricoeur demonstrates the fruitfulness of such an approach, which constitutes identity through the taking up of narratives, through an individual example, psychoanalysis, and a communal example, biblical Israel. Psychoanalysis most clearly demonstrates the importance of the narrative component of identity in its use of case histories. As was noted above, the goal of the "talking cure" is to take the unnarrated episodes, the pieces of a life that are "unintelligible as well as unbearable," and configure them into a narrative that allows the analysand to achieve a measure of *self-constancy*.[72] In working through sorrow, for example, "narrative constitutes an essential element of the work of mourning understood as the acceptance of the irreparable."[73] Israel stands as a unique example of narrative identity at the communal level because it has been "so overwhelmingly impassioned by the narratives it has told about itself."[74] There is a circularity to this relationship, in that Israel has achieved its singular identity precisely in its reception of the narratives of Exodus, Canaan, monarchy, exile, return, and so on, so that this community "has drawn its identity from the reception of those texts that it had produced."[75]

Recalling the objections that were given to the configuration of time by narrative, that the hermeneutical circle was "vicious," either because it accomplished nothing but a rearrangement of what was already there or because it artificially and thus violently imposed an order where there was none, Ricoeur argues that on the level of both the individual and the community, "we can affirm without hesitation that this circle is a wholesome one."[76] The key to this affirmation is "character," which encapsulates the entire mimetic triad. Prefiguration at the level of the individual refers to the "semantics of desire, which only include those prenarrative features attached to the demand constitutive of human desire." This responds to both sides of the objection: there is something that demands to be narrated, but the configuration of the narrative is not contained within it. Refiguration is then the result of an endless process of rectifying previous narratives. It is a measure of what Ricoeur takes himself to have accomplished that he refers to narrative identity as the poetic resolution of the hermeneutic circle.

The key to understanding Ricoeur's theory of narrative identity involves understanding at once both what it is and what it is not. He characterizes the two types of identity in terms of the Latin terms *idem* and *ipse*. *Idem* is the form of identity that is *sameness* (*Gleichheit, mêmeté*), while *ipse* is *selfhood* (*Selbstheit, ipséité*). Ricoeur clarifies the distinction as follows: "The difference between *idem* and *ipse* is nothing more than the difference between a substantial or formal identity and a narrative identity."[77] In practice, the latter form of identity is broader because it encompasses the former; the narrative of *ipse* identity is a configuration of the "substance" of the *idem* identity.

There are a number of ways in which *sameness* can be used with respect to *idem* identity. Ricoeur specifies three—quantitative, qualitative, and continuous—and each of these can also be understood in terms of what it is and is not. Quantitative identity refers to "uniqueness," the recognition that something is "one and the same thing," and its opposite is "plurality."[78] Qualitative identity, which Ricoeur also refers to as "extreme resemblance,"[79] is referred to when we say that two people are wearing identical outfits. The opposite to this kind of identity is "different." These two types of identity correspond to Kant's phenomenological categories and while "irreducible to one another," each can reinforce the other. In fact, the second serves to reinforce the first in the case of eyewitness testimony during the judicial process. The person I see in the courtroom today is the *same* person I saw at the scene of the crime (qualitatively, i.e., he looks the same), which supports the notion that we are talking about the *same* person in both cases (quantitatively, i.e., that person at the scene of the crime and this person in the courtroom are *one and the same* person). The problems that surround eyewitness testimony, especially as significant time passes, indicate the need for a third kind of identity. The person need not appear qualitatively identical in both cases if *uninterrupted continuity* can be established between the two occasions. The person may be thinner or taller or have different hair, but is still the same person. The opposite of this type of *idem* identity is "discontinuity." Thus the latter two types of identity serve as guarantors for the first, and the first type can be taken as the core meaning of *idem* identity.

But does uninterrupted continuity, in concert with similitude, establish that changes can occur without destroying identity? To recall a puzzle that has figured prominently in analytic philosophy, can a machine have all of its parts replaced over time without ceasing to be the same machine?

Ricoeur engages a specific example of the difficulties that are encountered when attempting to account for personal identity solely in terms of sameness. There are many such examples to choose from, since we have been in "the era of *puzzling cases*" since Locke invented the thought experiment of transplanted memories as a way of addressing the paradoxes of identity. In Derek Parfit's influential work, *Reasons and Persons*,[80] he constructs a futuristic scenario in order to call into question the viability of personal identity as a concept, and to ask whether it matters at all. A person's brain and body are completely encoded, transmitted through space, and then reconstituted, resulting in a precise double. Parfit explores variations on this scenario, the most interesting of which is that the original person is destroyed after the transfer takes place, which raises the question of whether the person "survives" in the replica. What Parfit wants to demonstrate is, in short: "Personal identity is not what matters."[81] Personal identity is merely a "supplementary fact" that is added on to the sheer existence of our brains, bodies, and experiences.

Ricoeur hones in on Parfit's drive to account for identity solely by means of impersonal description, and wonders whether Parfit is not guilty of presupposing precisely what he claims to put into question.[82] He notes the ease with which Parfit moves back and forth between the term "personal identity" and simply "our identity," whose possessive formulation raises the question of ownership. It re-introduces the overarching question of "who?" at the very point where it was decided that "who" did not matter:

> For really, how can we ask ourselves about what matters if we could not ask to whom the thing mattered or not? Does not the questioning about what matters or not depend upon self-concern, which indeed seems to be constitutive of selfhood? . . . The tenacity of personal pronouns . . . reveals something more profound than the rhetoric of argumentation: it marks the resistance of the question "who?" to its elimination in an impersonal description.[83]

In the very attempt to eliminate a selfhood that is not amenable to impersonal description, the persistence of that selfhood is reaffirmed. As Peter Welsen puts it in his summary of Ricoeur's position, "a description of the world exclusively based on the third person perspective presupposes a first person whose perspective is irreducible."[84] There is a *mineness* to selfhood that escapes any attempt to describe it from outside. "I am afraid, I believe, I doubt, I wonder if I am going to die or survive—in short, I am worried about myself."[85] This existential concern, this care for ourselves (*Sorge*), is altogether different from simple matters of fact.

Ricoeur argues that it is a fourth aspect of sameness, *permanence in time,* which underwrites both similitude and continuity (which in turn underwrite numerical identity): "[P]ermanence in time thus becomes the transcendental of numerical identity. The entire problematic of personal identity will revolve around this search for a relational invariant, giving it the strong signification of permanence in time."[86] The opposite of sameness as permanence in time is "diversity." But this new form of *idem* identity is also a form of *ipse* identity, and Ricoeur argues that the confusion between them necessitates a mediation by narrative identity:

> My thesis is consequently double: the first is that most of the difficulties which afflict contemporary discussion bearing on personal identity result from the confusion between two interpretations of permanence in time; my second these is that the concept of narrative identity offers a solution to the aporias of personal identity.[87]

As we saw above, it is precisely the task of narrative to mediate concordance and discordance, sameness and diversity. Because philosophy is oriented toward universals, there is a tendency to want to interpret permanence in time in terms of an unchanging underlying structure, such as the biological structure that is common to an acorn and an oak tree. But this is once again to collapse selfhood into sameness. There is no immutable core to *ipse* identity that needs to be protected.

A DIALECTIC BETWEEN SAMENESS AND SELFHOOD

The dialectic of selfhood and sameness can be established by looking at where they overlap and where they diverge. Ricoeur argues that sameness and selfhood converge in the area of *character* and diverge in the area of *promise keeping,* and further that narrative identity will come to serve as a bridge between them.[88] The phenomenon of character shows that sameness (*idem*) and selfhood (*ipse*) are connected, while keeping one's word shows that neither is reducible to the other.

It was noted above that character encapsulates the mimetic triad of prefiguration, configuration, and refiguration. Ricoeur defines character as "the set of lasting dispositions by which a person is recognized."[89] At this point, character seems merely to be an aspect of sameness, of the *idem* identity that is amenable to impersonal description. And indeed, character is the "what" of the "who."[90] But it is also more: "The identity of the character is comprehensible through the transfer to the character of the operation of emplotment, first applied to the action recounted; characters, we will say, are themselves plots."[91] Character in this narrative sense is something to be not described but interpreted. As the events of the story in which the character is involved change, so too does the character located within the context of these events change.[92]

On the other side of the dialectic of sameness and selfhood, where the latter escapes from the former, is the "keeping of one's word in faithfulness to the word that has been given."[93] The keeping of a promise involves a sub-sistence, but it is not a subsistence of sameness; it is a *self*-subsistence. "The continuity of character is one thing, the constancy of friendship is quite an-other."[94] There is a claim oriented toward the future in making a commit-ment that asserts one's own selfhood over against any variations in same-ness. This manifestation of *ipse* identity is a crucial component of Ricoeur's ethics, as we will see in the next chapter.

What holds the dialectic together is narrative. In the notion of "habit," a key aspect of character, we find that we are thrust into the temporal di-mension that will call for a narrative accounting. Acquired habits are to the person what traditional practices are to a community; what was once an in-novation undergoes a process of "sedimentation" that eventually conceals it. One can describe a habit in terms of the present, but the *acquisition* of a habit is a temporal process that cannot even be addressed without some recourse to narrative. Thus an acquired character *trait* is a function both of *idem* identity, "a distinctive sign by which a person is recognized, reidentified as the same,"[95] and also of *ipse* identity, in that a habit (as opposed to a simple behavior) is necessarily acquired over time. My character is my *self,* but is also the means by which I can be identified as one and the *same* person. The latter is easier to access because it is observable by anyone and is amenable to impersonal description, and it covers over the former but does *not* negate it. As Ricoeur puts it, "this *ipse* announces itself as *idem.*"[96]

Ricoeur identifies two significant limitations to the solution of narrative identity: instability and inexhaustiblity. The process of configuring one's life through plot is faced with the challenge that it is "always possible to weave different, even opposed, plots about our lives." Narrative identity draws on the categories of both history and fiction, and while the possibility of veri-fication of the historical component lends stability to narrative identity, the fictional component introduces imaginative variations that threaten to de-stabilize it. There is an equilibrium reached between sameness and selfhood, but that equilibrium is characterized by instability, and is thus a task as much as it is an achievement, "the name of a problem as much as it is that of a solu-tion."[97] Narrative identity is always incomplete, is perpetually being revised, and the so-called author is also narrator, character, agent, and patient within the narrative. But pure concordance is not what is sought:

> All these arguments are perfectly acceptable: the equivocalness of the notion of the author, the "narrative" incompleteness of life, the entanglement of life histories in a dialectic of remembrance and anticipation. The objections are valid only in opposition to a naïve conception of *mimesis*. . . . These are less to be refuted than to be incorporated in a more subtle, more dialectical comprehension of *appropriation*.[98]

With regard to the ethical "self-constancy" of a subject that narrative identity provides, it belongs to the field of imagination as much as that of action. There remains a gap between the reader and narrator of one's life and the "agent," who has the task of making choice from the ethical options that are raised through the act of reading. Narrative does have its own ethical component. The problem of translating the imaginative possibilities of action into actual ethical decisions is constitutive of narrative identity: "narrative theory can genuinely mediate between description and prescription only if the broadening of the practical field and the anticipation of ethical considerations are implied in the very structure of the act of narrating."[99] The transition from the narrative constitution of identity to the self-constancy of ethical responsibility remains problematic. To properly integrate narrative identity into an overall theory of personal identity, the issuance from narrative into ethics needs to be better accounted for, and this is the task that Ricoeur takes up in the prescriptive section of *Oneself as Another*.

5

Refiguration:
Ricoeur's "Little Ethics"

Oneself as Another began with Ricoeur's delivery of the Gifford Lectures at the University of Edinburgh in 1986, which explored the theme of the "capable person." A person can speak, act, and narrate, which formed the bases for the first six studies. But a person can also make promises and decisions. These capabilities were not covered in the original lectures, but four years after these lectures, Ricoeur wrote a further three studies, which he ironically calls his *"petite ethique, minima moralia,"*[1] for the publication of the book. It is this "little ethics" that constitutes Ricoeur's major contribution to the field of ethics, and while it does fit into the overall argument of the book, it could also easily be published on its own. The first chapter has an Aristotelian focus, asking what is meant when one speaks of the "pursuit of the good life." The second chapter takes a more Kantian approach, asking what it is to do one's duty. The third chapter breaks out of the context of a teleological/deontological opposition, reclaiming Kant for Aristotle by way of Hegel, and forges the tools to resolve entirely novel ethical problems.[2] The study on the ethical aim comes first because Ricoeur argues for "the primacy of ethics over morality—that is, of the aim over the norm."[3] The second study of the triad argues for the indispensability of a *detour* through moral norms as a necessary "sieve" through which ethics must pass. In the third, he reiterates that it is ethics to which morality must ultimately *return* when confronted with limit cases. In this, Ricoeur again retraces on a micro-level the journey of his philosophy as a whole. The move here is from the ethical aim (conviction, understanding), through moral norms (critique, explanation) and back to the deeper level of practical wisdom (second naïveté, appropriation). Each chapter has a specific task to accomplish in the overall arc of the argument:

> (1) the primacy of ethics over morality, (2) the necessity for the ethical aim to pass through the sieve of the norm, and (3) the legitimacy of recourse by the norm to the aim whenever the norm leads to impasses in practice—impasses recalling at this new stage of our meditation the various aporetic situations which our reflection on selfhood has had to face.[4]

Ricoeur is keenly aware that his discussion of ethical aims and moral duty puts him in the middle of a longstanding conflict of approaches. He explicitly rejects any concern with "Aristotelian or Kantian orthodoxy," although he takes freely from both, navigating by way of the now very familiar detour-and-return pattern.[5]

The first building block of Ricoeur's ethics is his working definition of the ethical intention: *"aiming at the 'good life' with and for others, in just institutions."*[6] He develops each of the three natural divisions in the definition in turn, and this sets the pattern for all three studies. The analysis in each study is distributed among the three grammatical persons (I/ self, thou/ other, he/she/each one), which makes for a three-by-three grid onto which we can map the little ethics.

THE ETHICAL AIM: OPTATIVE

Self-Esteem

In Ricoeur's definition, the term "good life" is enclosed in scare quotes, implying that he is aware that there is something troubling about the term. What is troubling in this case is the difficulty encountered in filling it with any content. It remains as "the nebulous realm of ideals and dreams of achievements with regard to which a life is held to be more or less fulfilled or unfulfilled. Ricoeur argues the formal nature of the claim is not to be confused with a *vague* claim; this is avoided by the Aristotelian grounding of the good life in praxis. Praxis is measured in terms of "standards of excellence,"[7] which are, as Ricoeur describes them, "rules of comparison applied to different accomplishments, in relation to ideals of perfection shared by a given

Table 5.1. Ricoeur's "Little Ethics"

Study	Self	Other	Each One	Mode
7. ETHICAL AIM	Self-Esteem	Solicitude	Sense of Justice	Optative
8. MORAL NORM	Autonomy	Respect	Principles of Justice	Imperative
9. PRACTICAL WISDOM	Dependent Autonomy	Critical Solicitude	Domesticated Sittlichkeit	Attesting

community of practitioners and internalized by the masters and virtuosi of the practice considered."[8] This is where the tools of the narrative arc come into play. In the *production* of the text that is a *life,* we interpret our actions through symbolic networks that precede us.[9] It is within the context of a *narrative identity* that these life plans are both formulated and continuously revised: "Our life, when then embraced in a single glance, appears to us as the field of constructive activity, borrowed from narrative understanding, by which we attempt to discover and not simply to impose from the outside the *narrative identity which constitutes us.*"[10] One is not hopelessly stuck in the traditions of the community, although one must in fact live in those traditions, which are the social fabric that forms one's context. This does not quell, but rather *enables* controversy and growth. A new virtuoso who does things that have never been done before is recognized *as* a virtuoso precisely because she is still recognized as excellent according to the standards already in place.

The discussion of "standards of excellence" applies to the ethical aim in two ways, which are again the two movements that we see everywhere in Ricoeur. We formulate our "life plans" with reference to these standards that *precede* us, and enable us to speak of the "internal goods" of a practice. That a doctor works to heal a wounded person is an *internal* good to being a doctor, in that a doctor who does such can appraise himself as in some way being a *good* doctor. The practices of doing so will inevitably be codified in rules and regulations, for both evaluative and pedagogical reasons. But the second application comes when the doctor is faced with limit situations. In these cases, the rules cannot stand on their own, but must have recourse to the *internal goods* that generated them. Thus, "life plan" is a continuous process: "moving back and forth between far-off ideals, which have to be made more precise, and the weighing of the advantages and disadvantages of the choice of a given life plan on the level of practice."[11] This process of weighing is not a deductive process, but rather an interpretive one. Ricoeur invites us to view our actions as texts to be interpreted, for two reasons: (1) our important decisions and our life plan are understood in terms of each other in the same way that part of a text and its whole are understood in terms of each other; and (2) interpreting an action as text enables us to consider the action's meaning *for us,* rather than its meaning in general. Searching for adequation between our life plan and our concrete decisions becomes an act of self-interpretation, which requires practical wisdom, or *phronesis:* "the search for adequation between our life ideals and our decisions, themselves vital ones, is not open to the sort of verification expected in the sciences of observation."[12] This interpretive task offers no apodictic certainty, but rather can aspire at most to a "plausibility" in the eyes of the community. The reflexive moment of such a task, when one has judged oneself to have provisionally achieved such an adequation, is manifested in *self-esteem.*

Solicitude

It is, of course, intrinsic to any relational anthropology that the "other" somehow be involved in the study of the self. In Ricoeur, this relational moment falls under the heading of solicitude, which "is not something added on to self-esteem from outside but that it unfolds the dialogic dimension of self-esteem."[13] It turns out that self-esteem is a complex, multi-stage task, one that cannot be realized alone: "[I]f one asks by what right the self is declared to be worthy of esteem, it must be answered that it is not principally by reason of its accomplishments but fundamentally by reason of its capacities. . . . The question is then whether the mediation of the other is not required along the route from capacity to realization."[14] Ricoeur answers this last question emphatically in the affirmative, and he asserts (following Charles Taylor) that understanding this is the only way to strike at the root of pernicious political atomism where the subject is first and foremost a subject of law, prior to any social relationships.[15]

The role of solicitude in realizing self-esteem is a delicate one. Drawing heavily on Aristotle's analysis of friendship, Ricoeur argues that friendship is not simply a psychology of cathectation but belongs rather to an ethics of reciprocity. Reciprocity can be broken down into three fundamental elements: reversibility, nonsubstitutability, and similitude. *Reversibility* refers to the nature of person-to-person designation, where every statement can be meaningfully turned around. We see this in the grammatical context when it is shown that when one says "you" to another, that person understands that as an "I" for themselves, and vice versa. *Nonsubstitutability* refers to the unique status of each person in the "I-thou" relationship. The other is valued, or esteemed by the self, and is not replaceable in that valuation and esteem, and the esteem that the other holds for the self is similarly irreplaceable. *Similitude,* which transcends the first two terms, refers to the fundamental recognition of likeness in the other, in spite of unavoidable discrepancies in the "equality" that is necessary for true friendship. It is only at this point that solicitude and self-esteem can finally emerge as a dialogical pairing. Ricoeur describes similitude as "the fruit of the exchange between esteem for oneself and solicitude for others."[16] It is the recognition that the other is a *self* and calls to be esteemed as such, as a self who also generates life plans, makes decisions, and esteems others. More particularly that other has an irreplaceable esteem for one's own self. Through this extension of solicitude one can now take the final step in the realization of self-esteem, which recognizes the equivalency of "the esteem of the *other as a oneself* and the esteem of *oneself as another.*"[17]

Solicitude gives voice to a fundamental lack in the self; we need to have others in order to be a self at all. There is in fact *no* self prior to this process, because the self is not posited, but is rather implied reflexively in the relationship. But just as that reflexive implication forces us to contextualize our reflection on the self, so too does the fact that all interpersonal relationships happen in a wider social setting force us to widen the scope even further to the question of *just institutions.*

A Sense of Justice

In our syntactical model, we have moved from considering the first-person "I," through the second-person "thou," and have now arrived at the third person, the "each one." Ricoeur's reflection on justice is founded on two basic premises: (1) that living well extends beyond interpersonal relations to the realm of *institutions;* and (2) that the measure of these institutions is *justice,* which is of a different ethical order than the solicitude of interpersonal relationships.

Institution is central to Ricoeur's notion of third person-relations. While interpersonal relationships can be governed by the free give and take of solicitude, these wider relationships require something more structured. Ricoeur defines the institution as "the structure of *living together* as this belongs to a historical community," whose fundamental characteristic is "the bond of common mores and not that of constraining rules."[18] The legitimacy of seeing institutions as enabling relationships rather than constraining them builds on Hannah Arendt's distinction between "power in common" and "domination." In contrast to the more pessimistic view of Max Weber, who sees domination and violence as intrinsic to political institutions,[19] Ricoeur (following Arendt) stresses the concertedness of human action that is embodied in institutions.[20]

Recalling the reversibility of the I-thou relationship, we can now add to reversibility "plurality," which acknowledges that each such relationship exists in a wider network of other such relationships, faceless people to whom we are also faceless. Just as a relationship to the other is necessary for me to realize myself, the consideration of these faceless others is necessary for me to have such relationships, and vice versa. The desire to act in concert on this project of enabling human relationships, and to give it permanence over time, cannot be actualized without the structure of the institution.

The success of an institution's enabling concerted action, or its corresponding failure to do so by degenerating into sheer domination, is governed by the virtue of *justice*. Ricoeur defends his treatment of justice in the ethical rather than the moral section of his analysis by pointing out that even the arch-deontologist John Rawls begins with a teleological moment, opening with a characterization of justice as "the first virtue of social institutions."[21] Ricoeur also distinguishes between two facets of justice: that which addresses the *good,* and that which addresses the *legal.* Ricoeur's ethical analysis deals only with the "good" facet of justice (the "legal" appearing under the aspect of the moral norm),[22] and again relies heavily on Aristotle's account in the *Nicomachean Ethics.* The most interesting part of the analysis is Ricoeur's insistence that Aristotle's limiting of the field of justice to *distributive* matters must be construed in the broadest possible sense. What is being distributed is not merely material goods and benefits, but also shares in participation and responsibility. The *justice* of this distribution is evaluated with respect to *equality* (*isotes*), which is not a brute arithmetic equality, but is rather a *proportionate equality,* which addresses both person and merit.[23]

Recalling Ricoeur's definition of the ethical perspective as *aiming at the good life with and for others in just institutions,* we can now see how the components fit together. One's aim for the good life is not a solitary project. Others do not constitute an intrusion into the project, but are in fact intrinsic to its very formulation as a project. Solicitude is the name given to this extension of esteem toward the other, which recognizes the other's esteem for oneself and makes possible one's ability to realize self-esteem. Justice is the virtue governing the realization of some form of equality, which, according to Ricoeur, "is to life in institutions what solicitude is to interpersonal relations."[24] A just institution enables interpersonal relations to flourish, both by providing a stable forum in which those relations can take place and by providing avenues of concerted action.

THE MORAL NORM: IMPERATIVE

While Ricoeur stands firm on his thesis that the ethical aim takes priority over the moral norm, he is nonetheless insistent that "it is necessary to subject the ethical aim to the test of the norm."[25] In keeping with the syntactical structure, he considers first how self-esteem becomes *self-respect* "under the reign of the moral law."[26] The second section addresses solicitude and the norm of respect for the other, while the third negotiates the transition from the *sense* of justice to the *rule* of justice.

Autonomy

The key to the norm is *universality,* the means by which "the norm puts the wish to live well to the test."[27] The presence of universality across both deontological and teleological tradition raises the question of how opposed those traditions in fact are. Ricoeur points to the criterion of *mesotēs,*[28] the golden mean in Aristotle's ethics, and asks whether this "acquires retrospectively the sense of a beginning of universality?"[29] While denying any attempt at syncretism, he points to the fact that there is within the teleological tradition a point of contact with the language of universal moral obligation.

The same is true for the deontological tradition. The great emblematic work is Kant's *Groundwork for the Metaphysics of Morals.* It is interesting then to note how this great work begins:

> It is impossible to conceive anything at all in the world, or even out of it, which can be taken as good without qualification [*ohne Einschränkung*], except a *good will.*[30]

It is remarkable that the seminal work of deontology begins by addressing the "good," although it should not be ignored that there is a break in assigning this predicate to the will instead of rational desire. Nonetheless, Ricoeur argues that "a certain continuity" is maintained: "While the predicate 'good' conserves its teleological imprint, the reservation 'without qualification' announces that anything that might lift the moral mark from the use of the predicate 'good' has been set out of bounds."[31] Ricoeur establishes that there is a point of contact, then differentiates between the two in terms of their mode of expression: the teleological uses the optative mode suitable to "expressions of desire," while the deontological uses the imperative mode suitable to a relation to the law.

Having identified universality as the key to the deontological approach, Ricoeur expands on how the "rule of universalization" manifests itself in Kant's work. He argues that "the idea of constraint, characteristic to the idea of duty," is "inextricably tied to the idea of universality."[32] This is most clearly seen in Kant's famous categorical imperative: "Act only on that maxim through which you can at the same time will that it should become a universal law."[33] What is constrained here (among other things) is the ethical aim itself, since the aim is an expression of desire, of inclination, and this cannot be universalized. Whatever is aimed at must be justified on other terms. The justification, however, is not made before an external arbitrator, but is rather an expression of *autonomy* that Ricoeur characterizes as "true obedience," since "when autonomy substitutes for obedience to another obedience to oneself, obedience has lost all character of dependence and submission."[34] The criteria of universality for any maxim are as much a question of *freedom* as of *duty*.

Ricoeur's own attempt to formulate a phenomenology of the will early in his career was very much in the Kantian tradition, but was never completed as planned. What spelled the end of the project, and initiated his "hermeneutical turn," was the resistance of the phenomenon of *evil* to empirical description. It seems that the exegesis of Kant in the section on the moral norm is designed in order to re-insert this question into the discussion. He argues that because Kant "exonerates" inclination of guilt, evil emerges precisely in the free choice of the will, in the formulation of maxims: "Because there is evil, the aim of the 'good life' has to be submitted to the test of moral obligation, which might be described in the following terms: 'Act solely in accordance with the maxim by which you can wish at the same time that what *ought not to be,* namely evil, will indeed *not exist.*'"[35]

Respect

The respect that is granted to other persons under the rule of the norm is intrinsic to autonomous self-respect, just as solicitude is intrinsic to self-esteem. Moreover, just as Kant's categorical imperative regarding the formulation of maxims encapsulated self-legislation, so the second formulation of the imperative, that all persons are ends in themselves and thus ought not be treated as means, encapsulates solicitude under the aspect of the norm. But in each case of the move from aim to norm there is a mediating term. Between the aim of the good life and the constraint of duty there was the "appraisal of the good will as unconditionally good."[36] The transition between solicitude and the norm of *reciprocity* is mediated by the various formulations of the Golden Rule. Doing as one would have done to, or *not* doing as one would *not* have done to, opens up a range of moral behavior; the latter under the aspect of constraint and the former under the aspect of benevolence.

What Ricoeur finds most interesting about these formulations is that there is both an active and a passive construction, implying that each injunction "stands out against the background of the presupposition of an initial dissymmetry . . . that places one in the position of an agent and the other in that of a patient."[37] Here the question of evil is once again in a central place. The unequal distribution of power ranges from the fairly benign forms of influence and manipulation to the very brutal forms of torture and humiliation. The latter two are taken as particularly grave because they destroy the *self-respect* of the "patient."[38] Similarly, Kant's intransigence regarding the non-universalizability of false promises is explicable when the betrayal of trust is understood as the opposite of the self-constancy that is intrinsic to selfhood.

Ricoeur is not an apologist for Kant here; he expresses serious reservations about Kant's use of the mediating concept "humanity" as a means of orchestrating the transition of respect owed by the autonomous self to the autonomous other.[39] This universalizing concept diminishes and even obliterates the other's alterity, withholding precisely what was to be given. Ricoeur argues, however, that Kant is partially successful in his task of respecting the other. The maxim of treating others as ends in themselves allows for an unlimited *plurality* of others, each with their own distinct alterity.[40]

Principles of Justice

The argument for the moral norm hits full stride when it moves to the third person, the faceless "each one" of justice. In the study on the ethical aim, Ricoeur established that justice was first applied to institutions, now defined as "the diverse structures of wanting to live together, which, to this end, secure duration, cohesion, and distinction."[41] The concept that orchestrates the transition from the ethical aim to the moral norm in the case of the third person is *distribution*. We saw above how Aristotle's distributive justice played out in the form of proportionate equality, but precisely what such an equality would actually look like is unclear; it is the task of the deontological perspective to clarify this. Nevertheless: "The principal legacy of ethics to morality lies in the very idea of the *just*, which henceforth looks both ways: in the direction of the 'good' as the extension of solicitude to 'each one' of the faceless members of society; in the direction of the 'legal,' to such a degree does the prestige of justice appear to dissolve in that of positive law."[42] The deontological perspective seeks to *formalize* the principle of justice by shedding its teleological heritage, and it does this by interpreting justice *procedurally.*

Historically, the deontological tradition found its place in politics through an alliance with the contractualist traditions of Hobbes, Locke, and Rousseau, and Ricoeur argues that this is no accident.[43] This latter tradition centers around the "procedure of an imaginary deliberation," which occurs before, and thus takes priority over, "any prior commitment to an alleged common good."[44] Ricoeur is quick to emphasize that this social contract is an imaginative *fiction*—"a founding fiction to be sure, as we shall say, but a fiction nonetheless"[45]—that puts the foundation of the republic on uncertain ground. The social contract is not a *fact,* in the same way Kant could refer to autonomy as a fact of reason, and the gauntlet laid down for deontology is to justify the existence of the contract, the sovereignty of the people, without recourse to religious or cultural forms of life that would relativize the contract itself.

As an entry into this project, Ricoeur engages the work of John Rawls, especially his magisterial *A Theory of Justice,* as the most influential attempt to defend the deontological approach in politics. Rawls's argument is that justice conceived of as "fairness" is best able to secure justice in institutions, avoiding utilitarianism (another teleological position) without any recourse to any comprehensive theories concerning the good life. He posits a reasonable individual in an "original position," situated behind a "veil of ignorance," who then must choose what kind of society she wishes *without* knowing what her place will be in that society. Every reasonable person, Rawls maintains, that is put in such a position would choose the same thing: a society in which basic rights are non-negotiable and in which the lot of the person in the least advantageous position would be maximized. Inequalities are minimized but not eliminated because inequalities could well serve to ameliorate the life of the least (maximin).

Ricoeur maintains that there is much to be learned from Rawls's theory but that it does not accomplish its primary goal, which is to detach justice from any anchoring in the good:

On the one hand, one can show in what sense an attempt to provide a strictly procedural foundation for justice applied to the basic institutions of society carries to its heights the ambition to free the deontological viewpoint of morality from the teleological perspective of ethics. On the other hand, it appears that this attempt also best illustrates the limits of this ambition.[46]

Rawls has many things in common with the social contract theorists, not the least being the grounding of their respective theories in an imaginative fiction. The original position behind the veil of ignorance is ahistorical, speculative "fable," which raises the question as "to what extent an 'ahistorical' pact can *be binding on* a 'historical' society."[47] It also imports a great deal of information into it, not least of which is knowledge of the various theories of justice from which to choose. Rawls explains the key principles of his theory of justice *before* his treatment of the original position, implying that the position might not be quite so *original*.

But Rawls has even more in common with Kant. The entire project of shedding all teleological baggage from a theory of justice is a political extension of Kant's universalizable maxims.[48] This unifies the entire approach to moral norms as one of employing *formalism* to achieve a *universality* that is legitimated by *autonomy*. Here it is worth quoting Ricoeur at length:

> Formalism therefore amounts to setting (something) aside, as this will be expressed in each of the three spheres of formalism: setting aside inclination in the sphere of rational will, excluding the treatment of others simply as means in the dialogic sphere, and, finally eliminating utilitarianism in the sphere of institutions. In this regard, one cannot emphasize too strongly that the exclusion of utilitarianism in the original situation has the same signification as the other two exclusions and is in a sense constructed on the base of these prior two exclusions. Finally, the deontological viewpoint is founded thrice over on a principle that provides its own legitimation: autonomy in the first sphere, the positing of the person as an end in himself in the second, and the social contract in the third. Here again, it must be strongly asserted that autonomy governs the three spheres: the idea of the person as end in himself is held to be the dialogic expression of autonomy, and the contract is its equivalent on the plane of institutions.[49]

Rawls's attempt to eliminate any empirical data in his political theory of justice is thus ultimately grounded in Kant's attempt to eliminate empirical data (inclinations) from personal moral decision making. This is legitimized at the personal level by the freedom and dignity that demands that the person be a self-legislating agent. This autonomy is extended to the interpersonal and institutional spheres through the concepts of person-as-end and social contract, respectively.

The limits of the formalism of the deontological perspective are found on both sides: in its grounding and in its application. It is central to any formal approach to morality that it be self-grounding, but Ricoeur argues that it cannot fulfill its promise. It is at the institutional level that it is particularly weak, while being strongest at the level of personal autonomy, so he focuses first on the latter. Autonomy is legitimate only if it can draw legitimacy from the "fact of reason," but Ricoeur argues that this so-called fact can only be *attested* to. He again cites the opening affirmation of Kant's *Groundwork* to drive home that this is an attestation that "roots the deontological viewpoint once more in the teleological perspective."[50] Regarding reciprocity, the formal person-as-end criterion is an attestation to the conviction that "things have a price and persons, worth."[51] On the level of institutions, Ricoeur argues that the fictional social contract, which Rawls simply carries to "a higher level of refinement,"[52] is generated to compensate for the *forgetting* of an original "will to live together" that grounds the deontological in the teleological.

In its application, the deontological perspective proves to be insufficient at all three levels when the claims come into conflict. This can happen both when two claims compete on the same level—be it personal, interpersonal, or institutional—or when different levels are at play in the same decision. To resolve these, there needs to be recourse to the ethical aim to which the moral norm attests, and this is what Ricoeur calls "practical wisdom."

PRACTICAL WISDOM: CONVICTION

Any ethico-moral theory that attempts to maintain a dialectic between the teleology of the ethical aim and the deontology of the moral norm will eventually have to come to terms, even if only negatively, with Hegel's *Sittlichkeit*.[53] Given the role that this concept has played in granting moral authority to the state, and the horrendous consequences that resulted from its appropriation by twentieth-century totalitarianism, there is every reason to shy away from it. But this would be to throw out the wheat with the chaff. Ricoeur does not want to do away with the concept, describing the aim of practical wisdom as "reconciling Aristotle's *phronesis,* by way of Kant's *Moralität*, with Hegel's *Sittlichkeit*."[54] He explicitly rejects, however, any notion of *Sittlichkeit* as a master category that is capable of resolving the conflicts generated by the application of rival moral norms: "it is not a matter of adding a third agency to the ethical perspective and to the moment of duty, that corresponding to the Hegelian *Sittlichkeit*."[55] Ricoeur's more modest version "takes the risk of depriving itself of the resources of a philosophy of *Geist*,"[56] which leaves *Sittlichkeit* "stripped of its pretention [*sic*] to mark the victory of Spirit over the contradictions that it itself provokes."[57] This domesticated *Sittlichkeit,* this *critical phronesis,* "would no longer denote a third agency, higher than ethics and morality, but would designate one of the places in which practical wisdom is exercised."[58]

Ricoeur is also intent to note that while the deontological pretense to *sufficiency* has been exposed both on the plane of ultimate grounding and on the plane of application, this does not undermine the *necessity* of the deontological moment: "this manner of referring morality back to ethics is not to be taken to mean that the morality of obligation has been disavowed. . . . If we did not pass through conflicts that take a practice guided by the principles of morality, we would succumb to the seductions of a moral situationism that would cast us, defenseless, into the realm of the arbitrary."[59] The role of morality in the scheme of ethical reflection is "to connect two levels of ethical life, the basic one and applied one."[60] The basic, ethical aim is often so deeply embedded in our daily lives that it requires some method of bringing it out into the open so that it can be examined, and the moral norm fulfills this task.

The place where moral rules come into conflict and finally emerge into critical *phronesis* is in the realm of *tragic situations.* Ricoeur follows Hegel in choosing *Antigone* as the laboratory of practical wisdom.[61] The tragic grandeur of Antigone is that she chooses the duty to her family over the duty to her city, but Ricoeur argues that Antigone is no better than Creon in this, in that both adopt a "strategy of avoidance." Antigone is not interested in any nuance that might threaten her absolute duty to her brother, just as Creon is not interested in any nuance that might undermine his duty to his city. The source of ethical conflict, according to Ricoeur, "lies not only in the one-sidedness of the characters but also in the one-sidedness of the moral *principles* which themselves are confronted with the complexity of life." And the solution to this is found in not rules or principles, but actions: "in the conflicts to which morality gives rise, only a recourse to the ethical ground against which morality stands out can give rise to the wisdom of judgment in situation."[62] It is in practical wisdom that the twin specters of absolutism and relativism, the "ruinous alternatives of univocity or arbitrariness," can finally be avoided. Martha Nussbaum notes that in practical wisdom as a solution to tragic conflict, Ricoeur clearly surpasses Kant, "who simply denied that such conflicts ever arise," but also surpasses the ancients, because "he is able to relate his solution to the distinction between the teleological and the deontological in a way that no premodern writer would have been able to do."[63]

Domesticating *Sittlichkeit*

The difficulty in writing about practical wisdom is that it mediates in so many different ways that it is difficult to structure the discussion. Ricoeur confesses that this study "still looks like an appendix, and it should become the crucial chapter."[64] The study reverses the order of the previous two studies, beginning with the institutional rather than the personal, at least partly because it is the most convenient way to engage *Sittlichkeit*, but also because it best fits the structure of a "return" movement, both in the context of the little ethics and in the movement of the work as a whole.

The central figure is still Rawls. While his attempt to legitimize his theory of justice without reference to the good does not succeed, the way in which he modifies his theory to meet his critics is of interest to Ricoeur. Already in *A Theory of Justice* itself, Rawls advances the notion of a "reflective equilibrium" between the rules generated from the original position and our "considered convictions."[65] This is clearly an at least partial grounding of the moral norm in an ethical aim. There is also the use of "primary social goods," a frankly teleological concept, which inevitably gives rise to conflicts in the estimation of how these social goods are in fact "good." He invokes the work of Michael Walzer to drive home just how inevitable such conflicts are.[66] But the inevitability of such conflicts only undermines the pretension of Rawls's theory of justice to be freestanding; the theory itself remains very useful, and even indispensable. The aim is not to rid ourselves of conflicts, but to deal with them wisely as they arise. As Ricoeur puts it: "Democracy is not a political system without conflicts but a system in which conflicts are open and negotiable in accordance with recognized rules of arbitration."[67] The task of critical *phronesis* at the institutional level is conflict management, not conflict avoidance.

Conflicts can arise, and indeed do arise, at the very deepest levels: the legitimation of the government itself, or the means by which a government can be labeled "good." Such conflicts are inevitable, giving rise to what Ricoeur calls the "grand words of politics," such as security, prosperity, liberty, equality, and many others.[68] These words are so emotionally laden, and thus so misused, that one is tempted to declare them useless except for purposes of propaganda. Ricoeur, however, sees two ways to rehabilitate them:

What may have led us to believe that these concepts could not be rescued is that two major phenomena have not been taken into account, phenomena which a hermeneutical-style philosophy of action is prepared to recognize; first, each of these terms has an insurmountable plurality of sense; second, the plurality of ends of "good" government is perhaps irreducible; in other words, the question of *the* end of "good" government is perhaps undecidable.[69]

It is this admission of "undecidability" that ultimately claims *Sittlichkeit* on behalf of *phronesis,* as "a plural, or rather public, *phronesis* resembling the debate itself."[70] The state can make no univocal claims as to its role in society simply because there are no such univocal claims to be made. This is finally an expression of Aristotelian "equity," where public decision makers rectify what previous legislators either could not or did not anticipate due to the tendency to oversimplify in generating "universal" laws.[71] This tendency is not a failure, however, for it is only through the conflicts between laws that attempt to be universal that the conditions for true *critical phronesis* can be reached.

Critical Solicitude

Ricoeur takes promise keeping to be emblematic of *ipse* identity, and he uses it as the key example to explore the conflicts that arise in the attempt to universalize respect for the other. This is strengthened by Kant's famous response to the problem of altruistic falsehoods in defense of truth telling as a perfect duty to others. Although the deontological norm will be surpassed, Ricoeur is intent on pursuing the moral detour to the very end, and he defends Kant against some of the more commonplace attacks on the "vacuity" of formalism:

> Two points should be recalled here: first, the rule of universalization is applied to the *multiple* maxims which are already behavioral regularities; without them, the rule of universalization would, so to speak, have no "grist to grind," nothing to test. Next, and this remark is more novel, there are maxims that successfully pass the text of universalization; these are the very ones that Kant calls duties (in the plural).[72]

Kant does not attempt to build morality from scratch, and the formal sieve through which he passes existing "potential" maxims is not so tight that nothing gets through. The duty to tell the truth is presented by Kant as a perfect duty to others, but Ricoeur argues that others are *not* really taken into consideration in Kant's treatment of false promising, especially his reply to Benjamin Constant.[73] Rather the argument is that it is one's own personal integrity at stake, and the other is only a cipher representing humanity. Ricoeur is aware that this potentially poses problems for his own construal of selfhood: "Have we not ourselves made self-constancy through time the highest expression of the identity of *ipse* in contrast to that of *idem*, that is, in opposition to the mere permanence or perserverance of things (a permanence that is found on the plane of selfhood only in character)?"[74] The self-constancy that characterizes *ipse* identity is similar enough to Kant's argument for personal integrity that it risks absorbing the alterity of the other into its own calculations. But Ricoeur argues that the other is implied from the very moment that one makes a commitment to which one will remain constant. Otherwise the self-constancy would become trivial: "a commitment that did not involve doing something that the other could choose or prefer would be no more than a silly wager."[75]

Here Marcel surfaces once again at a crucial point in Ricoeur's reflections. Marcel's famous assertion that "all commitment is a response" is used by Ricoeur to introduce the notion of *disponibilité*,[76] which is "the key that opens self-constancy to the dialogic structure established by the Golden Rule."[77] In the context of the dissymmetry of the Golden Rule, I am the agent who will actively "do unto" another and the other will passively "have done unto" them. To take advantage of this dissymmetry is to do violence: "the false promise is a figure of the evil of violence in the use of language, on the plane of interlocution."[78] In this way, the injunction against falsehood rests not solely on a logical contradiction, as it did with Kant, but also on a prohibition against violence to the other. I give my word, and the other *counts on* me to keep it, which results in my taking on a burden of fidelity not only to my integrity but to the other who is counting on me. "This *counting on* connects self-constancy, in its moral tenor, to the principle of reciprocity founded in solicitude."[79]

The specificity of the other's demand opens the door to precisely what Kant so carefully tried to avoid: competing universal demands. The tragedy of action on the level of institutions is also present in interpersonal relations, and at this level they are felt with even more force.[80] An exception to one of at least two conflicting duties must be made, and one is declaring not *oneself* to be the exception, but the other. Addressing the difficult case of medical practice and euthanasia, Ricoeur again returns to the ethical aim of solicitude to guide his way between competing norms. The injunction not to increase suffering all too frequently comes into conflict with the duty to tell the patient the truth: "Practical wisdom consists in inventing conduct that will best sat-isfy the exception required by solicitude, by betraying the rule to the smallest extent possible . . . one must have compassion for those who are morally or physically too weak to hear the truth."[81] To say that one must in all cases tell the patient the whole truth because not to do so would violate her human dignity is to retreat into Kantian formalism and refuse to see the patient in her concrete, specific alterity. It is to pretend that there is not another claim (not increasing suffering) that comes into conflict. "Generally, the most se-rious moral decisions consist in drawing the dividing line between what is permitted and what is forbidden in zones which themselves are 'median' and resistant to familiar dichotomies."[82] Serious moral decisions *are* serious pre-cisely because they resist dichotomization, and require what Ricoeur calls a *critical solicitude*. In formal terms, respect for others as ends in themselves is an absolute claim that admits of no exceptions, but when different forms of the claim conflict in application, the moral norm of respect must have recourse to the ethical aim of solicitude if a wise decision is to be made.

Dependent Autonomy

The construal of the person as a self-legislating free individual is the centerpiece of Kant's philosophical anthropology, so it is fitting that it serves as the terminus of the return move in Ricoeur's little ethics. Here the crux of the dialectic is clearly articulated: "a confrontation between the *universalist claim* attached to the rules claiming to belong to the principle of morality and the recognition of positive values belonging to the *historical and com-munitarian contexts* of the realization of these same rules."[83] Both the claim and the contexts must be affirmed, or the phenomenon of tragic action is stripped of its tragic element, by either reducing it to merely misguided be-havior or denying the seriousness of the conflict.

Ricoeur reinforces Kant's anthropology in order to surpass it, and he does so by honing in on three concepts: the self-sufficiency of autonomy, the criterion of universalization, and transcendental pragmatics. Regarding autonomy, Ricoeur argues that only an autonomy that is "contaminated" by an "egological thesis" can claim self-sufficiency, and this would be simply to revert to the positivism of the *cogito* philosophies. But by taking the return move from justice back through respect to autonomy, the *auto* can rid itself of egological contamination and reclaim its reflexive status. This comes at a price, however, since "an autonomy that is of a piece with the rule of jus-tice and the rule of reciprocity can no longer be a *self-sufficient* autonomy."[84]

But there is no corresponding loss of freedom or dignity. Recalling with Gadamer that authority is not coextensive with domination, a dependent autonomy is, ideally, a *liberated* autonomy.

The second line of approach is to question Kant's strict use of the criterion of universalization in judging maxims. If the attempt to universalize a potential maxim results in an internal contradiction, the maxim self-destructs. But Ricoeur sees this as needlessly harsh: "Reducing the test of universalization in this way to noncontradiction gives us an extraordinarily poor idea of the coherence to which a system of morality can aspire."[85] Noncontradiction is too narrow a platform on which to build a moral philosophy. Ricoeur proposes the process of judicial reasoning in the common law tradition as a better example of the kind of coherence that is sought in moral reasoning. Using the system of precedent cases and deliberating about what each case has to offer the issue under consideration allows for a "productivity of thought" that nonetheless respects the laws as written. In this model, "every conception of justice requires a coherence that is not merely to be preserved but to be constructed."[86] There are obvious differences at the level of the individual, but there is a strong analogy. Personal "laws" that have been self-legislated come to bear on the process of moral decision making, but it is acknowledged that the laws may not have perfect applicability in each case.

The greatest difficulty with this "judicial" approach to moral decision making is that the so-called laws that motivate moral behavior often operate below the surface. Ricoeur finds Habermas's transcendental pragmatics, itself a retrieval of Kant's transcendental deduction, to be of particular value in uncovering the hidden ideologies operative in moral decision making: "between discourse, power (in the sense of domination), and possession, the ties are so inextricable that a social therapeutics of the systematic distortions of language has to be added to a simple hermeneutic incapable of curing by its discourse alone the misunderstanding in discourse."[87] It is worth stressing at this point that we have not strayed from the first-person perspective. This would be the case only if we were dealing with a self-sufficient autonomy rather than a dependent one. The self-sufficient *cogito* need not consider the question of "social therapeutics," but the hermeneutic self who recognizes that his ethical reflections are saturated with language and concepts that he did not develop cannot pretend to such a lofty isolation. Habermas's ideal speech situation, which we will see more of in the next chapter, is conducive to Ricoeur's project because it recognizes discourse as a practical, performative act that takes place in a context. Its primary role is to safeguard the autonomy of each person in the discourse, but it demands that claims be redeemed through argument.[88]

Argumentation is not the nemesis of convention, but rather a necessary detour that *convictions* must pass through to become *considered convictions*.[89] Recovering Rawls's notion of "reflective equilibrium," Ricoeur argues that in all important discussion, there is this detour through the argumentative demand for universality. Regardless of how specifically contextual the matter at issue is, "it remains that it is the plea for *universality* that gives full weight to the problems tied to the *historicity* of concrete morality."[90] But a universal norm that is articulated within the context of an ethical aim, is always *on the way*; universal formulations are either struggling for articulation from their contextual origins, "potential or inchoate universals," or they are struggling to make themselves applicable to a particular situation, "universals in context." This sense of universality, according to Ricoeur, "best accounts for the reflective equilibrium that we are seeking between universality and historicity."[91]

David Kaplan concisely summarizes the deployment of practical wisdom in the resolution of novel ethico-political situations as follows:

> (1) It always upholds the moral norm, although it may be applied differently according to the particulars of the situation; (2) it is a search for an Aristotelian mean, less in the sense of a compromise than an attempt to find common ground; (3) so as not to appear arbitrary, it should seek the advice of others, especially competent, wise, experienced people.[92]

The third point reinforces the notion of *dependent autonomy* as separate from self-sufficient autonomy in the Kantian tradition. Others are implied in very structure of practical wisdom at all three levels.

DESIGNATING THE SELF

We have now followed Ricoeur through the largest arc of detour and return, the critical arc that proceeds from a phenomenology of the will through the detour of linguistic mediation and returning to a hermeneutics of the self. We have also followed him through the narrative arc that is inscribed within the return, from a *description* of the acting and speaking self through the *narration* of identity to the *prescription* of ethical behavior. Furthermore, we have followed him through a more precise critical arc, from the ethical aim to *live well with and for others in just institutions* through the universalizing imperatives of the moral norm to the contextual universals of practical wisdom. By proceeding backward through the middle, narrative arc, we are able to see what has been learned about the self in the process of detours within detours. This will also address the three guiding problematics of Ricoeur's hermeneutics of the self: reflexive mediation, sameness and selfhood, and the self and the other.

Recognition

The critical arc of the little ethics positions the universal moral norm between a simple and a critical *phronesis*. On the one hand, the norm finds its *source* in the ethical aim, as both Kant and Rawls implicitly concede when they open their respective works with explicit references to *good* and *virtue*. On the other hand, the norm cannot be applied in novel or difficult situations without *recourse* to the ethical aim, as when the injunctions to minimize suffering and to tell the truth conflict in the case of caring for terminally ill patients. The mediating norm works at all three levels: at the personal level, the desire for self-esteem passes through the imperative self-respect to a considered conviction of dependent autonomy; at the interpersonal level, solicitude for others (and for oneself as an other) passes through the imperative to respect others as ends to a critical solicitude; and at the general level, a sense of justice as cooperative, empowering institutions passes through the rule of justice as legal injunctions, which forms the paradigm for practical wisdom as a *Sittlichkeit* that has been reclaimed by *phronesis*.

Of the three problematics around which *Oneself as Another* was organized, the critical arc of ethics is designed to speak to the third, the relation of the self to the other. Ricoeur is of the opinion that there is a "discouraging banality" to the conversation on "alterity" in French philosophy,[93] and this would seem to be justified. Especially in the wake of Levinas's *Otherwise than Being*,[94] there is such a reaction against the *cogito* that the Other becomes an external master through the injunction forced upon the self by the Other's face. A variation on the Cartesian motto could be proposed: *spectus ergo sum, tu regardes donc je suis*. This reduction of the self to such complete passivity is, for Ricoeur, "hyperbole, to the point of paroxysm."[95]

Ricoeur contends that there is no conflict between the self moving toward the other and the other moving toward the self.[96] He offers the term "recognition" as a way of understanding what has been accomplished:

> Recognition is a structure of the self reflecting on the movement that carries self-esteem toward solicitude and solicitude toward justice. Recognition intro-

duces the dyad and plurality in the very constitution of the self. Reciprocity in friendship and proportional equality in justice, when they are reflected in self-consciousness, make self-esteem a figure of recognition.[97]

The key to recognition is *solicitude,* the open regard for the other within the context of the ethical aim. In recognizing the other as a self, I am able to accept and absorb that other's regard of me.[98] This is a precondition of a fully appropriated reflexive selfhood; there is no way for this to occur within the confines of a posited ego. Only in the act of regarding the other's regard for me can I *esteem my self as an Other.* It is not a question of my choosing to regard others so that I might learn to regard myself; this would be to reverse the order. Rather, it is implied reflexively in the very operation of self-esteem that this dialectic between the self and other is in play. An appropriated selfhood merely *recognizes* the operations for what they are.[99]

Responsibility

The narrative arc of the hermeneutics of the self finds its microcosm in its own mediating term: narrative identity. The dialectic between sameness and selfhood, between empirical perseverance and self-constancy, is held together by narrative identity. The two overlap in the area of character, where the sedimentation of the habits formed in self-constancy eventually appears as acquired character traits that are identifiable through their empirical perseverance. The two diverge in the area of keeping one's word, where a permanence of the self is asserted over and against any empirical instability, be it psychological or physical.

The term Ricoeur selects as most helpful for understanding this dialectic is *responsibility.* There are three temporal aspects to responsibility, corresponding to the three tenses. The future is most intuitive, the example of promise keeping being an obvious case. I will accept the consequences of my actions, claiming things that are to my credit and making restitution for actions that are my fault. Claiming the action now entails taking responsibility for it in the future, regardless of unintended consequences. Responsibility to the past, on the other hand, involves the recognition that the thing which I claim for myself, *my past,* is not strictly mine. As Ricoeur says, "we assume a past that affects us without being entirely our own work but that we take upon ourselves as ours."[100] These two types of responsibility converge in the present. For moral identity to be based on narrative identity, I must accept that I am held as *self-constant,* "the same today as the one who acted yesterday and who will act tomorrow."[101] I behave responsibly in the present when I am aware that I am held to the past to which I am indebted and to the future in which I will be held accountable.

Imputability

The opening task of Ricoeur's hermeneutics of the self was to establish the reflexive self, "the primacy of reflective mediation over the immediate positing of the subject." This was accomplished first through a hermeneutic retrieval of the story of the *cogito* from Descartes to the present. The exaltation of the *cogito* is countered by its humiliation in Nietzsche, which opened the way for a humbler, wounded *cogito*. No longer an *ego,* this *self* could not be addressed directly but only could be implied reflexively through its operations. This necessitated a *detour* through analysis because what this self *is* could be discovered only by passing through what can be ascribed to it. The ascription of action to an agent is both semantic and pragmatic, and the first four studies of *Oneself as Another* explored the analytical resources of speech and action.

Ascription, however, could be applied only to an "agent," a form of identity that can appear only under the aspect of *sameness.* With the tools of narrative identity, together with its ethical implications, ascription is transformed into *imputability:* "the ascription of action to its agent, *under the condition of ethical and moral predicates* which characterize the action as good, just, conforming to duty, done out of duty, and, finally, as being the wisest in the case of conflictual situations."[102] While an action can be *ascribed* to an agent, it can be *imputed* to a self. This is the self of self-esteem that aims for the good life with and for others in just institutions, that passes through the sieve of the universalizing moral norm and ultimately accepts responsibility for making decisions in conflictual situations.

Attestation

Ricoeur closes out his hermeneutics of the self with an exploration of the ontological implications of the first nine studies. He reiterates the critical arc in an attempt to articulate his accomplishment in terms of *attestation.* Attestation is "the assurance—the credence and the trust—of *existing* in the mode of selfhood." It finds its opposite in suspicion, but the two stand not in contradiction or paradox, but rather in a critical arc: "It [suspicion] is not simply the contrary of attestation, in a strictly disjunctive sense as being-false is in relation to being-true. Suspicion is also the path *toward* and the crossing *within* attestation."[103] Truth in the sense of attestation is not the same as in the sense of adequation. Opposites relate dialectically in the mode of attestation. This is why, when taking up the question of the relationship between the self and the Other, Ricoeur is so critical of Levinas's seeming self-abnegation. While the collapse of the self/other dialectic is a perennial and grave danger, collapsing it in the direction of the Other is not a viable solution. The Other can still be "the necessary path of injunction" without overwhelming the Self.

This is the culmination of Ricoeur's detour-and-return dynamic. Multiple variations of both the critical and narrative arcs are in play at once. The critical arc is operative in the engagement of the other as a source of injunction to the self, a *moral* moment of critique in one's *ethical* life plan. Simultaneously, the other functions as a *configuring* moment in the self's quest to exist as a self. The Other who regards herself as a Same and me as an Other is a *productive* detour through which I must pass to move from a pre-figured sense of "I" to a fully developed self. Both arcs operate at the level of ethics, which is itself the end of a narrative arc that passed from description through narration to prescription. What was described was the "wounded cogito" that had to pass through the detour of analytic semantics and prag-matics before narrative identity could appear. This "wounded cogito" was the result of the critique of the *cogito* by the anti-*cogito* philosophies in yet another critical arc, and was also the departure point for a hermeneutics of the self that began with eidetic identity and passed through the detour of sign, symbol, and narrative.

The largest arc remains to be completed. In the second chapter, we em-phasized Ricoeur's "double life," his resolute intention to keep his biblical faith and his philosophy on separate tracks. This is not an aesthetic prefer-ence, but a restraint. Ricoeur insists that he would that it were otherwise: "I am, in a certain sense, also very keen to unify myself and not to stay in division, but I am constrained by my fear of confusion."[104] This is an odd fear for Ricoeur, who moves so comfortably between apparently incompat-ible disciplines with his critical hermeneutics. But what all the arcs of the previous paragraph have in common is that they were detours either *for* or *within* hermeneutics. Hermeneutics moves with much less assurance when the shoe is on the other foot, when *it* is the potential detour. This configura-tion of hermeneutics as a detour for faith helps to explain the sharp retreat from speculation that closes out *Oneself as Another:*

> Perhaps the philosopher as philosopher has to admit that one does not know and cannot say whether this Other, the source of injunction, is another person whom I can look in the face or who can stare back at me, or my ancestors for

whom there is no representation, to so great an extent does my debt to them constitute my very self, or God—living God, absent God—or an empty place. With this aporia of the Other, philosophical discourse comes to an end.[105]

Ricoeur refuses to say anything further on the Other, for the Other transcends the boundaries of philosophical discourse. This places sharp limits on what he can say about the Self. But this is not the end of the story. Although philosophical discourse comes to an end, this does not mean that all discourse comes to an end. It remains to be seen what kind of discourse can take up the conversation where Ricoeur leaves off.

Part Three   Return

Having completed our philosophical detour, we now return to the question of theology's struggle to manage the tension between *integrity* and *relevance*. We have new tools to think through this problem: both the critical arc and the narrative arc can mediate theology's attempt to open to the disciplinary "Other" without sacrificing its own identity. But the question remains very broad. Disagreements inevitably arise as soon as either "integrity" or "relevance" gets defined with any precision. Just how relevant does theology have to be, and what constitutes its relevance? Conversely, at what point does theology begin to lose its integrity, and what criteria are used to make that judgment? To take philosophy, theology's perennial conversation partner, as an example: can theology agree to do its work according to philosophical criteria of argumentation and still maintain its theological integrity, or will theology's very identity become lost in a "network of alternating takeover attempts," as Habermas warns?[1] In terms of "theology" and "philosophy" as disciplines, neither can be defined with enough precision to make the tensions productive. Nor is there a third, neutral position from which we could make such generalized judgments.

Perhaps it is too much to expect such clarity at the disciplinary level. But if we narrow the scope to a single theologian and a single philosopher, and observe the interaction on a more concrete level, perhaps a beginning can be made. There is, after all, no way to read "theology" as such, only particular theologians who attempt to practice it, and likewise with philosophy. Individual points of contact are thus not only the most fruitful, but actually the *only* way such authentic interactions can occur; generalizations come later. Even when speaking in broad disciplinary terms, one is forced eventually to appeal to the arguments of individuals of that discipline. The individuals that will be used in this case are the "major powers" referred to in part 1: Karl Barth and Paul Ricoeur. Thus far in the North American conversation, Barth has been too closely linked with an inappropriate philosophical model (the

Wittgensteinian cultural-linguistic model) and Ricoeur too closely linked with an inappropriate theological model (Tracy's correlationist model).

The tools we now have at our disposal make the task more manageable. Taking the original Christian witness in the Gospels, we now have the conceptual vocabulary to speak of how they *configure* the story of Christ with a view toward *refiguring* the world of those who listen. Each time this Word is proclaimed in sermon or sacrament, the participatory retelling of the story is a continuing configuration of what has been received, in order to refigure the lives of those who participate. As Barth will insist, "the fundamental form of theology is the prayer and the sermon."[2] Theology as an academic discipline is a critical detour from this fundamental theology, abstracting from the concrete practices in order to better understand what is happening and should happen. But as a detour, its goal is first and last to return, to have its conceptual insights appropriated back into the lives and practices of Christians. Theology, however, needs a conceptual language in order to accomplish this, and thus must take its own critical detour through philosophy.

The sixth chapter will concern itself with arguing for the structural compatibility between Barth and Ricoeur on the theoretical level by emphasizing the similarity of pattern between the two, as well as the hospitable but distant attitude of each toward the other's discipline. The final chapter will concretely demonstrate the compatibility by using Ricoeur as a hermeneutic detour for Barth in the interplay of anthropology and ethics, making use of Ricoeur's theory of narrative identity, his distinction between selfhood and sameness, and the self-other relationship of the ethical aim.

6

Chalcedonian Hermeneutics

Here I attempt to cash in the wager I made in the introduction, that Barth's theology and Ricoeur's philosophy will prove compatible. In one sense, this is a natural pairing because of their similarities: they share not only a Christian faith, but also a background in the Reformed tradition, a dialectical method, an appreciation of narrative, and a concern for the integrity of both philosophy and theology. In another sense however, Barth may seem an odd choice for a pairing with Ricoeur. Barth's massive influence on the postliberal theology and Ricoeur's association with the home of revisionist theology at University of Chicago Divinity School place the two on opposite sides of a highly polarized debate. The postliberals are anxious that Ricoeur's hermeneutics will colonize theology, and the revisionists are concerned that Barth's Christocentric theology is too narrowly exclusivist. The polarization of this debate has led to falsely dichotomized options when considering the claims of both Ricoeur's hermeneutic philosophy and Barth's Christocentric theology.

As we saw in the second chapter, David Tracy and Hans Frei have dominated the reception of Ricoeur in North American theology, characterizing the initial positive and negative responses to Ricoeur's hermeneutics. Tracy goes so far as to say that hermeneutic philosophy should be the new ally for theology (replacing Platonism, which is now "in its twilight"), because it "provides the kind of contemporary philosophy needed by a revelational theology."[1] Frei registered strong objections to the "application" of philosophical hermeneutics to theology, which would reduce theology to a mere regional application of a general theory. Those who follow Frei's interpretation tend to accept his projection of those methods onto Ricoeur as well. We have seen, however, that this *rejection* turns out to be a view of Ricoeur through the partially distorting lens of Tracy's *use* of Ricoeur. Moreover, Frei and the "Yale School" are not the only representatives of Barth.[2] Even if there is an incompatibility between Ricoeur and Frei, it need not follow that there is a similar incompatibility between Ricoeur and Barth.[3]

RICOEUR AND BARTH ON SCRIPTURE

Mark Wallace is the first to undertake a sustained argument in favor of the compatibility of Barth and Ricoeur.[4] His contention is that Ricoeur and Barth have the same three phases in their "hermeneutical arc," although they draw their terms from different traditions. Barth draws his three stages from the medieval formula of *explicatio, meditatio, applicatio* (updated to *Beobachtung, Nachdenken, Aneignung*),[5] while Ricoeur opts for the terms naïve understanding, objective explanation, and appropriation. By examining Wallace's treatment of how Ricoeur and Barth *read*, we will gain some insight into the similarities in their pattern of thought.

Naïve Understanding, Observation

For both Barth and Ricoeur, the first stage is to allow the text to unfold through a simple reading, with no limits on what the text can or cannot mean. The primary loyalty of the reader is to the text, not to any foreign system of meaning. Ricoeur calls this moment "naïve understanding," referring to the fact that in this first, naïve moment of reading, the reader can only make a provisional "guess" at the text's meaning. This is far removed from the process of determining the authorial intention of the text, for "correct understanding can no longer be solved by a simple return to the alleged situation of the author."[6] What the author may have meant to say is subordinated to what the author actually *said,* the verbal meaning of the text. The reader's estimation of the meaning of the text can at first be no more than a guess because the whole can be known only through its parts, and the parts can be understood only in terms of the whole. There is no escape from this hermeneutic circle, but a provisional guess allows the reader to get into the circle in the right way.[7]

Likewise, Barth urges the reader to "stop and listen to what the New Testament actually says," before we move to any judgment of its validity or decision regarding application.[8] The impetus toward fidelity to the text is even stronger in Barth because the reference of the text in this case (the incarnate Word of God), is *more real than we are,* a point we will return to in the next chapter. Barth also emphasizes that *what* is said cannot be separated from *how* it is said. In his famous confrontation with Bultmann—who wanted to *demythologize* the Gospel so that the core message (*kerygma*) could appear more clearly and be translated into language more accessible to the contemporary reader—Barth emphasized that such translation is a secondary process, which, if it is to be done well, depends on the prior task of exegesis.[9] Without first pursuing the meaning of the text through exegesis, Barth wonders what criteria are being used to differentiate the "outward imagery" from the "actual substance" of the biblical witness.

Both Ricoeur and Barth are against Bultmann on this point of form and content. They argue (albeit in different ways) that the content of the biblical message cannot be separated from the form in which it is presented. Ricoeur is more sympathetic to the existentialist tenor of Bultmann's hermeneutics than Barth, but argues that Bultmann short-circuits the process by moving too quickly to the moment of existential decision, predetermining what *is* and *is not* important before engaging the text. The world of the text must be allowed to unfold, with the self as one of the things interpreted, before these existential questions can be addressed.

Objective Explanation, Reflection

The second, explanatory moment of Ricoeur's method must be treated with care, for it is here where philosophical hermeneutics threatens to overwhelm its subject matter, leaving biblical hermeneutics as a mere "regional application" of a general hermeneutic theory. Ricoeur has always been sensitive to this issue, and was aware that because he *begins* the explanatory moment with a straightforward application of his philosophical hermeneutics, those who are attuned to the danger of the colonization of theology by foreign systems of thought would immediately accuse him of such a transgression (which is what happened in the case of Frei). But Ricoeur argues that the explanatory moment is necessary, is distinct, and must be given room to work. The biblical text is in fact a *text,* and thus falls at least partly under the rules of reading and interpreting texts. As we saw in the second chapter, Ricoeur warns against constructing a biblical theology "which does not include initially and in principle that passage from speech to writing."[10] Texts are like artifacts, constructed according to deliberate patterns that enable them to be interpreted in different times and places. This does not reduce Scripture to a mere application, because whatever it is that makes Scripture unique, "it is nothing that belongs to the relation between speech and writing as such."[11] It is the rigorous precise work of this second stage to construct possible interpretations that do not do violence to the text as it is structured.

Perhaps Wallace's most important contribution in comparing Barth and Ricoeur is his debunking of the notion that Barth is hostile to philosophy as such, although Wallace himself finds his discovery of pro-philosophical statements in Barth both "remarkable" and "surprising." There is a difference between being hostile toward philosophical colonization and simply being hostile toward philosophy, and Barth is clearly not the latter:

> We must remember that we are definitely ranging ourselves with those who "explain" the Bible, i.e., read it through the spectacles of a definite system of ideas, which has the character of a "world-view" and will in some way make itself felt as such when we read and explain the Bible. If we hold up hands of horror at the very idea, we must not forget that without such systems of explanation, without such spectacles, we cannot read the Bible at all.[12]

Barth clearly recognizes the hermeneutic fact that our prejudgments are always and necessarily a part of the interpretative process.[13] What Barth combats is the tendency to allow these prejudgments to become systematized as criteria by which Scripture is judged. Thus Barth encourages a heuristic, ad hoc approach to the use of philosophy in biblical interpretation. It is heuristic so that the philosophical concepts never rise to the status of criteria, and it is ad hoc so that competing philosophical systems can always keep each other in check.

This insistence on the explanatory moment argues against any kind of biblical literalism or fundamentalism. Because texts are deliberately structured, they need to be interpreted in a way that takes account of that structure. As Barth puts it: "At the start of this attempt, we still find ourselves wholly on the plane of general hermeneutics."[14] This is part of Ricoeur's overarching project, but it is no less important to Barth. A responsible interpreter of the Bible, no matter how threatened she may feel by the colonization of higher critical methods, can never afford to ignore them altogether. This form of rigorous explanation is a necessary detour in the hermeneutic process.

Appropriation

The word "appropriation" carries with it connotations of the mastering subject who autonomously chooses from the possible meanings disclosed by the text and applies them at will. Were this the case, the scriptural Word would at best be a useful tool in the subject's search for enlightenment. Ricoeur argues that this is only one side of the story: "What is appropriated is indeed the matter of the text. But the matter of the text becomes my own only if I disappropriate myself, in order to let the matter of the text be. So I exchange the me, master of itself, for the self, disciple of the text."[15] Having gone from the original guess through the difficult, painstaking work of scientific investigation, the reader must now surrender the mastery if the full matter of the text is to appear.

Barth is substantially in agreement with Ricoeur on the importance of self-dispossession; if anything, he makes the point more strongly. He finds the correlationist theologians of the day (e.g., Tillich) to be, in Ricoeur's terms, masters of the text. They had important ethico-political questions of their own, and *appropriated* the biblical text as a way of answering those questions. As he did with Bultmann, Barth objects that this allows *our* concerns to rule our reading of Scripture, and predetermines what is and is not important in the biblical text. The question is not whether we can successfully determine the meaning of the text and appropriate it, but whether we can openly encounter Christ in the text and *be appropriated* by him. "When the distinctions have been made they can be pushed again into the background and the whole can be read (with this tested and critical naivete) as the totality it professes to be."[16] Wallace nicely juxtaposes this with Ricoeur's own formulation of appropriation as "second naïveté " to emphasize the similarity.

Here the common foe for Barth and Ricoeur is the historical critic. Both consciously employ the full range of historical-critical tools, but both object to the notion that a thorough *explanation* of the circumstances surrounding the text somehow constitutes an *understanding* of the matter of the text. The text is not a mere veil to be torn aside in search of the real "facts," but rather a mediator of Revelation, with a positive role to play in the process. If there is no move back toward the text's implications for the reader, the text has been only explained, not understood.

COMPLEMENTARY PATTERNS

Wallace successfully demonstrates that there is a striking similarity between the hermeneutic approaches of Ricoeur and Barth in their reading of Scripture. He also goes on to point out some divergences, which will be addressed later. I would emphasize the similarity as one of *pattern,* and I would suggest that this points to an even greater affinity between Barth and Ricoeur. The work of both is stamped with a discernible pattern of thought, and while these patterns are not identical, they are similar, and perhaps similar enough to be compatible. Ricoeur's pattern is detour and return (in this case the critical arc), while Barth's pattern can be characterized as "Chalcedonian."

The Chalcedonian Pattern in Barth

Reading Barth is a daunting task. His method of recapitulating an argument as each new point is added often leaves the reader confused as to which direction the argument is moving. George Hunsinger addressed this problem by pointing out a number of motifs and patterns that recur throughout Barth's work. While there is no unifying system to be found, attention to these motifs and patterns can help the reader make that provisional "guess" as to the text's meaning. The most prominent of these is the Chalcedonian pattern, named after the Christological definition (without separation or division and without confusion or change) issued from the council of Chalcedon in AD 451.[17]

Perhaps the most striking thing about the Chalcedonian definition is its minimalism. Considered historically, it might be seen as a compromise position, mediating the excesses of the high Alexandrine and the low Antiochian Christologies of the fourth and fifth centuries, finding a middle ground that more or less satisfied both factions. Considered doctrinally, however, it is a unifying recognition that there were essential truths on both sides that needed to be affirmed, but in a way that did not say more than was possible to say. Thus, the Chalcedonian definition operates not as an exhaustive definition, but as a hermeneutic construct; it is quite positive in its affirmations of Christ's divinity and humanity, but offers no specifics beyond those of perfection and completeness, which makes the definition dependent on the sacred text to which it refers.[18] If either the full divinity or the full humanity of Christ is denied, any account of His saving work will be insufficient, but the very lack of specification of divinity and humanity points us back to Scripture. As Hunsinger puts it, "Chalcedon offers no more and no less than a set of spectacles for bringing the central witness of the New Testament into focus."[19] There are two natures in the one person of Christ, and one cannot be asserted to the exclusion of the other.

Chalcedon maintained the tension by employing three basic procedures, two explicit and one implicit. Explicitly affirmed are both *unity* and *differentiation,* while an asymmetrical ordering is implicit in the presentation. "The Chalcedonian pattern, formally speaking, is a pattern of unity ('without separation or division'), differentiation (without confusion or change), and asymmetry (the unqualified conceptual precedence of the divine over the human nature of Jesus Christ)."[20] In Barth, this pattern is pervasive because his theology is resolutely Christocentric; the patterns of Christology will inevitably appear wherever they are relevant, and for Barth, there is no place where they are *not* relevant. It is in his anthropology that the Chalcedonian pattern is most prevalent: "Through the Spirit of God, man is the subject, form and life of a substantial organism, the soul of his body—wholly and simultaneously both, *in ineffaceable difference, inseparable unity, and indestructible order.*"[21] Hunsinger explains that over the whole of the *Church Dogmatics* this pattern "governs the discussion at every point virtually without exception,"[22] and moreover that each element protects against particular doctrinal traps that would lead to a lack of coherence with the biblical witness.[23] Therefore, whenever there is a discussion in Barth of the relationship between the divine and the human, these three elements will be present and active.

INEFFACEABLE DIFFERENCE

The element of ineffaceable difference protects against the fatalistic tendencies toward determinism or monism, a tendency that Barth sees as characteristic of "metaphysical dogmas" that attempt to unify divine and human action into a single, rational system.[24] Such systems, as laudable as their aims may be, inevitably end up somehow circumscribing God *within* the system. The very generality that characterizes systematic theology excludes the particular divine-human person of Christ—who performed a particular redemptive act in a particular time and place as is witnessed to in a particular canon of Scripture—from being the central core of theology. It attempts to make sense of God without recourse to the concrete particularities of Christ, and thus paints over the miraculous intervention of God in history. That such an occurrence be an instance of *no* class, that it is a singular *event* that is described and not an example of a state of being, cannot be accounted for within a metaphysical system.

Any attempt to unify Christ's work and our situation according to some higher principle loses the "biblical center" of the Christian faith, which results in *confusion and change* because everything must then be accounted for within a single calculus. God and the human creature can no longer be in a relationship of freedom and grace, because the absolute freedom of God can be exercised only at the expense of negating human freedom. It becomes a zero-sum game. Only by maintaining the ineffaceable difference between God and the human creature can their unity be conceived in a way that is degrading to neither.

INSEPARABLE UNITY

The element of inseparable unity protects against a Pelagian or semi-Pelagian positing of independent human autonomy. Were the human ability to freely cooperate with God fully, or even partly, a product of something inherent in human nature itself, the human creature's complete dependence on the special operation of divine grace would be negated.[25] What would also be negated is the radicality of sin, and thus the radicality of Christ's work on the Cross. To be sinful is to have "completely lost the capacity for God,"[26] and thus to be completely dependent on the grace of God as it is offered in the person and work of Christ. A sinful human creature that is somehow a cooperator in the process of redemption, a co-redeemer, is, for Barth, "a self-contradiction."[27] Using a geometric metaphor, Barth argues that while the Pelagian and semi-Pelagian positions take human freedom as the second focal point of an ellipse, the true relation is conceptually *asymmetrical*, "the circumference around one central point of which it is the repetition and confirmation."[28] Human freedom, insofar as it is achieved, is participatory, both mediated by and completely dependent on the person and work of Christ. We can repeat and confirm, but never initiate or complete; to be human is to be utterly dependent.

INDESTRUCTIBLE ORDER

The element of indestructible order protects against the use of "dialectical identity" to avoid the theological pitfalls of Pelagianism and determinism. Dialectical identity is a strategy that resolves the paradoxical relationship between divine grace and human freedom by casting them as two sides of the same coin. As Barth puts it, "what is seen from one side as grace is freedom when seen from the other side and *vice versa*."[29] This in turn leads to a positing of a "secret identity" between divine and human capacities.[30] Barth emphatically rejects any position of identity or complementarity between the human and the divine. To posit such a coordination would be to imply that both can be studied together to the point where they can be identified as "one and the same reality."[31] This would require either the anthropomorphizing of God or the partial deification of the human creature. Without the insistence on indestructible order, the unity-in-difference that enables a "mutual ordering in freedom" cannot be maintained.[32]

This threefold pattern is at work in Barth's biblical hermeneutic. The moment of reflection, the explanatory moment, is a distinctly human moment, and it cannot be avoided. Indeed there is no wish to avoid it, provided it is situated within the larger hermeneutic context, and not given primary importance. The moments of observation and appropriation are dominated by Scripture itself with the human in a more receptive, even "naïve" role. The emphasis on the Word in the outside stages and the emphasis on the human in the middle stage underscore that the receptive moments and the critical moment cannot be separated—Barth might here use Ricoeur's dictum: to explain more is to understand better—but neither can they be confused. More importantly, the receptive moments have precedence over the critical moment; the point of reading Scripture is never simply to explain it or use it for our own ends. If this last element is missing, it will all fall apart. Either the reader will be left with an impoverished literalist reading (separation and division), or the critical methods will overwhelm the process (confusion and change). All three elements of the Chalcedonian pattern are mutually interdependent.

The Detour-and-Return Pattern in Ricoeur

In the previous chapters, we have seen the detour pattern in operation throughout Ricoeur's work, both in the overall structure and as a continuing leitmotif. But in the linear progression through the various manifestations of the pattern, one can lose sight of the forest for the trees, so it is worth pulling back to see how pervasive it is.

Ricoeur first gained recognition for his work on the phenomenology of the will, a projected trilogy that never saw completion because the pure phenomenological method was insufficient for the task. Following the *Symbolism of Evil* (and even during the work itself), Ricoeur recognized the need to engage the forms in which human culture is expressed, and embarked on what is now referred to as his hermeneutic turn. This "detour" occupied him for the next quarter century, engaging psychoanalysis, semiotics, structuralism, metaphor, and narrative. The question of personal identity was once again broached in the conclusion of the final volume of *Time and Narrative,* and taken up in detail in *Oneself as Another.*

The scope of the detour/return motif in Ricoeur's thought might even be wider. His first collection, *History and Truth,*[33] was born of his political activism prior to the Second World War, which itself stemmed from the political ambiguity of his own father's death in the First World War. His entire corpus can be seen as an extended detour from the initial ethico-political question of how to remember those who died in war (especially if their nation's role was not honorable), and how the past in general should be remembered by those who live. The detour goes through all the stages described above—with the history/fiction relation explored in *Time and Narrative II* as the crucial point in the detour—and finally returns to the original area of interest in *Memory, History, Forgetting* and *The Course of Recognition.*

The detour/return pattern is even more prominent in the methodological choices that Ricoeur has made following the *Symbolism of Evil.* We have already seen in Wallace's account of Ricoeur's biblical reading a move from naïve understanding that *detours* through objective explanation and *returns* to a second naïveté in appropriation. Wallace goes on to list the terms that other authors have applied to that particular detour/return move, but we need look no further than Ricoeur himself. The titles of his books are notable for portraying this: narrative as a necessary detour from cosmological time to human time in *Time and Narrative;* text as a way of recounting action that also returns to action in *From Text to Action;* the other as an indispensable part of becoming a self in *Oneself as Another;* and most importantly, critique as a middle moment between naïve and sophisticated conviction in *Critique and Conviction.* Within the books themselves there are myriad examples of this pattern at work. Chief among these is the narrative arc of threefold mimesis, comprising prefiguration, configuration, and refiguration. As we saw in the previous two chapters, the pattern is even stronger in *Oneself as Another,* appearing several times and on different scales.

The omission of the two studies on natural theology from *Oneself as Another* suggests the very broadest possibility of detour and return with respect to Ricoeur. The suggestion that his philosophical work *as a whole* constitutes a detour will be addressed in detail in the next section. For now, it is sufficient to note the similarities between the detour-and-return movement and Barth's Chalcedonian pattern. The two poles of the detour-and-return dialectic exhibit the same quality of unity-in-distinction, or "mutual enveloping,"[34] as the first two elements of the Chalcedonian pattern. More important to note is that a detour is just a detour; it is not the main road. A detour has both an origin and a terminus, and it is positioned with respect to the main road in a way that the main road is not positioned with respect to the detour. Thus there is a clear *asymmetry* between the two poles of the detour-and-return movement.

PHILOSOPHY AND THEOLOGY

Divergences: The "Christological Lodestar"

According to Wallace, Barth and Ricoeur part ways when it comes to anthropology and Christology, and Wallace clearly sides with Ricoeur in both instances.[35] Wallace argues that Barth's "anthropocentrism" prevents him from fully developing the importance of creation in the story of salvation. Barth interprets Scripture as primarily concerning God's relationship with humans: "In practice, the doctrine of creation means anthropology—the doctrine of man."[36] Wallace contends that this special relationship is construed at the expense of all other life, and shows a lack of ecological sensitivity that has pervaded the tradition. Such an anthropocentric view "narrowly shrinks the biblical world."[37] Ricoeur's more "cosmological" hermeneutic, on the other hand, allows for the "full display" of the world of the biblical text, "with all of its nonanthropological coordinates."[38] The second phase of Wallace's argument addresses the centrality of Christ in Scripture:

> While they formally stand together in according the biblical world a primacy in interpretation, Barth and Ricoeur interpret the material content of this world differently. According to Barth, the subject matter of the Bible is plainly Jesus Christ. . . . Ricoeur's theological hermeneutic, on the other hand, operates with no such christological lodestar, and herein lies a major area of disagreement between the two thinkers.[39]

Ricoeur and Barth part ways on the overarching importance of Christ in Scripture, with Ricoeur allowing for a more "polyphonic" rendering of Revelation. Wallace's argument seems to depend a great deal on the intrinsic superiority of diversity over unity. Characterizing Ricoeur's position are glowing terms such as pluralistic, polysemic, multiplicity, imaginative, and plenitude; while Barth's position is more starkly characterized as Christocentric, homogenizing, and narrow.[40] When this is coupled with the former allegation of anthropocentrism, the inescapable conclusion of all this is that Ricoeur has the more adequate theological hermeneutics.

There are a few problems with such an assessment. The first is whether Ricoeur himself has a "theological hermeneutics" in the first place, any more than Barth has a philosophical hermeneutics. What both *do* have is a biblical hermeneutics, but the fact that each has a different approach is hardly problematic. Barth is a theologian, while Ricoeur is a philosopher, and each employs the tools appropriate to his respective discipline. The fact that Barth is not adequately philosophical or that Ricoeur is not adequately theological need not imply that either is failing in his task, or even that the two are in serious disagreement. Ricoeur is reading the Bible primarily (but not only) as a cultural classic that has had an unparalleled impact on Western civilization, which brings it to the attention of philosophical hermeneutics, while Barth is reading the Bible as Holy Scripture, the sacred text that bears witness to the Word of God, which is the primary source of dogmatic theology. Personally both read as committed Christians, but professionally they are not participating in the same conversation. Barth is in dialogue with a theological tradition, while Ricoeur is in dialogue with the philosophical tradition, with no *philosophical* allegiance to the received interpretations (e.g., the ecumenical councils) of the role of the person of Christ in biblical interpretation. He demonstrates a clear personal preference for the Old Testament writings because of the multiplicity of literary forms, while Barth gives more weight to the New Testament witness simply because he is a Christian dogmatic theologian. Thus, what we see in their dissimilarity is not necessarily a "major area of disagreement," but rather the consequence of a difference in vocation.

Given such differences in vocation, there is no surprise in finding a difference in approach. Ricoeur begins with a philosophical anthropology while Barth begins with a theological anthropology. These starting points prefigure their readings of Scripture, which has a significant impact on how their interpretations develop. What *is* surprising is that their interpretations turn out to be as similar as they are. The difficulty arises only when one begins to treat Ricoeur primarily as a *theologian*. Wallace is certainly correct in noting that Ricoeur and Barth do not hold the same doctrinal positions, but it is fair to neither Barth nor Ricoeur to hold them to the same standard. Wallace seems to cast Ricoeur's as the superior *theological* position, while in reality it is superior by the standards of *philosophical* hermeneutics. By the criteria of dogmatic theology, Ricoeur's positions are not only inferior but occasionally outright heterodox. Nor is Ricoeur unaware of this, allowing that such divergences are "perhaps where the philosopher that I am acts upon the apprentice theologian that moves within me."[41] Here Wallace, despite his great service in bringing the two together, has unwittingly contributed to the overall misconstruing of Ricoeur's relevance for theological reflection.

I am suggesting that instead of placing Barth and Ricoeur on the same ground, which cannot but fail to do justice to neither, they can better be understood as operating in distinct spheres, which can then be related within a Chalcedonian or detour/return model. Moreover, such a relationship should occur quite naturally if the congruence in their scriptural hermeneutics is indeed an instance of a more encompassing congruence in their overall thought. Fortunately, both have addressed the issue, and although it is never the central point of an argument for either, what is there fits into this pattern.

Convergences: Humility before the Word

As the *Church Dogmatics* is a work that seeks to articulate a dogmatic theology that is faithful to Scripture, it does not take up the issue of the formal relationship between philosophy and theology.[42] However, in his earlier lectures on ethics, Barth did address the formal relationship between theological and philosophical ethics, which can be taken as a guide for the larger relationship.[43] As the main moves of Ricoeur's philosophy are also contained within his ethics, this is a fruitful point of contact. Barth notes that the "summary rejection" of theological ethics by the philosophical ethicist is "a very natural one" because the world of theological ethics is so "alien."[44] This disregard by philosophy is provocative, and Barth examines several strategies with which the theologian might address the philosopher. In his treatment of these strategies, we will once again see the Chalcedonian pattern at work.

The first strategy he takes up is the one of apologetics, which he defines as "the attempt to establish and justify theological thinking in the context of philosophical, or, more generally and precisely, nontheological thinking."[45] His negative appraisal of apologetic tendencies in theology is well known. Barth vigorously opposes any theological capitulation to philosophy's rules and methods. He advises the theologian not to begin on the defensive: "he cannot regard the supposedly original inhabitants of the land as a court to which he is commanded or is even able to give account."[46] Apologetic strategies not only betray the original loyalty to theological reflection, but also are doomed to failure. A theological ethics that tries to prove that it is implicit in philosophical ethics, that philosophical questions are better answered when "religious symbolism" is taken into account, might sneak into discussion, but "would still be irritating to the philosopher."[47] This is what we saw in the first chapter. Tracy's apologetic approach culminates with the assertion that the secularist and the theologian share the same fundamental conviction, but the former lacks the "existentially appropriate symbolic representation."[48] Philosophy inevitably sees the "gift" for what it is: a Trojan horse. Philosophy thus opens the horse, empties all the "theological" soldiers outside the gates, then takes the horse. The theologian gains entrance, but without any theology.

But Barth also opposes with equal vigor the strategy of isolation, which he characterizes as the "crowning of apologetics in much the same way that war is the continuation of politics by other means."[49] This "diastasis," which is opposed to the "synthesis" of apologetics, is where the theology takes the pretentious high road, "as though theology knew secrets which philosophy . . . neither knows nor ought to know." Barth denounces this approach, arguing that this "must be abandoned no less than that of apologetics."[50] There are strong tendencies toward this in the postliberal position, as we saw when Frei was so intent on protecting the *sensus literalis* from a perceived philosophical threat. Philosophical reflection on theological topics is welcomed by Barth.[51] Apologetics violates the element of ineffaceable difference, while isolation violates the element of inseparable unity.

The most "refined" error that Barth identifies, one that successfully avoids apologetics and isolation, is the Roman Catholic position. While Barth ultimately opposes this position, he finds much to learn from it, and characterizes the dominant Protestant approach as "coarser" and "crass" in comparison.[52] Moral philosophy and moral theology, "united in the person of the Roman Catholic theological ethicist,"[53] simply divide up the task of *Christian* ethics. Moral philosophy operates in the light of natural reason (hence the appropriation of Aristotle's philosophical virtues), while moral theology, the higher of the two, avails itself of Scripture and tradition, culminating in the theological virtues. The difficulty Barth sees is that by coordinating the work of God's grace and the human striving for God within the framework of a metaphysics of Being, the Catholic position ultimately is forced to abandon the radicality of both sin and grace. Barth argues that "God's grace . . . is either full, total, and exclusive grace or it is not divine,"[54] which is another expression of the Chalcedonian element of indestructible order. As Barth sees it, the Thomist model gives the human creature part of the initiative, thus violating that order. As a result, grace is no longer really grace, and sin is no longer really sin. As with all cases of the Chalcedonian pattern, a violation of the third element inevitably leads to a collapse of the entire pattern.

Barth conceives of the relationship of philosophical and theological ethics in terms of the relationship between the possible and the actual. Both disciplines have as their focus the Word of God and the repercussions of his self-revelation, but philosophy and theology contextualize it within different categories, possibility and actuality respectively. Barth emphasizes that what he intends to relate is a *Christian* theology with a *Christian* philosophy, the Christian element being understood as "the Word of God," by which he means "our Lord from and by and to whom we are what we are."[55] Neither the theologian nor the philosopher has *control* over this element, but both presuppose it and bear witness to it. But while theology takes up this confession as its actual theme, philosophy need not address the matter directly, but only as possibility. In fact, Barth argues that a Christian philosophy "must fundamentally refrain from confessing whenever this possibility arises."[56] The subject matter of a proper philosophy is not the Word of God itself, but rather the human creature *understood* in its relationship of inseparable unity, ineffaceable difference, and indestructible subsequence to the Word of God. As a result, such a philosophy will be identified by its awareness of its limits:

> Naturally it is a very definite philosophy, not that of a particular school or tendency, but one determined by its presupposition, that will be demanded by theology and acknowledged by it to be justified. . . . It can be determined absolutely only by the knowledge of the Christian element, the Word of God, that precedes self-reflection . . . , by its awareness that in practicing that reflection it cannot say the last word that solves the question of man but that the question can be put in merely penultimate words only after and as the last word has been and is spoken.[57]

The question that remains is whether there is a philosopher who will accept these terms. It is important to note that Barth does not put philosophy in a position of indestructible subsequence with respect to theology, since "theology, too, is an act of human reflection and understanding."[58] Philosophy, just like theology, is a reflection on the truth that is in Christ. "Nor is it called to do so, indeed, at a lower level than theology."[59] The relationship of unity, distinction, and order is to the object of the Christian faith, the Word of God. The priority that theology exercises over philosophy is only the priority that is analogous to that of actuality over possibility.[60] "Philosophy is *not* ancillary to theology. With philosophy, theology can only want to be ancillary to the church and to Christ."[61]

The philosopher who best satisfies the requirements of a Christian philosophical ethics as articulated by Barth is Ricoeur. This should not be surprising, given the impact that Barth had on the young Ricoeur. Barth's role in opposing the Nazis earned him a moral credibility and popularity that reached its zenith in the late forties and fifties. Like many young Protestants, Ricoeur was deeply influenced by Barth during this time.[62] As François Dosse notes in his wonderful biography, Ricoeur's later divergence from Barth "would change nothing on a certain number of fundamental points."[63] Chief among these is the role of the subject as *responsive:* "It was in fact Karl Barth who first taught me that the subject is not a centralizing master but rather a disciple or auditor of a language larger than itself."[64] Another significant appropriation was the Word as a stark singularity that prevented the closure of any system. With the development of this theme in the *Church Dogmatics,* Barth "allowed an escape from the choice between a culturally liberal subjectivity and submission to papal authority."[65] But it was not only Barth who influenced Ricoeur on this point. An even stronger push came from Marcel: "I was confronted from the beginning with the polarity between philosophy and religion, at first because Gabriel Marcel was quite anxious to distinguish what was religious from what was philosophical in his thought."[66] Whatever Ricoeur's *natural* impulses might be, he was certainly *nurtured* to distrust the merging of philosophical and religious thinking. As we saw in the second chapter, Ricoeur has also had a professional interest in being respected as a philosopher in an environment where theological influences were not welcome, and his appreciation of genre has sensitized him to the dangers of conflating modes of discourse.[67] What I have called his "double life" opens him to accusations of inconsistency, but he prefers that to "confusionism."[68] This last term points most obviously to Ricoeur's "Chalcedonian" concern to avoid confusion and change.

However, Ricoeur, like Barth, sees the isolationist strategy of "diastasis" as equally untenable. Between biblical exegesis and philosophy of religion, he has written scores of essays on explicitly religious topics. Against the "regional application" criticism that theologians were beginning to level against him, Ricoeur clarified that although the Bible *begins* as a regional instance, there is a much more complex relationship of "mutual inclusion" at work. Scripture is an instance of a text for the perusal of philosophical hermeneutics; so too philosophical hermeneutics is itself a theory of understanding at the disposal of theology: "By turns, one envelops the other."[69] Hence Ricoeur's insistence: "We can arrive at a philosophical reading of religious texts."[70] A pure separation or division is not an option for Ricoeur any more than it was for Barth.

The thorniest question will of course be the question of order. While Ricoeur might be content to assent to the unity-in-diversity of a Christian philosophy and theology, will he be willing to allow theology the priority Barth accords to actuality over possibility? That the theologian would put philosophy in the back seat is to be expected; for the philosopher to agree would be remarkable. But here again the structural organization of *Oneself as Another* is informative. The first study proposes a "sort of armistice" between religious and philosophical language. Ricoeur commits himself to pursuing an "autonomous" philosophy, but allows that at the profound level of "motivation," his Christian convictions are not without their effect. By motivation, he means "something that I do not master," a source that escapes his control. And the book closes on an agnostic note, noting that there is an Other who calls without being able to name who that Other is. Ricoeur likens this to Moses, who can see the promised land without being able to enter. There are clear reasons why this is the case: "Faith is indeed the limit of all hermeneutics, while at the same time standing as the non-hermeneutical origin of all interpretation . . . the thematic of faith eludes hermeneutics and attests to the fact that the latter has neither the first nor the last word."[71] It is the surrender of both the first and last word that makes hermeneutics itself the ideal detour for theology. Barth wanted the Christian conviction of being confronted and called by the Word of God to be active yet unnamed in Christian philosophy. He also identified a Christian philosophy not by its material principle or method, but by its willingness to forgo the last word. What Barth cast in terms of actuality and possibility, Ricoeur casts as a difference between faith and hope:

> If there is something like an *intellectus spei* (as a parallel to the expression *intellectus fidei*), it may be that this *intellectus spei*, this intelligibility of hope, does not consist in pointing to a specific object but to a structural change in the discourse. This structural change could concern what we might call the act of closing the discourse.[72]

Ricoeur both acknowledges the Word as his unmastered source and explicitly refuses to include it in his philosophical reflection. He also voluntarily gives up the last word because to go further would be to stop doing philosophy. Thus Ricoeur's entire philosophical anthropology can be regarded as a detour that can neither master its origins nor fully articulate its conclusions.

A Natural Alliance?

Barth's attitude toward the role of philosophy in theological reflection is demanding but not unreasonable: [T]he use of a scheme of thought in the service of scriptural exegesis is legitimate and fruitful when it is determined and controlled by the text and the object mirrored in the text. We might simply say: when it really becomes contributory to reflection."[73] While this would tend toward an ad hoc approach, as both Frei and Lindbeck advised, what if we were to find a philosophical approach that was tailor-made for sustaining such an authentic encounter because it was designed with that in mind? Would we not then have a natural alliance, as Tracy proposed? Tracy argues that Ricoeur does keep the philosophical distance appropriate to the relationship, and we have seen that Ricoeur is aware that his critical reflection occurs within a larger framework of conviction.

Theology, if it is to maintain its integrity, must take great care not to allow confusion or change to occur by blurring the boundaries between philosophy and theology. But the dangers of separation and division are equally great. Theology needs a vibrant and critical philosophy to converse with and be challenged by if it is to remain vibrant itself. Within the confines of theology, certain questions cannot be pursued to their fullest extent without betraying the fundamental loyalties of the theologian to the church in which they function. The absence of a vibrant Christian philosophy leads either to an intellectually arid theology that cannot respond in any meaningful way to the live and urgent questions posed to it or to a theology that sacrifices its integrity by ignoring its loyalties and following its questions through to the end, even if the end is heresy. The strength of philosophy is that it cannot *be* heretical; there are no authoritative creeds or texts against which it can transgress. It is a detour, a necessary detour that functions according to its own rules, but one that can ultimately return to theology.

As we have seen, there must be an ordering principle if this is to work. If there is no order to the relationship, theology will either absorb philosophy and become arid or be absorbed and become heretical. But this asymmetrical ordering cannot be the "unqualified precedence of the divine over the human" that is characteristic of the Chalcedonian pattern. That pattern refers to the relationship between the human and the divine. While the Word of God is divine, and thus cannot be encompassed by any human system of thought, theology is a human activity, albeit with a divine reference. Insofar as it is human, that is, it is expressed in human language, it can be addressed and considered from a philosophical perspective. This is why Barth allows that theology is "a sort of philosophy"; it is human creatures who engage in philosophical reflection. Thus, the pattern of interaction is one of *qualified* conceptual precedence: the precedence arising from the absolute priority of God over world, and the qualification arising from that fact that both are human endeavors. It is the sort of qualified precedence that a main road has over a detour.

Even the assertion of a qualified precedence comes only from the perspective of theology. It is that philosophy cannot tell theology how its work is to be done, not that theology's work is inherently more worthwhile.[74] Barth the theologian insists on this more than Ricoeur the philosopher. Both Barth and Ricoeur are intent on setting the limits to their own discourses because both operate within a Chalcedonian framework, where the Word of God is in a relationship of inseparable unity, ineffaceable difference, and inde-structible order to our all-too-human endeavors. Barth would be at one with Ricoeur, who situates the entire academy within this larger framework:

> To take up the cross of Jesus, for me, a member of the university, the commu-nity of knowledge, means not to overevaluate my knowledge, caught up as it is in questions of proof and guarantees, before this necessity—higher than any logical necessity: "It was necessary that the Son of Man should suffer and be crucified."[75]

7

Theological Anthropology:
Removing Brackets

In chapter 5, we saw Ricoeur define the ethical aim as "the good life with and for others in just institutions," but it remains to be seen what constitutes a good life. This definition is the main road of what is perhaps the most accessible example of Ricoeur's critical arc, the move from the ethical aim through the detour of the moral norm and back to a lived practical wisdom. But the titles of Ricoeur's three studies on ethics all begin with "The Self," because his ethics as a whole is the return moment of a narrative arc that moved from description through narration to prescription. This self that is the holder of this ethical aim is constituted in narrative, and the narrativity of selfhood is crucial to making sense of any ethical aim. The constitutive narrating and re-narrating of a life story does not happen in a vacuum, but will draw on the narrative sources that are at the disposal of the teller. Moving further back through the arc to description, the pre-narrative components that are the raw material that is configured by emplotment, the actual lived events about which the story is told and retold, are not ethically neutral. Nor are the conceptual networks and symbolic structures that allow concepts such as "action" and "event" to be distinguished from sheer physical movement.

While Ricoeur follows his mentor Marcel in allowing that "my life is not a story," but he counters that "the story" he tells to himself and others "is the story of my life," because "the demand for a story comes from the depths of life in order to clarify itself."[1] There is an "ontological priority" to the life that is told in the story, but there is an "epistemological priority" to the story itself. Our experience of the world is structured by language, and our experience of our own lived history is temporal and thus structured by narrative.

In making the judgment of a good life, Ricoeur provides us with the tools to identify the narrative structure, but offers little when it comes to the content of the *story* that will be structured by narrative. His ethics presents us with the formal notion of a "good life" without telling us what constitutes such a life. To be sure, the good life must somehow be "with and for other in just institutions," and there will be some reference to existing "standards of excellence," but there is little in Ricoeur's ethics that would enable us to judge a life "good" in the broadest sense. At best, we could offer the appraisal of "well done," just as one could affirm that one had done well in one's career without being able to judge whether the career choice itself was a good one.

The thinness of Ricoeur's account of the good life is a strength rather than a weakness, a humble admission that the "good life" cannot be defined with greater specificity without going further than philosophy can go. This could be read as a philosopher who is aware of and beholden to the call of Christ, but formally refuses to explicitly confess because it would violate the standards of the discipline. While Ricoeur's ethics was the return movement of a hermeneutic arc that began with description and passed through narrative, the entire anthropological project was framed in terms of human capacities, and the prescriptive return can delve no deeper than the descriptive point of origin. For a comprehensive theological anthropology this is insufficient, but Ricoeur's unwillingness to transgress the boundaries of philosophy is precisely what makes his philosophical hermeneutics so fruitful for theological reflection.

Yet the judgment needs to be made, and here there need be no such constraints. We have the conceptual tools to define an explicitly Christian narrative identity, a good life with no phenomenological brackets surrounding it. We could, for example, begin to define the good life as that which glorifies the God who revealed himself in Christ, an explicitly theological statement. Ricoeur's hermeneutic anthropology would then be called upon as a detour that helps us navigate the path from the confession of Christ as Lord to a life that is lived for Christ. This could in some sense appear arbitrary, for hermeneutics could as easily be deployed in interpreting how the words "Christ" and "Lord" are used, and how they have come to mean what they mean today. But there is no way out of the circularity, and as Heidegger advised, we must simply try to get into the circle in the right way.

Having demonstrated the compatibility of Barth and Ricoeur, we can now complete the return movement and re-enter a fully theological mode. Rather than take our cue from Tracy, who defined fundamental theology in terms of the academy, with the theologian as a mediator who uses "openly public arguments" that appeal to "all intelligent, reasonable and responsible persons," we take our cue from Barth, who argues that "the fundamental form of theology is the prayer and the sermon."[2] Theological reflection will necessarily be reflecting most fundamentally on Christianity as it is practiced in the lives of Christians, not a set of creeds or concepts. Here Barth converges with Marcel in distaste for the "spirit of abstraction," in this case any theological reflection that forgets the concrete, embodied existence from which it arose, that, as Marcel puts it, "ceases to be aware of these prior conditions that justify abstraction and deceives itself about the nature of what is, in itself, nothing more than a method."[3] The propositions, arguments, and systems of academic theology are the inevitable detour of Christian reflection; they are indispensable, but are neither its origin nor its goal. In Ricoeur's language of critique and conviction, it is the lived convictions that are the main road, and critical distance that provides the detour.

It might be asked whether Barth *needs* any philosophical explication, or whether his own philosophical categories are sufficient. Certainly Rudolf Bultmann, his longtime conversation partner, thought there was a problem:

> You have failed to enter into (latent but radical) debate with modern philosophy and naively adopted the older ontology from patristics and scholastic dogmatics. What you say (and often only want to say) is beyond your terminology, and a lack of clarity and sobriety is frequently the result.... It seems to me that you are guided by a concern that theology should achieve emancipation from theology. You try to achieve this by ignoring philosophy. The price you pay for this is that of falling prey to an outdated philosophy.[4]

The danger that Bultmann describes is real, though it is not clear that Barth falls into it to the extent that Bultmann thinks. There is a fair bit of what Bultmann wanted Barth to adopt that has already fallen out of philosophical fashion, and Bultmann's use of the quintessentially modern pejorative "outdated" betrays an overarching commitment to the Enlightenment narrative of progress. However, it also seems clear that it was not an informed choice on Barth's part, and the ensuing postliberal preference for the ad hoc method of incorporating philosophy into theology has its roots there. No one philosophical model is given too much conceptual sway, a decision based not on an assessment of the merits of the model, but on the principle of protecting theological autonomy by keeping philosophy weak. This is again reminiscent of Marcel's endless battle against the spirit of abstraction, the seductive power of working with abstract concepts that prevents a return to the concrete, and Gadamer's concern the methods of the natural sciences were overtaking the humanities and impeding the search for truth. Similarly, Barth fears that any philosophical system, if given free rein, will seduce theology away from its roots in the Word.

It is difficult to fault Barth for this, for at the time there was little in the way of viable philosophical models that did not find their root in the radicality of Cartesian doubt. To be sure, there were trenchant criticisms of modernity going back at least as far as Nietzsche—whom Barth, it should be noted, engages beautifully as a courageously coherent choice for "Dionysius against the Crucified"[5]—but those were criticisms of modernity's *positive* project, not its penchant for doubt. In a philosophical culture where doubt was held in such high esteem as an indicator of rationality, there was little that one of Barth's convictions do but keep it at arm's length in the name of preserving the integrity of theological reflection.

But Ricoeur can be deployed here to extend Barth's project with much the same creative fidelity used to extend the projects of Marcel and Gadamer. A careful, patient engagement of disciplines that suffered from the spirit of abstraction (e.g., structuralism) could be productive, provided it was treated *as a detour* from which there would be a return, a *réflexion seconde*. Similarly, he extended Gadamer's project by adding his "critical supplementation" to Gadamer's hermeneutics of tradition. The difference here is that Ricoeur's own hermeneutics of the self will be taken as the detour for Barth's anthropology. He of the endless detours will become a detour himself.

There can, of course, be no question of passing Barth's entire theology through the detour of Ricoeur's hermeneutics. Even if this were possible, it would be the work of not just a book but many books. Nor is it desirable, for that would realize the very fears of Barth and the postliberals (and Ricoeur, and even Habermas) regarding the colonizing threat of philosophy. By concentrating solely on one aspect of Barth's anthropology, however, we can find out if the compatibility that we have seen in theory is likely to be borne out in practice. The task here is thus first programmatic: it is not primarily to flesh out Barth's theology, although the hope is that it will indeed be enriching, but to demonstrate how Ricoeur's philosophical hermeneutics can be productively appropriated into theology, and be suggestive of further applications. Building on the point of contact between Barth and Ricoeur in the previous chapter at the level of philosophical and theological ethics, anthropology is a natural extension of the engagement.[6]

BARTH'S THEOLOGICAL ANTHROPOLOGY

In §44 of III/2 of the *Church Dogmatics,* Barth takes up the question of the human creature before God. Here we see the pattern of detour and return at its clearest in Barth. It is divided into three subsections, each of which maps cleanly onto the points of the critical arc. The first section, "Jesus, Man for God," entrenches the fundamental premise that humanity is not something that Jesus participates in, but rather the reverse. But while this Christological point acts as a foundation for the question of the human creature, Barth argues that Christology cannot answer or even properly address anthropology: "Anthropology cannot be Christology, nor Christology anthropology."[7] We are separated from the person of Christ not only by our sin but also (and more so) by His identity with God. There is an "irremovable difference" between the man Jesus and all other human creatures. Thus the study of humanity in general, which Barth addresses in the second section, "Phenomena of the Human," is not only appropriate but necessary. Barth critically examines three non-theological anthropologies, and is most amenable to the existentialist anthropology of Jaspers, although he constantly reaffirms that the study of the *phenomena* of the human is "condemned to abstractions" as long as we are only considering humanity in general. In the third section, entitled "Real Man," Barth returns to his adamant insistence that a study of the *real* human can be done only by taking the man Jesus as its starting point. Otherwise, we will find ourselves "confusing the reality of man with mere phenomena of man."[8]

Main Road: The Royal Jesus

Much confusion about Barth's anthropological stance can be avoided by differentiating between the term "human *creature*" and the more common term "human *being*." The latter term denotes what Barth calls the *phenomenal* human, while the former denotes what Barth calls the *real* human. Anthropology and the other human sciences can study only the phenomenal human, whose definition as human must be defined in terms of accessible traits, be they rationality, genetic lineage, or other capacities. But if creatureliness is constitutive of true human identity, "not as something fortuitous, contingent and temporary, but as a necessary and constant determination of his being,"[9] then we will have to look elsewhere for a truly comprehensive anthropology. A theological anthropology (where the *theos* in question is the God revealed in the person of Jesus and not the conceptual placeholder of philosophy) cannot help but choose a different starting point, and that point is the person of Jesus Christ. Jesus is the true human because of his identity with God. "It would be impossible to see and think about man, i.e., the man Jesus, if we did not at once see and think about God also."[10] That God elects to become incarnate in the person of Jesus means that God has unconditionally placed himself in solidarity with every human being: "He is not a man for nothing, not for Himself. He is a man in order that the work of God may take place in Him, the kingdom of God come, and the Word of God be spoken. . . . The basis of human life is identical with its *telos*. Deriving from God, man is in God, and therefore for God."[11] This last sentence refers explicitly to the person of Jesus, not to humans in general as they stand now. And it is this general case that must be considered for Barth to articulate his theological anthropology. But what is established first is that our cue for what it is to be truly human is to be taken from the only true human. It is not merely the apophatic insight that a human alone or humanity itself cannot gain knowledge of God—we cannot even gain knowledge of real humanity. If we start with the phenomenal human, we cannot even get to the real human. As Barth puts it, "We can never acknowledge the genuinely godless man to be real man."[12]

Part of the difficulty of Barth's reception in contemporary theology is that he takes as given what many wish to contest. That Jesus is fully God, or that Scripture is authoritative in its testimony to God's revelation in the person of Jesus Christ, is analyzed, reflected on, and expounded, but it is not called into question. This lack of suspicion toward his own theological sources might be taken as either naïve or arrogant, but in fact it is both sophisticated and humble. He is a dogmatic theologian who takes it as his task to elaborate on the doctrines of the Church so that Christians might better understand themselves and thus live more fulfilled Christian lives. He is not engaged in apologetics, and is not concerned with making this theology plausible to those who do not share his faith. If Jesus is not the self-revelation of God in the world, then Barth's is the most thoroughly wrongheaded theology that could be imagined, because he is so fully committed. He does not have one foot on the dock; if his theological ship sinks, he has no recourse. And he is aware of it. Speaking of his insistence that we cannot be real human creatures without reference to Christ, he makes it question of courage:

Theological anthropology must not be so timid that it does not firmly insist on this simplest factor of the situation. Nor must it be so distracted that it suggests every possible and impossible foundation for its thesis except the simplest of all, namely, that every man as such is the fellow-man of Jesus. The biblical message to which we must keep is neither timid nor distracted in this respect . . . [it] never addresses man on any other basis. It does not appeal to his rationality or responsibility or human dignity or intrinsic humanity.[13]

Whatever failings Barth may have, he does not succumb to the theologically timid temptation to practice theology under the sign of modernity's radical doubt. There is a humility that infuses the entire *Church Dogmatics* that is absent in any work that it is less committed to this central Christological premise. As Eberhard Jungel puts it: "A proper theology makes no compromises. . . . Barth's doctrine is free of any compromise, yet it is also free of any unfortunate dichotomy between the deity of God and the humanity of humankind. . . . A resolute refusal to compromise in theology does not at all mean a forced choice between two abstract alternatives."[14] In refusing to consider the human creature apart from the Word of God, Barth also refuses to consider God himself apart from the Word of God that is also the real human. Because God chose to become human and freely bind himself in covenant with human creatures, and because our knowledge of God is acquired first and foremost through God's revealing of himself in history through the person of Christ, any elaboration on the study of God necessarily entails an anthropology:

"Theology," in the literal sense, means the science and doctrine of God. A very precise definition of the Christian endeavour in this respect would really require the more complex term "The-anthropology." For an abstract doctrine of God has no place in the Christian realm, only a "doctrine of God and man," a doctrine of the commerce and communion between God and man.[15]

Neither humanity nor God can be considered in isolation from the other, for to do so would be to consider them in the abstract. This is not a premise that is or even seeks to be rationally grounded in some general system; it does not take Christians to be somehow more intelligent or insightful than those outside the faith.[16] Those who do not follow Barth in his *confessional* affirmations are not his intellectual inferiors, but neither are they are his conversation partners in this explicitly theological discourse. He is reflecting on the Christian faith as testified to in Scripture and expounded on throughout the Christian tradition. Even in the above passage, Barth lists off a variety of other plausible anthropological starting points: reason, responsibility, dignity, or humanness as such. He rejected these starting points for his anthropology because they are inappropriate for a *theological* anthropology. He does, however, accept other anthropologies as legitimate, though limited, and engages each in turn.

Detour: The Phenomenal Human Being

BARTH AND THE PHENOMENAL

Of the three non-theological anthropologies that Barth engages—Darwin's naturalism, Fichte's idealism, and Jaspers's existentialism—he has the most affinity for Jaspers's existential anthropology.[17] The "lasting merit" of Jaspers's anthropology is its openness to otherness, and thus the otherness of God. It aims at an interaction with "a being which is not identical with man but confronts him and yet is for man the solution to the conflict of his existence."[18] But Barth also finds Jaspers's existentialism limited, "at the point where it has to lay a concrete foundation and give specific support for its programme of demonstrating that human existence is actualized only through its relation to the transcendent." The limits of an existentialist anthropology are so serious because, Barth argues, to think about the human creature apart from God is to no longer think about the real human creature, who "exists only in his relation with God. And this relation is not peripheral but central, not incidental but essential to that which makes him a real man."[19] This, for Barth, raises the issue of potentiality and actuality:

> Necessarily, therefore, it leaves indeterminate the whole idea of human freedom, understanding the freedom which it takes to characterise humanity in purely formal terms as a capacity to seize this or that possibility . . . there can result only the general truth that in some way or other man is a reasonable and responsible being, personal, historical and capable of decision. But if this is the case, it must be pointed out in conclusion that, although the concept speaks of actuality, its true reference is only to potentiality . . . it does not actually attain the real which it seeks to attain and seems to denote. . . . It speaks abstractly of *capacity* or disposition.[20]

This paragraph could easily have been written with Ricoeur in mind, as he shares all these limitations with Jaspers. The language of capacity and capability is the very language that Ricoeur utilizes in his own anthropology; it is indeed the category of capability that organizes the studies of *Oneself as Another*. Ricoeur's hermeneutic anthropology is notable for being overtly sensitive to its own lack, but is unapologetic about it. From the perspective of the philosopher, if this is the most that can be done, it is also the least that must be done. And Barth does affirm that such philosophical projects are important to a theological anthropology:

> [A] knowledge of man which is non-theological but genuine is not only possible but basically justified and necessary even from the standpoint of theological anthropology. . . . It will then see them [human phenomena] more modestly, less metaphysically, but for that reason so much the more precisely and strictly and completely. Theological anthropology is prepared to welcome all such general knowledge of man.

Of course, all welcoming of non-theological anthropologies comes with the recognition that they are radically incomplete. He argues that insofar as they prescind from confession, "they are all bracketed, and no decisive enlightenment about man is to be expected from within these brackets, but only from a source outside. This source is God."[21] Recall Ricoeur's closing summation from *Oneself as Another,* that "with this aporia of the Other, philosophical discourse comes to an end,"[22] and his earlier assertion that faith is "the limit of all hermeneutics, while at the same time standing as the non-hermeneutical origin of all interpretation," and therefore that hermeneutics "has neither the first nor the last word.[23] Ricoeur accepts that his philosophical anthropology is bracketed, and will ultimately seek its decisive enlightenment from a source outside. It is precisely the kind of anthropology that Barth welcomes, for what Barth is asking for here is a *hermeneutic* phenomenology of the human being. Taking our cue from Ricoeur's anthropology, where "the detour by way of objectification is the shortest route from the self to the self,"[24] we can say that the detour by way of the phenomenal is the shortest route from the real to the real.

RICOEUR'S HERMENEUTICS OF THE SELF

As Ricoeur's hermeneutics of the self has already been presented in detail, here we will rehearse only the most relevant points. As we saw in the second part, Ricoeur's hermeneutics of the self is organized around the human capacities to speak, act, narrate, and be held responsible. It is in the latter two capacities that identity as "selfhood" (*ipse*) emerges from the analysis of the speech and action of the substantial and formal identity as "sameness" (*idem*). The *ipse* is the "who" rather than the mere "what" of *idem*. The crucial aspect of selfhood that needs to be recalled here is that it is constituted by narrative. It is in this narrative structure that we will find the resources to express Barth's "real" human, so this narrativity must be developed further.

Narrativity

To be human is to be not only an agent (who acts in the world) and a patient (who is acted upon), but also a narrator. Most fundamentally, this is because we live *in time*. If we are to make sense of the facts and events in our lives, if we are to have a coherent identity, we must select what is important and arrange it in some meaningful order. As Ricoeur notes in the first volume of *Time and Narrative*, cosmological time is very different from human time— it is a function of space and motion, where innumerable things occur simultaneously. Narrative is the means by which we translate cosmological time into human time, the means by which we take the innumerable sensations that we experience and unify them into something that can be understood.

In any narrative configuration of a "true" story—and let us keep for the sake of simplicity to stories that make a claim to historical veracity—there must be both selection and arrangement. For example, consider the everyday storytelling when one colleague asks another: "How was your weekend?" When the story is told, many things that happened will not be included because it is impossible to include everything, and even trying to include too many of the possibly relevant details could make the story incomprehensible. Therefore the narrator must select the most "important" parts for purposes of telling an intelligible story. Some of what is selected will be talked about at length, even if it actually lasted only a very short time, because it is judged to be somehow important to either the teller or the listener. Conversely, the teller may know that some of what is rejected is both important and interesting to the listener, but there is no way (or the teller lacks the skills) to tell all of the relevant details in a single account. But it is crucial to note that when this selecting and arranging is being done, the narrator is making *choices*.

The question then becomes: what narrative paradigms are available for narrating one's actions—not only or even primarily to others—but to *oneself*? This question leads to another, more difficult question: are the narrative paradigms that we have at our disposal—be they provided to us by culture, community, or family—appropriate for the detour that takes us from description to prescription? There is commonly a great deal of attention paid to the content of books and films and heated arguments about what should and should not be in curricula. But the content of the stories influences the formation of the self much less than the do the narrative structures that organize those stories.

The problem is that there is a lack of normative criteria by which to evaluate these modes of discourse. A story may be true factually, but the narrative structure still distorts reality and lead to injustice and suffering. Ricoeur acknowledges the danger of this normative vacuum at the level of politics in *The Course of Recognition:*

> It is worth noting that ideologies of power undertake, all too successfully, unfortunately, to manipulate these fragile identities through symbolic mediations of action, and principally thanks to the resources for variation offered by the work of narrative configuration, given that it is always possible, as said above, to narrate differently. These resources for reconfiguration then become resources for manipulation.[25]

The political problem of the ideologies of power penetrate right down to the first-person task of narrating oneself to oneself. But there are additional resources within Ricoeur's own work that allow us to begin an evaluation of narratives according to their truth, though the final judgment will once again go beyond the boundaries of philosophy.

The conventional assessment of truth involves the judgment of whether a particular statement is adequate to the reality it purports to address. But long before Ricoeur developed his theory of narrative identity, he was already dissatisfied with the narrowness of this approach. It was in the context of defending religious language as meaningful he introduced a second type of truth: "[We] are confronted by a mode of discourse that displays claims both to meaningfulness and to fulfillment such that new dimensions of reality and truth are disclosed, and that a new formulation of truth is required."[26] The new mode of truth as *manifestation* or *disclosure* (Heidegger's *aletheia*) is opposed to the more conventional view as *adequation*. A form of discourse such as a narrative, or any form exhibiting "indirect reference," makes an implicit claim to somehow manifest something new in reality, to disclose new meaning. But if this is the case, there is a criterion for judging indirect reference—how well it discloses reality—and this will enable us to make judgments about the truth of narratives. A true *story* (content) is one that makes no false statements; the account of the events is adequate to the reality. A true *narrative* (structure) will be evaluated differently, according to its disclosive value, whether it conceals or reveals it. The story could be less true factually while being far more disclosive of reality.[27]

Judging narrative truth is further complicated by recalling that the narrative arc moment of configuration (the detour from prefiguration through configuration to refiguration) is an act of the *productive imagination.* Narratives (as well as metaphors) do not merely *refer* to reality, they *refigure* it. There is an act of creative agency involved in using a narrative structure to disclose truth, and this act necessarily conceals as well as reveals by foregrounding some aspects and omitting others. What I am suggesting here is that the decisions we make in the act of narrating are the most profoundly ethical decisions we make in our lives. This is not simply because the conversations of friendship are often in the narrative mode, as we share our experiences with one another. More profoundly, it is because of the perpetually operating internal narrative: the story I tell myself about myself is not simply *about* who I am, *it is who I am*. It is my *self*. And if the story I tell myself about myself constitutes my selfhood, the narrative paradigms used to structure that story and make it intelligible will also structure my selfhood.

The model for judging the truth of narrative configuration comes not from impersonal description (a true statement), but from personal evaluation (a true friend). When a person narrates their suffering to themselves or others, there is a common tendency to distort the account in order to minimize discomfort. For example, upon receiving a rejection notice for a much-desired position, one copes with the rejection by saying, perhaps, "I didn't really want that anyway," and focusing the narrative on the now negative aspects of the position. The act of *narrative anesthesia* takes what was keenly desired and attempts to render it undesirable, thus functioning as an anesthetic that dulls the pain of the disappointment. But if narration is an intrinsically *ethical* act, it is all the more so when one is narrating actual events, and uniquely so when one is narrating events from one's own life to oneself. There is a fundamental dishonesty to this anaesthetized narrative; crucial elements are being omitted, not because they clutter up the narrative or interfere with the disclosure of reality, but because they disclose *too much* reality, and are thus too painful. There is a way in which anaesthetized narrative is simply *false*, but in the sense of a false friend.[28] A distorted narrative is false because one is not being true to one's self.

This can be made clearer by applying it to actual friendship. When a friend tells a story of distress, a common response is to offer narrative configurations to support why "it's not really so bad," or even the odious "it wasn't meant to be." Is this really an attempt to help the person work through (*Durcharbeitung*) their suffering, or is it an attempt to avoid expending the emotional energy required to help them do the work? In the latter scenario, the choice of distortion over disclosure in the narrative covers over the truth and disfigures the self, and is an act of *false* friendship. In the former, one might judge that the friend is falsely dramatizing the suffering, in which case the "it's not so bad" reconfiguration would be the appropriate corrective to a distorted narrative that would disclose more truth, and thus be the act of a *true* friend.

This simplified and seemingly trivial example of narrative distortion becomes anything but trivial when one considers that one is narrating and re-narrating constantly, and that the possibilities of distortion are endless. Such isolated acts of distortion can quickly grow into habits. What is at stake in such a case is not a transient emotional state, but a piece of one's narrative identity, one's selfhood that emerges through the narration of the event.

The word we use to give our ethical assessment of the self that emerges in this process of narrating is itself a literary-narrative term: we talk about *character*. In the fourth chapter, we noted first that character is at the intersection of *ipse* and *idem*, of selfhood and sameness. As selfhood, character is itself a story with a plot, as with a character in a novel. But in the narrative of a life, character can also be assessed as "the set of lasting dispositions by which a person is recognized,"[29] the sum of the sedimented habits acquired over time. In character, the narrative self reveals itself as something amenable to third-person description, "the *what* of the *who*, where *ipse* announces itself as *idem*."[30] But character is first and foremost part of selfhood, not sameness.

This narrative self is not posited like the Cartesian *ego*, but comes to be reflexively through relationships of mutual esteem with others. The ethical assessment of character was inscribed in a critical arc that moved from the *ethical aim*—defined as the "good life with and for others in just institutions"—through the detour of the universalizing *moral norm* to the *practical wisdom* of a self that cannot be posited, but only attested to. As noted above, the "good life" is framed in formal terms by Ricoeur, but no matter the content, it will be lived in relationships of solicitude with others. It is indeed in these relationships of mutual esteem that one learns to esteem oneself (as an Other) and thus becomes a self at all. Moreover, these relationships are constitutively narrative, where we tell stories to and about one another. A child's narrative identity, her selfhood, first begins to emerge in stories told *about* her, either to her or in her presence. Bringing solicitude and narrative together further reinforces the importance of narrative truth, where one learns not only to esteem oneself as an Other, but also to be true to one's self as an Other. One's life that is narrated makes the same demands for nonviolence that the Other makes, precisely because one learns to esteem oneself as an Other.

These relationships of solicitude necessarily exist within the structures of institutions that extend to those who are distant, but who have their own relationships of solicitude in becoming selves. One of the measures of justice for such institutions was the extent to which they enabled concerted action, allowing those who participated to hold power in common. This can be extended to narrative paradigms, for it is the role of institutions to retrieve and preserve stories, and more importantly to provide the cultural space in which new narrative paradigms can be constructed and applied to existing narratives as a way of increasing truth by disclosing more reality.[31] Of course, as Ricoeur noted above, political institutions are the natural home of the "ideologies of power" that seek to manipulate narratives, especially historical ones, in turn sanitizing or aggrandizing their own pasts in order to increase their hold on power in the present. This application to *collective* narratives is an issue taken up by Ricoeur in *Memory, History, Forgetting,* and *The Course of Recognition,* as well as by Richard Kearney in *On Stories.*[32]

As we prepare for the return move to a theological anthropology, we can begin to see the points of contact where Ricoeur's philosophical anthropology will be appropriated. In the distinction between *ipse* and *idem,* it is the *ipse* identity that will be needed to describe the "real" human creature, since the *idem* can never pass beyond the merely phenomenal. Thus, the relationship between the human and God will be constitutively narrative. Furthermore, the real human creature will exist in relationships of solicitude with others who are not only phenomenal but real, and these relationships are cultivated within the institution of the Church.

Return: The Real Human Creature

To return to a theological anthropology is, for Barth, always first to return to the person of Jesus, who is "the Archimedean point given us beyond humanity, and therefore the one possibility of discovering the ontological determination of man." There is "no choice in this matter," for any other approach "is not yet or no longer theological anthropology."[33] So when Barth asserts that the "being" of the human creature is a "being with God" and this being "derives from God,"[34] it is because Jesus himself is "the creaturely being who as such not only exists from God and in God but absolutely for God instead of for Himself."[35] Jesus is not human because he participates in the same humanity we do. Rather, we are human because we participate in his true humanity, which is to be from, with, in, and for God. This culminates in the statement that the being of the human creature is a *history:* "It is the existence of the man Jesus which teaches us that the being of man is a history. What happens in this existence, *i.e.,* that the Creator shows his concern for His creation by Himself becoming a creature, is the fullness and sum of what we mean by talking about history."[36] This history is contrasted with a "state," where the being acts according to capacities "intrinsic to itself." A being's history, on the other hand, "begins, continues and is completed when something other than itself and transcending its own nature encounters it, approaches it and determines its being in the nature proper to it, so that it is compelled and enabled to transcend itself in response and in relation to this new factor."[37] The elucidation of what it means for our very being to be a history is clearly a hermeneutic task, and a philosophy that is first concerned with interpretation can provide the necessary tools.

Considered in terms of Ricoeur's distinction between selfhood (*ipse*) and sameness (*idem*), the real human being cannot be expressed in terms of the substantial *idem*. The identity of the real human creature, defined as a *history* of being from, with, in, and for God, is constitutively narrative, and thus an *ipse* identity. There is no core non-narrative identity for the real human creature to which the narratives refer. If we remove all the narrative components from the real human creature, we are left with nothing real. The recipient of salvation is not a "what" but a "who." The real human creature is a story, not an otherwise stable phenomenon about which a story is told. Salvation itself comes to us through narrative.

Ricoeur's understanding of character as the intersection between *idem* and *ipse* is also important for understanding the distinction between the real and the phenomenal human. Character as the expression of selfhood is emplotted and thus narrative, but character is also the "what of the who," the protrusion of selfhood into sameness. So when Ricoeur says that in character, "*ipse* announces itself as *idem*,"[38] we can extend that to say that in character the real human creature announces itself as the phenomenal human being. Rather than character being phenomenal first, a thing about which we tell a story, it is the sedimentation of the lived story into habitual patterns. Selfhood is not epiphenomenal, but rather real in a way that is other than the phenomenal, a history, not a state.

The reality of selfhood extends past the death of the phenomenal human. Whatever the reality may turn out to be of the human's postmortem fate with respect to God, it cannot be meaningful in any sense of the word unless it is part of the same story. With Derek Parfit's "transplanted brain" analogy, Ricoeur demonstrated the quandary of identity could not be resolved through recourse to *idem* identity alone. Transpose this analysis into the glorified body of the resurrection of the dead confessed in the Nicene creed. In both cases, it is an insoluble problem if human identity is conceived of only in the *idem* sense. But if the *ipse* is introduced—selfhood, the whonness, the narrative unity of the person—then we can say that whatever else is true about what comes after death, it is a continuation of the same story. If that is not the case, then it is meaningless.

We can now return to the question that first organized our discussion of narrativity: what narrative paradigms enable me to recount my "real" self in a manner that is true to my real self? In this theological context, my own story cannot provide the organizing narrative structure of my selfhood. This *individualist* narrative cannot describe the real human, but rather will approach God instrumentally, with a view toward how the relationship will benefit me. While railing against individualism is common because it is so obviously self-idolatrous, the stories of one's community or one's nation cannot mediate the "real" self either. These *communitarian, tribalist,* and *patriotic* narrative paradigms can account for the relationality of selfhood, but only for the phenomenal human being. Alone they cannot get at the real human creature, and will inevitably reduce the real to the phenomenal. Beyond that, the world's narrative cannot be the primary narrative in which to locate my sense of selfhood, for *humanist* and even *ecological* narratives cannot get past the phenomenal.

Rather, the narrative identity of the true human creature will take God's self-disclosure in history in the person of Christ as the hermeneutic key to a story that begins with the creation of the universe and ends with the eschaton, locating all other narratives within its narrative logic. Merold Westphal refers to this as a "meganarrative," importantly distinguishing it from the metanarratives that have been so successfully attacked by postmodern philosophers:

> "[M]eta" suggests a change of level. A metalanguage is a second-order discourse, a language about another language. Modernity's metanarratives, on Lyotard's account, are about modernity's scientific and political discourses. But the biblical meganarrative is a first-order discourse. Its recital in homily and liturgy (both in the biblical text and in subsequent worship) is kerygma and not apologetics.[39]

It is its resistance to the spirit of abstraction, its grounding in the concreteness of "homily and liturgy," that saves the Christian story from metanarrative status. This meganarrative does not explain my real self from above, but rather contextualizes and anchors my real selfhood by providing a story that I can live *within.*

Hauerwas, a postliberal very much inspired by Barth and Frei, struggled to articulate this, arguing, "descriptively the self is best understood as a narrative, and normatively we require a narrative that will provide the skills appropriate to the conflicting loyalties and roles we necessarily confront in our existence."[40] He goes on to argue that "the self is a gift," and as a separate point suggests, "we need a story that helps us accept that gift."[41] Despite the privileging of narrative and story in Hauerwas's account, he cannot escape casting the self in *idem* (Ricoeur) or phenomenal (Barth) terms. The story is not simply a mechanism to accept the gift, the gift *is* a history to be told. But though Hauerwas lacked the conceptual vocabulary to express the self as narrative—admitting that his claims "obviously require a defense more elaborate than I can hope to develop here," and further admitting, "I am unsure I even know how to defend such a claim or know what [a] defense would or should look like."[42]—he nonetheless follows Ricoeur's path that ethical concerns are inscribed into the very act of narrating. The configuration of the narrative is but the *detour* of the narrative arc and must *return* to prescription. The ethical self that aims at the good life with and for others in just institutions could do worse than reside in Hauerwas's community of character.

The subsumption of one's personal narrative into the Christian meganarrative would be done according to Barth's Chalcedonian pattern. My life story is a truly human life story only as it participates in the story of Christ's person and work (inseparable unity). There is no question, however, that it is *my* life story (ineffaceable difference). Yet my life story can be a truly human life story only insofar as it *participates* in the humanity of Christ (indestructible order). In such a story, I can no longer cast myself in the intuitively obvious role of protagonist, even though it is still my story. This is captured in the apostle Paul's famous formulation, "I have been crucified with Christ; it is no longer I who live, but Christ who lives in me."[43] My self as protagonist of my own story is dead; it is no longer my story, but Christ's story that constitutes me as a self.

The choice for Christ over oneself as the protagonist of one's narrative has far-reaching effects. Returning to our example of narrative anesthesia and its effect on selfhood, we can extend the example from suffering to sin. The phenomenon of narrative anesthesia intensifies in the case of sin, particularly in the recounting of one's own sinful behavior. While the working through of suffering is a difficult process, an adequate account of one's own sinfulness is simply impossible. Only in the safety of the absolute love (esteem) of God in Christ can one even begin to accept, and thus narrate, the *true* depths of one's own sinfulness. And it is only if one abandons oneself as protagonist (i.e., dies to oneself) and positions the story of one's life in the larger story of Christ's loving work of redemption that one can narrate one's life truly without recourse to narrative anesthesia. Even when one is displaced as protagonist, narrative unity is a limited endeavor because sin is an open wound that cannot be accounted for systematically.

At the level of institutions, this extends from tribal and national narratives to narratives of the Church. The explorations of political narratives undertaken by Ricoeur offer many resources, both to ecumenical conversations and to the narrative identities of ecclesial communities. For churches too can suffer from identity crises that result from considering the community only in terms of *idem* identity. Part of learning to inscribe one's narrative into the narrative of Christ is to recognize the Body of Christ as having a history whose identity is constituted in narrative. Here Ricoeur's ethical formula of "with and for others in just institutions" is particularly helpful. We cannot appropriate our real humanity without the esteem of our real humanity—created by God and redeemed in Christ—by others, whom we esteem in the same way. And the space in which these relationships of mutual esteem take place is the institution of the Church that has carried this narrative through time. The redemptive work that would allow us to tell ourselves the truth about ourselves without recourse to narrative anesthesia can take place only within these relationships.

The difficulties faced by personal sinful narratives are magnified when applied to collective narratives in the broadest sense, and are particularly acute in theological accounts of evil. Here Ricoeur's philosophy can again function as a detour for Barth's theology. While Ricoeur questions Barth on his account of evil,[44] it is important to remember that it is a philosopher addressing a theologian (although Ricoeur does pose some tough questions). Barth approaches evil from the viewpoint of sin, while Ricoeur comes from the perspective of suffering, which occasionally puts them at cross-purposes. This can once again be accounted for in terms of detour and return. Barth's "Christological lodestar" (to use Wallace's term) allows him to approach the question of evil in the world with the confidence that the problem of evil can be addressed, although only paradoxically and only in terms of the person and work of Christ. Ricoeur pushes the question much further, seeing the question of evil as a challenge for both philosophers and theologians. As a philosopher, Ricoeur probes the question of evil, the "surplus of suffering" in the world, far more thoroughly than Barth. Ricoeur has no sense that this will be resolved to anyone's satisfaction, and wonders whether theologians do not paint over this problem. The philosopher's service to the theologian in such a conversation is as corrective detour, a warning not to indulge in *narrative anesthesia* when giving an account of evil in the world. There is rough road to be traveled in the account of evil, and no eschatological hope can excuse theologians from the journey. Evil cannot be accounted for systematically, and yet must be narrated *truly*. The theologian, however, cannot allow the philosopher to declare this difficult detour the main road. The problem of excessive suffering may be a legitimate starting point for philosophy, but it is not the starting point for theology. Christian theology does not exist to be an answer to the question of evil. But just as Ricoeur preferred to detour through disciplines that overdid the abstraction so that he could be assured that he was going far enough, a confident theology will engage philosophy in the same way.

This suggests further potential applications of the hermeneutical detour to theology. Propositional doctrines would be properly positioned as the critical detour from the narrative of God's redemptive work. They are not diminished by this, for Ricoeur's critical supplementation to Gadamer's hermeneutics creates a positive role for this critical distance, namely that it enables us to explain more, and thus understand better. Doctrinal disputes could never become truly intractable without recourse to the stories that form the world in which those disputes take place. Much as the ethical aim is universalized in the propositions of the moral norm, which in turn must have recourse to the aim when those norms are in conflict, the propositional statements of the faith would have recourse to the narratives in cases of conflict. If the second- or third-order doctrines of sin, God's omnipotence, and God's omnibenevolence cannot coexist systematically, then they must have recourse to the meganarrative from which those doctrines are drawn.[45] The debates on, for example, free will and determinism would look far different situated within the hermeneutic arc, with both the sovereignty of God and the dignity of the human evaluated within a narrative logic rather than a merely propositional one. There is no area of theological reflection—historical, ethical, systematic, liturgical, pastoral—into which this hermeneutical refiguration would not penetrate.

As we complete the return movement of the overall project, it is worth noting that this application of Ricoeur's philosophical anthropology as a detour for Barth's theological anthropology is by necessity incomplete. The application serves primarily to demonstrate how Ricoeur's hermeneutics of detour and return can be refigured as a detour itself, available to be appropriated by theology. While one of the tasks was to show that Ricoeur's anthropology and ethics can function as a concrete detour for Barth's doctrine of the phenomenal and real human creature, the larger task was to complete the argument that theology, if it chooses its partners wisely and structures the engagement carefully, has little to fear and much to gain from fully engaging philosophy.

Conclusion

There have been a great many detours. We began by articulating the tension between integrity and relevance as it applied to an increasingly disestablished theology. Because theology has been perpetually under attack—and when it is not under attack it is often because it is dismissed as too weak or irrelevant to be worth attacking—much of theology has been practiced *in response* to an external set of rules that is hostile to religious belief because of its deep-seated bias toward doubt. The question of that chapter addressed the best way for theologians to behave, not the abstract-judgment best way to do theology. Theology is an abstraction in a way that theologians are not, and to consider one without the other threatens to fall victim to Marcel's spirit of abstraction. This is why a particular philosopher and a particular theologian were engaged as part of this project rather than, for example, hermeneutical philosophy and postliberal theology as abstractions.

One of the dangers, as exemplified in Tracy, is that the stance of appeasement, if assumed for long enough, will become the natural posture for the theologian. Theologians would then become so concerned with appealing to all intelligent, reasonable, and responsible persons that fundamental loyalties gradually shift from the Church to the academy. Calling on the criticisms of philosopher Jürgen Habermas and postliberal theologians George Lindbeck and Stanley Hauerwas, I called into question the nature and role of

Fundamental Theology in Tracy's model, suggesting that it ultimately robs theology of its distinctive identity.

The second aspect of Tracy's importance is his advocacy for Ricoeur's hermeneutics in the contemporary theological conversation. The postliberal hostility to Tracy's revisionist model, coupled with Frei's repeated conflation of Tracy with Ricoeur, has led to the ejection of Ricoeur's hermeneutics from postliberal conversation, a condition that continues to the present day. Frei's misreading (or even non-reading) of Ricoeur has taken root in postliberal theology. This disdain for any independent philosophy, anything that seems too much like a conceptual system, is a protectionist strategy, practicing theology in a perpetual defensive crouch, alert for attack on all sides, risking incoherence if it guarantees that theology will not be colonized.

Fortunately, postliberal theology as it exists today is not quite so constrained. At the end of the first part, we noted DeHart's metaphor of the postliberal "river delta," where the main river of Frei and Lindbeck branch out into numerous separate and smaller branches. Even grouping Frei and Lindbeck into a single stream is suspect. DeHart quite usefully attempts to group these various offshoots into something intelligible: (1) Hauerwas's countercultural ethic and critique of modernity; (2) the resurgence of communally formed spirituality over and against individualist and/or intellectual approaches; (3) the quest for a postcritical hermeneutic of Scripture; (4) the quest to balance Scripture and community, retrieving premodern theology in the name of a "catholic and evangelical theology"; and (5) an attempt to reappropriate Barth, both in understanding his texts and in standing with him in defense of the integrity of theological reflection. DeHart notes that many of the theologians in these branches are somehow developing the broad strokes of what Frei and Lindbeck seemed to stand for, but aren't that interested in the particular methods that Frei and Lindbeck used. Insofar as there is still a postliberal theology, it is an extremely wide-ranging phenomenon.

James Fodor is more optimistic about inscribing theologians into the annals of the "highly internally differentiated" postliberal theology, even including those he knows would reject the label, such as Milbank, Ward, and Pickstock from the Radical Orthodoxy movement. In his excellent entry in the third edition of *The Modern Theologians*,[1] he asserts that among many aspects of postliberal theology are its deployment of narrative and its emphasis on the "peculiar grammar of the Christian faith," as well as the more negatively phrased non-constitutive, non-essentialist, non-foundationalist, non-apologetic approach to theology. He sees the movement as growing steadily in influence, with the wide variations unproblematic because post-liberal theology was never a school to begin with.

My own admiration for Barth's theology puts me broadly in line with the postliberals, except that another common feature they share is rejecting the philosopher who shared their concerns and was most keen to continue in dialogue with them. The "allergy to German Idealism" (as Schner once described it) led them to miss the fundamental shift that took place in philosophical hermeneutics that took it past modernity without being transformed into what is more generally labeled "postmodern." Some of Gadamer's most significant accomplishments were to unmask the Enlightenment's "prejudice against prejudice," to rehabilitate tradition and authority as rational sources of judgment, and to inscribe self-understanding in the context of effective history. This, as Tracy rightly argues, makes hermeneutics uniquely suited as a counterpart to theological reflection. It does not see the traditions, authorities, or faith stances of theology with an immediate structurally dictated condescension, as is common with analytic or deconstructionist philosophy.

With Ricoeur extracted from the Chicago-Yale conflagration, we could look at hermeneutics afresh in part two. Gabriel Marcel's tireless fight against the "spirit of abstraction," using *réflexion seconde* as a concrete counterpart to the more conventional critical reflection, set Ricoeur on the path that would first lead him to deploy Husserl's eidetic reduction as a critical detour to Marcel's own project that returned to a richer sense of participation in Gadamer's hermeneutics of tradition. This set off a series of critical detours (and returns) through Habermas's critique of ideology, structuralism, and analytic philosophy. This last detour also set the stage for a return to the anthropological question first engaged in Ricoeur's philosophy of the will.

Among the areas that Fodor identifies for the development of postliberal theology is its treatment of narrative. He argues that despite the centrality of narrative to postliberals' reflections, they are curiously vague about precisely how it actually shapes communities, absorbs worlds, and relates to more systematic theological discourse. This concern is addressed in the second iteration of the detour-and-return pattern, the narrative arc, which was articulated in the fourth chapter. The productive imagination that enables a metaphor to refigure reality coupled with an analysis of temporality leads to Ricoeur's threefold *mimesis,* the narrative arc of description-narration-prescription. It is in the interplay of this arc with the critical arc that Ricoeur generated his theory of narrative identity that is the core of his hermeneutics of the self. Key to this was the distinction between sameness (*idem*) and selfhood (*ipse*), and narrative constitution of selfhood. These would later be used as a detour to refigure Barth's distinction between the real and phenomenal human.

The self, *described* by the analytic fields of semantics and pragmatics and configured in *narrative*, completes its return in the *prescriptive* moment of Ricoeur's "little ethics." In these three studies the critical arc was once again deployed to take us from the optative mode of the ethical aim ("the good life with and for others in just institutions") through the universalizing imperative mode of the moral norm, returning to the mode of attestation characterized by practical wisdom. The solicitude of the relationships of mutual esteem allowed the self to emerge (as an Other), and also provided the paradigm for evaluating the justice of institutions. This also would function as a detour in the configuration of a Christian narrative identity.

In the introduction, I claimed that I would be "willing to *dis*-appropriate my own project in the act of appropriation, in much the way that the self must cease to possess itself in the act of appropriating a text." To some extent, that is what happened in part three. There was the preunderstanding that the philosophy of Ricoeur would function as the minor term in a Chalcedonian pattern, available to be fully appropriated by theology. Surprisingly, one of the primary reasons that this did not work is that this would be opposed by Barth. For Barth, both philosophy and theology stand in a Chalcedonian relationship to the Word, and thus cannot stand in such a relationship to one another. But this does not mean that there can be no appropriation. Theology has a freedom to explicitly confess the Word that philosophy does not. Particularly in anthropology, this leaves theology in a position of qualified precedence without denying philosophy's autonomy or indispensability. Just as Ricoeur can read biblical texts philosophically, so too can his philosophical texts be read theologically. His entire philosophical work can be used as a *detour*.

This was put to the test in the final chapter by taking a small part of Barth's theological anthropology through the detour of Ricoeur's philosophical anthropology. Barth and his followers are suspicious of any talk of independent capacities in humanity because the true human is defined in relationship to God. But what the detour helped articulate is the structure with which this relationship takes place, the point of contact in the human where God speaks to us. This point was in our capacity to narrate precisely because, as Barth insists, the revelation of the Word is a decisive act in history and not merely a general revelation. The Word confronts us as a history because to be human is to have a history that needs to be told in order to become a self, and this cannot be done without narrative. The selfhood of the very Word made flesh that stands at the center of Barth's theology was constituted in narrative.

Christianity is not first and foremost written or thought; it is lived. This is the concrete existential ground that must always be at the forefront of theology if it is to avoid Marcel's *spirit of abstraction*. Fundamental theology, as Barth said, is in the prayer and the sermon. It is first a move through not the critical arc, but the narrative arc. The *main road* is the ordinary Christian who has confessed Christ as Lord, be it in the act of conversion or of confirmation. We can work backward and recognize that as the moment of appropriation where the story of Christ's history, configured in a narrative where Christ becomes the protagonist of the Christian's story, is then allowed to refigure the self and thus the world of the Christian. The confession is the return moment of the narrative arc. That confession must then be contextualized by the community of Christians. The regular proclamation of the Word in the life of the Church gives the Christian further narrative configuration, which continues to refigure the Christian's life as lived. The preaching and practices of the Church are thus designed to take the Christian on a *detour* through the narrative arc that begins with confession and ends with a refigured life that is appropriated and lived for Christ. The arc closes into a circle as that refigured life becomes the basis for a deeper confession that will undergo an ever deeper and richer contextualization, in turn leading to a more mature living of the Christian life.

One of the reasons that it must be first a narrative arc rather than a critical one is that it is our *ipse* identity, our selfhood that is structured by narrative, that receives whatever salvation is offered in the Christian message. We saw how Ricoeur examined Derek Parfit's hypothetical experiments with identity as a way of prizing apart *idem* (sameness, answering the question "what?") from *ipse* (selfhood, answering the question "who?"). Only if we appreciate the magnitude of what was accomplished there can we appreciate the importance of the narrative arc in the task of theology. When addressing the Word that confronts us, "this revelation brings its own historical location, its own reality in space and time."[2] It is first and foremost a story that confronts us, and engaging the narrative structure story does not merely alter how we view ourselves, it actually changes who we are. Selfhood is not epiphenomenal. There is no core "self" about which the stories are told; the narrated stories constitute the self. There is therefore no self that is the object of salvation apart from one's participation in the story of salvation. Whether we speak of the evangelical emphasis on the moment of conversion or the Catholic emphasis on the reception of the sacraments, these are first instances of participation in the narrative. To appropriate better the narrative of salvation is not first to understand what is happening, but to actually have it happen. The confession that is appropriated through narrative is lived, then that life is told about through the narrative configuration of salvation, leading to a still deeper appropriation.

Theology that does not help us through this narrative arc is ultimately of no value, but this in no way means that the critical arc is dispensable. The act of proclamation also contains within it reflections on what this story that has refigured means and attempts to explain. These propositional doctrines are only detours, because they are engaged in a mode of critical distance rather than lived participation, but they are also indispensable, because to explain more is to understand better. Doctrines do not point to the "real" truth behind the narrative, but are the only way to explain the world that unfolds in front the narrative. But the critical detour always originates in and is for the sake of better configuring the story, and the better configuration is always for the sake of a refigured life. To treat any detour as an end in itself, whether it be the critical distanciation of the critical arc or the productive configuration of the narrative arc, is to forget that the detour is always at the service of lived participation; it is to fall victim to the spirit of abstraction.

A great deal of theological reflection must be done that does not address this *directly*. The task of the critical theologian is taken from this fundamental theology of worship and liturgy, which is both the source and the goal of its reflection. But those charged with proclaiming the Word must go deeper into its meaning if they are to guide others through these detours that lead to a refigured life. For this, they rely upon theologians who do not work directly (or at least not primarily) with shaping the proclamation that will shape the lives of ordinary Christians. This theology delves deeply into both the narrative and the doctrines that are drawn from it, forever seeking out new elucidations of doctrines that would allow the narrative to be recounted more truly, that is, in a way that discloses more truth. But this critical theology, while indispensable, can never be more than a detour. It can be a very extensive detour, but it must never lose its moorings by thinking that it can be divorced from either its origin in lived participation or its goal in enriching that lived participation. If it becomes disconnected from this, it falls victim to the spirit of abstraction. It remains connected by being critical as part of being hermeneutical, the detour of the critical arc.

A hermeneutical theology will undergo many of its own critical detours if it is to be effective. As we saw in Barth's engagement of non-theological anthropologies, other disciplines must be engaged for the theology to understand itself better. It would not do justice to the task of enriching the proclamation that will shape the lives of Christians if detours into these other disciplines were not taken. If the detours are not rigorous and pursued to the end, the appropriation will be shallow. Philosophy must be engaged, if only because the conceptual language that a critical theology uses to express itself must be drawn from somewhere, and to ignore philosophy will lead to a lack of rigor and theological self-awareness about the language that is used. Anthropology, sociology, and psychology must be engaged to better understand human beings in their relationships. Nor can these detours be cursory. There is a need for theologians who are also well versed in these disciplines, and even more so for Christians in these other disciplines to pursue these detours to their furthest point. Recall how Ricoeur preferred to engage those disciplines that suffered from the spirit of abstraction, because in going too far, they gave him the perspective to judge what was far enough so that the appropriation might be as rich as possible. A critical hermeneutical theology is by necessity interdisciplinary and will engage those theories that go too far afield, as a way of ensuring that they are going far enough. The key problem of the postliberal preference for the ad hoc approach to philosophy is that it discourages engagement with the very modes of thinking that will lead to the richest appropriation. Ricoeur's hermeneutical philosophy is, as Tracy said, a "natural alliance" for this kind of theology, helping to mediate the interactions with other disciplines so that these interactions are both more productive and less dangerous to the integrity of theology.

To recapitulate: confessing Christians will gather together to both narrate and live out the stories that shape their salvation, and in doing so shape themselves. Key to this practice is the proclamation of the story in homily and liturgy that will enable them to better live out that story. The pastors in charge of this must have gone through the detour of critical theology in order to have a deeper understanding of the warp and weft of the story, the better to guide the congregants through the detours that will enable them to understand and live the story better. The critical theology that will be drawn upon for this must itself have gone through detours through the human sciences to better understand the human creatures who are confronted with this narrative of salvation. Having delved deeply into the human sciences (or engaged those who have), the critical theologian returns, appropriating that knowledge into a theology that is still grounded in the kerygmatic proclamation with a view toward enriching the understanding of those charged with proclaiming it. The pastors in turn take their richer understanding and use it to better configure the story so that it will better shape the lives of those who hear. Finally, those who hear will take their refigured lives back into the world in which they live, returning the next time with new experiences, questions, blessings, or problems that need to be configured within their narrative of salvation. And the circle continues.

These are merely a few of the potential applications of Ricoeur's hermeneutics to theology, using the pattern of detour and return. It is too much to say that this pattern of interaction can resolve the tensions between the integrity and relevance of theology, if such a resolution is even possible. It does, however, open up a possibility. If a philosopher such as Ricoeur can productively interact with a theologian such as Barth using this pattern, with neither having to sacrifice the integrity of their respective disciplines, then perhaps this pattern points to a possible mode of interaction for the disciplines as wholes. Other patterns may work as well or better for other theologians and philosophers; what is imperative for the future of theological reflection is that there be such productive interactions at all.

NOTES

INTRODUCTION

1. Milbank, "Foreword." Milbank also claims that theology is being revitalized, with more students reading (majoring in) the discipline. He provides no data, though it is possible that the greater "religiosity" in North America means that theology has yet to hit bottom as it did in the UK, and thus is not yet ready to bounce back.

2. Reagan, *Paul Ricoeur,* 91.

3. See Raynova, "All That Gives Us to Think," 671.

4. Ihde, "Paul Ricoeur's Place in the Hermeneutic Tradition," 64.

5. Thompson, *Critical Hermeneutics.*

6. Kearney, "Between Oneself and Another," 149–60.

7. For other accounts of the "arcs" in Ricoeur's thought, see Stiver, *Theology after Ricoeur,* esp. 56–78; Bontekoe, *Dimensions of the Hermeneutic Circle.* Bontekoe offers schematics for a remarkable *forty* variations of the "hermeneutic circle" from Schleiermacher to the present. On Stiver, see note 20 below.

8. Wiercinski, "Introduction," ix.

9. See Ricoeur, "The Model of the Text: Meaningful Action Considered as a Text," in *TA,* 144–67.

10. See Ricoeur, "Life in Quest of Narrative," 20–33.

11. *FS,* 205.

12. Ricoeur, "Reply to David Stewart," 448–49.

13. Ricoeur has recently referred to himself as an *"intellectuel chrétien,"* a Christian intellectual. See Ricoeur, "L'attribution de la mémoire à soi-même, aux proches et aux autres: un scheme pour la theologie philosophique?" 21.

14. Mudge, "Introduction," 3.

15. My thanks to Jean Greisch for pointing out this parallel to me.

16. Tracy, "Ricoeur's Philosophical Journey."

17. *FS* was published in 1995, fifteen years after the Mudge collection.

18. Ricoeur with LaCocque, *Thinking Biblically.*

19. Raynova, "All That Gives Us to Think," 643–44.

20. See Mark I. Wallace's *SN,* which will be addressed in detail in chapter 6. See also Vanhoozer, *Biblical Narrative in the Philosophy of Paul Ricoeur;* Fodor, *Christian Hermeneutics.* Fodor's book (with which this book unwittingly shares a structure) delves deeply and critically into Ricoeur's philosophical conception of reference, truth, and meaning, but ultimately judges Ricoeur in theological terms. Most importantly there is Dan R. Stiver's excellent *Theology after Ricoeur: New Directions in Hermeneutical Theology,* the book that most overlaps with this one, in that it takes Ricoeur's so-called theology as tangential to his more important philosophical contributions. Stiver's articulation of the two arcs (which he labels "hermeneutical" and

"mimetic") is extensive, but is treated as one aspect among many. The book is richly suggestive of many aspects of Ricoeur's philosophy, approaching each one topically, and seems to be in dialogue with an evangelical Christian tradition that is both fascinated and repelled by all things "postmodern." See Stiver, *Theology after Ricoeur*, 2n2. Ricoeur himself disliked the term "postmodern," arguing that there is actually very little clarity on what "modern" means.

21. Mudge, "Introduction," 3.

22. See Cohen and Marsh, *Ricoeur as Another*; Venema, *Identifying Selfhood*; Kaplan, *Ricoeur's Critical Theory*. Theological concerns come to the surface at the end of Venema's work.

23. *TN* 3, 248.

24. Ricoeur, "Sorrows and the Making of Life-Stories," 322–24, also in Manoussakis and Gratton, *Traversing the Imaginary*; Ricoeur, "Paul Ricoeur, Religious Belief."

25. I would argue that the lack of recent discussion in no way implies a resolution, just as an old couple who no longer argue simply because they no longer speak to one another can hardly be said to have resolved their differences. Furthermore, that discussion is the closest that the ostriches and the fighters of the long defeat get to one another. The moderate stance of each side stands in for the more extreme approaches, with fundamentalism at one pole and secular a-theologies at the other.

26. Tracy, "Ricoeur's Philosophical Journey," 203.

27. Kearney, "Narrative Imagination," in *Paul Ricoeur*, 181.

28. *OA*, 115.

29. See *OA*, studies 7–9, "The Self and the Ethical Aim, the Self and the Moral Norm, the Self and Practical Wisdom: Conviction," 169–296.

30. Barth, *Ethics*, 19–45.

31. Wiercinski, "Seeking Understanding," xiv. For more on the hermeneutic reading, see Wiercinski, *Inspired Metaphysics*, esp. "The Hermeneutic Reading of Siewerth," 1–15.

32. Gadamer, *Truth and Method*, 270.

33. Ricoeur, "Myth as the Bearer of Possible Worlds," 27.

34. Hunsinger, *How to Read Karl Barth*, 207.

35. Ricoeur, "Reply to David Stewart," in *PPR*, 449.

36. Barth, *Church Dogmatics* III/2, 325.

37. *OA*, 25.

38. *FS*, 189.

1. FUNDAMENTAL LOYALTIES

1. For an example of Hauerwas's abrasive style, see Stanley Hauerwas, "The Importance of Being Catholic: A Protestant View," *First Things* (March 1990). For a heatedly sarcastic response to Hauerwas's "usual discernment and tact," see Dennis P. McCann, "Natural Law, Public Theology and the Legacy of John Courtney Murray," *Christian Century* 107 (Sept. 5–12, 1990): 801–803.

2. Tracy, *The Analogical Imagination*, 57–58.

3. Ibid., 57. While *Analogical* shies away from the catchphrase "common human experience" that drew so much attention in *Blessed Rage for Order*, the second hermeneutic constant is strikingly close to the "phenomenology of the religious dimension" that typifies common human experience. See Tracy, *Blessed Rage for Order*, 52.

4. Ibid., 7.

5. Ibid., 8–9.

6. Ibid., 13, 246.

7. Habermas, *Moral Consciousness and Communicative Action,* 65–66.

8. This presents a problem, since the rules are to be purely formal, without any ethical content. However, since styles and topics of discourse are excluded de facto, the rules themselves act as a negative ethic.

9. Habermas, "Transcendence from Within, Transcendence within this World," 240.

10. Ibid.

11. Despite its centrality, it is difficult to see how a fundamental theologian could ever talk about the Trinity within these rules.

12. Tracy, "Theology, Critical Social Theory, and the Public Realm," 19.

13. Ibid. Tracy gives an admirably concise and helpful summary of the postliberal position, but then abandons the issue and never returns.

14. Ibid., 35.

15. Ibid., 36.

16. Habermas, "Transcendence from Within, Transcendence Within This World," 233.

17. Ibid., 230.

18. Ibid., 230–31, 233.

19. For a helpful summary of the various strands of postliberalism, see Dorrien, "The Future of Postliberal Theology"; DeHart, *The Trial of the Witnesses,* esp. 1–56; and Pecknold, *Transforming Postliberal Theology.*

20. Lindbeck, *The Nature of Doctrine.* See James M. Gustafson, "The Sectarian Temptation"; his assessment of the postliberal position as "a pernicious, sectarian temptation" was only one of the many heated responses to *The Nature of Doctrine.*

21. Lindbeck, *The Nature of Doctrine,* 125–26.

22. Ibid., 47.

23. Ibid., 33.

24. Hauerwas presents artistic creativity as an analogy, noting that the mastery of any given art form invariably precedes any alteration that an artist makes to that form. Playing a jumble of notes that has never been played before is not musically "creative" unless one is deliberately pushing the limits of a form that has been mastered.

25. Hauerwas, *Against the Nations,* 8.

26. The extent to which Christianity *is* disestablished is a significant one. It would seem that even from a liberal perspective, it is clear that Christianity is on the fringes, else why appeal to modern versions of intelligence and reason rather than arguing from an explicitly Christian perspective? The question is then a strategic one: do Christians attempt to positively influence the societies in which they live by trying to bring Christianity into the conversation, or do they instead concentrate on maintaining their own communities in isolation? Are the two even separable? This is further complicated by the (at least) implicit presence of the Christian tradition in Western social structures. There are many elements in modern liberal democracy that are heartily endorsed by Hauerwas, but the extent to which they require a citizenry familiar with Christian "logic" is a complex question.

27. Hauerwas, *Against the Nations,* 24.

28. Ibid., 44.

29. The notion that one who is maximally different will offer the most insight is a curious one. In personal decision-making situations one often looks for an advisor

who has "distance" from the situation, so that they can be "objective." This is always a limited possibility, because objective distance becomes a hindrance if the advisor is so "distant" that there is no understanding of the issues involved. The tension between proximity and distance is one that anyone seeking advice must address in selecting an advisor or a conversation partner.

30. Hauerwas, *Against the Nations*, 44.

31. Ibid., 13.

32. Lindbeck, *The Nature of Doctrine*, 128. As we will see in the final chapter, this statement can be affirmed in part, with the additional acknowledgment that external disciplines may provide better tools to express those intratextual outlooks. The conceptual vocabulary must come from somewhere.

33. Hauerwas, *Against the Nations*, 42.

34. Ibid., 24.

35. Ibid., 25.

36. Habermas, "Transcendence from Within, Transcendence Within This World," 230. See p. 21 above.

37. Perhaps the first casualty of this mode of interaction is *hell*, which has virtually disappeared from the theological landscape. See D. P. Walker, *The Decline of Hell* (London: Routledge and Kegan Paul, 1964); Martin Marty, "Hell Disappeared. No One Noticed. A Civic Argument," *Harvard Theological Review* 78 (1985): 381–98. For a historical survey and the possible "comeback" of hell, see George Hunsinger, "Hellfire and Damnation: Four Ancient and Modern Views," in *Disruptive Grace*, 226–49.

38. Knitter, *Jesus and the Other Names*, 35.

39. Paul Knitter, "Toward a Liberation Theology of Religions," in Hick and Knitter, *The Myth of Christian Uniqueness*, 8, 123.

40. It is indeed an *application* of Tracy, who is the single most quoted author in *No Other Name?* often at length.

41. David Tracy, "Catholic Classics in American Liberal Culture," in Douglass and Hollenbach, *Catholicism and Liberalism: Contributions to American Public Philosophy*, 197. Tracy lumps the postliberals in with the neoscholastic Catholic theologians as exceptions to this "consensus."

42. Tracy, *The Analogical Imagination*, 3, 63, 86.

43. Thomas, "Public Theology and Counter-Public Spheres," 456.

44. It is unfortunate that Hauerwas's regrettable reputation for personal rudeness overshadows his more defensible lack of academic manners. The two are not logically interdependent.

45. Tracy, *The Analogical Imagination*, 63.

46. Tracy might correctly note that this is a "typically situational analysis," and use it as a defense against an anti-correlationist attack. But the rejection of external plausibility structures is perennial; only the particular application requires a situational analysis. See Tracy, "The Uneasy Alliance Reconceived," 548–70.

47. Milbank, "Foreword," 11–12.

2. THEOLOGY, HERMENEUTICS, AND RICOEUR'S DOUBLE LIFE

1. See Wiercinski, "Introduction," in *BHD*, xiv–xvi.

2. *OA*, 25.

3. Ricoeur, "Reply to David Stewart," in *PPR*, 448–49.

4. This reaches its apotheosis in his *Types of Christian Theology*, where Tracy is taken to be under the "hermeneutical tutelage" of his "mentor" Ricoeur. See Hans

Frei, *Types of Christian Theology* (New Haven and London: Yale University Press, 1992), 6, 32. It should be noted that when criticizing Tracy's model, I avoided referring to Frei's use of Tracy as exemplar of one of his five types of theology on the grounds that his typology as a whole distorts far more than it explains. As Paul DeHart notes, the use of Tracy is particularly problematic for three reasons: (1) Tracy's thought develops over time; (2) Tracy persuasively contests Frei's reading of his work, and (3) Frei passed up the obvious choice of Hegel. See DeHart, *The Trial of the Witnesses*, 225–39. This last may be because there would be an uncomfortable tension in casting Barth's favorite philosopher in the villainous role of type two. Gordon Kaufmann, the exemplar for type one, once noted with genuine melancholy after a seminar that he wished Hunsinger and Placher had never edited *Types of Christian Theology* for posthumous publication because it artificially froze categories and cut off conversation.

5. *TA*, 53.

6. *TA*, 298.

7. The purpose of this exposition is to situate Ricoeur's critical supplementation to Gadamer's hermeneutics, not to analyze Ricoeur's reading of the hermeneutic tradition. All the relevant texts, including Habermas's review of *Truth and Method*, have been collected in a single, very helpful volume. See Gayle L. Ormiston and Alan D. Schrift, eds., *The Hermeneutic Tradition*. For another more theologically driven reading of the same tradition, see Westphal, "Hermeneutical Finitude from Schleiermacher to Derrida," 50–65; also Jeanrond, *Theological Hermeneutics*, 44–77, and Stiver, *Theology after Ricoeur*, 31–50.

8. *TA*, 55.

9. *TA*, 56.

10. Schleiermacher, *Hermeneutics*.

11. While Ricoeur is more positive than Gadamer about the accomplishments of Schleiermacher and Dilthey, his analysis nonetheless depends heavily on Gadamer's. See Gadamer, *Truth and Method*, esp. part 2, sec. 1, "Historical Preparation," 173–264.

12. *TA*, 56.

13. For another reading of Dilthey that places him in proximity with Ricoeur, see part 2 of Anthony Thistleton, *Interpreting God and the Postmodern Self*.

14. *TA*, 62. Dilthey makes the following distinction regarding the "subject matter" of the *Geisteswissenschaften*: "What is given always consists of expressions. Occurring in the world of the senses, they are manifestations of mental content which they enable us to know." This distinction between the mental content and its manifestations is at the core of the dichotomy between explanation and understanding in Dilthey. See Dilthey, *Selected Writings*, 218.

15. *TA*, 58.

16. *TA*, 54.

17. *TA*, 65.

18. *TA*, 68.

19. For another account of the move from Heidegger to Gadamer, see Palmer, "Heideggerian Ontology and Gadamer's Hermeneutics," 113–21.

20. *TA*, 272.

21. Gadamer, *Truth and Method*, 278–79.

22. Ibid., 253.

23. *TA*, 72.

24. *TA*, 272.

25. Gadamer, *Truth and Method*, 358.

26. Ricoeur, "Philosophical Hermeneutics and Theological Hermeneutics," 15. It is worth noting that this essay has been substantially revised and retranslated; see "Philosophical Hermeneutics and Biblical Hermeneutics," in *TA*, 89–101. I have chosen the earlier version here, first, because it is one that Frei could have had at his disposal, and second, because the essay was compressed in the revision, with many interesting paragraphs removed.

27. *TA*, 71.

28. *TA*, 73.

29. Ricoeur, "Philosophical Hermeneutics and Theological Hermeneutics," 15.

30. Ibid., 16.

31. Ibid., 22.

32. Ibid., 25.

33. *TA*, 93.

34. *TA*, 88.

35. Frei, *Theology and Narrative*. See also Lindbeck, *The Nature of Doctrine*. Tracy understands how Lindbeck comes to label him an "experiential-expressive" theologian, but he finds the term as applied to Ricoeur simply "bizarre." See Tracy, "Lindbeck's New Program for Theology: A Reflection."

36. Tracy, "A Theological View of Philosophy: Revelation and Reason," 154.

37. Ibid., 155.

38. Ibid.

39. Ibid., 155–56.

40. Ibid., 156.

41. See figure 1 in chapter 1 above.

42. Tracy, *The Analogical Imagination*, 68–69.

43. William Placher offers the following astute assessment of Tracy: "A scholar of astonishing erudition and great generosity, he seems to have read everything and to have found something of value in everything he has read. Amid all this appropriation, sometimes of writers who strongly disagree with each other, it is often hard to get clear on just what Tracy *rejects*." See Placher, *Unapologetic Theology*, 155. In light of this, it is all the more shocking that Frei continued to cast Ricoeur in the role of Tracy's "mentor." Not only might Ricoeur not crack the top five influences, but Tracy is too eclectic and original to be anyone's disciple.

44. Frei, *The Eclipse of Biblical Narrative*, 104.

45. Frei, *Theology and Narrative*, 103.

46. Ibid., 104.

47. Ibid., 143.

48. Frei, *The Eclipse of Biblical Narrative*, 130.

49. Frei, *Theology and Narrative*, 118.

50. Ibid., 125.

51. Ibid., 126.

52. This shift from Ricoeur to Tracy, as though the two were interchangeable, is the first instance of the Ricoeur-Tracy conflation.

53. Frei, *Theology and Narrative*, 130.

54. This use of the "post" prefix is highly suspect when applied to hermeneutics, which is itself a form of postmodern thought. For a situation of Ricoeur within "postmodernism," see Madison, *The Hermeneutics of Post-Modernity*. As mentioned above, Ricoeur disliked the term "postmodern" immensely.

55. This is not to deny that Frei makes some keen observations, but to refer to his own assessment: "in the company of historians I always insist that I am a theologian but when thrown with theologians I identify myself as a historian. I deny that this is either evasive or confused because under all circumstances I am clear about one fact: *I am not a philosopher.*" Hans Frei, "Letter to Jane Beck: Feb 15, 1977," *Collections* (Yale Divinity School Library, 1–4), as quoted in M. Higton's "Hans Frei: An Annotated Bibliography," emphasis mine. See http://people.exeter.ac.uk/mahigton/frei/bib3.html#bib.

56. Most notably, Frei's attempt to use Derrida to undercut Ricoeur relies on the perceived antipathy between Ricoeur's hermeneutics and Derrida's deconstruction. But as Leonard Lawlor persuasively argues, Ricoeur and Derrida (and their respective adherents) have for decades had a heated but highly productive discussion precisely because of the similarities in their thought. See Lawlor's "Introduction: A Barely Visible Difference," in his *Imagination and Chance.* The appendix (131–63) is a transcript of a 1971 conversation that clearly demonstrates the similarities.

57. Tracy, "Lindbeck's New Program for Theology," 469. The "experiential-expressivist" label gained even more currency in Frei's posthumously published *Types of Christian Theology*, which sets a five-point continuum that goes from a Kantian rationalism (represented by Gordon Kaufmann) to a Wittgensteinian fideism (represented by D. Z. Phillips).

58. Stiver points out that there is a similar lack of clarity in the postliberal metaphor of the biblical text *absorbing* our world: "it does not include a critical way of distinguishing what can and cannot be absorbed, or between what should and should not. On the surface, it is preposterous to suggest that Frei and Lindbeck are suggesting that we emulate cultural details of the ancient world, such as giving up cars and TVs in favor of donkeys and scrolls. Obviously, they mean something different—but what?" Stiver, *Theology after Ricoeur*, 51.

59. Frei, *Theology and Narrative*, 118.

60. For a discussion of the problems with the postliberal homogenization of the tradition, see T. W. Tilley, "Postmodern Theologies," in Joy, *Ricoeur and Narrative.*

61. For a sustained discussion on the problems of Frei's own "foundationalist" hermeneutics, see Comstock, "Truth or Meaning."

62. This would be supported by Paul DeHart's argument that Frei was influenced to reject hermeneutics by the work of one of his students: "The 1972 dissertation of his student Charles Wood was an important influence here, a Wittgensteinian critique of the entire tradition of hermeneutical philosophy from its origins in Heidegger to its culmination in Gadamer." See DeHart, *The Trial of the Witnesses*, 16.

63. "I am deeply persuaded that *materially* philosophy must not govern the curriculum or the spirit of modern seminary education, but that *formally* its thorough-minded, disciplined probing is one of our few protections against the regnant confusion of Christian depth with a soft and addle-brained mentality." Hans Frei, "Letter to Roger L. Shinn, Aug 26, 1981," *Collections* (Yale Divinity School Library, 4–86), as quoted in Higton, "An Annotated Bibliography."

64. Tracy, "Ricoeur's Philosophical Journey," 202. See also Mudge, "Introduction," 3.

65. Ricoeur, "Philosophical Hermeneutics and Theological Hermeneutics," 17.

66. *TA*, 90.

67. Ricoeur, "Philosophical Hermeneutics and Theological Hermeneutics," 19.

68. Ibid.

69. Ibid., 20.
70. Ibid., 22.
71. Ibid., 26.
72. Ibid., 27.
73. Ibid., 28.
74. Ibid., 30.
75. Ibid.
76. *TA*, 99.
77. *OA*, 25.
78. *TA*, 99.
79. *OA*, 24. In this statement are the seeds of a hermeneutic response to Milbank's Radical Orthodoxy.
80. *CC*, 150. See also Reagan, *Paul Ricoeur*, 119–21.
81. See Ricoeur, *Essays on Biblical Interpretation*; Ricoeur with LaCocque, *Thinking Biblically*.
82. *CC*, 90–91.
83. For example, see Merold Westphal's frustration with "the discrepancy between the book written and the book we might claim to have a right to expect," in Westphal, "Review of *Oneself as Another*." Henry Venema expresses similar concerns: "if conviction and certainty of self cannot be produced by rational analysis, shouldn't Ricoeur articulate how the particularity of his own religious tradition stimulates the production of an imaginative vision that affects what appears to him as philosophically necessary . . . ? Not to give consideration to that which can only be received as gift and is worthy of risking one's whole life, excludes too much." See Venema, *Identifying Selfhood*, 162.
84. Ricoeur, "Reply," 449.
85. See Fergus Kerr's discussion of Wittgenstein on Barth in his *Theology after Wittgenstein*, 152–53. It should be stressed that there is no antipathy here for Wittgenstein, one of the great philosophers of the twentieth century. His philosophy is of incalculable importance in addressing the analytical problems of logic, denotation, certainty, and other important philosophical problems of the analytic tradition, *problems Karl Barth does not have.*
86. See DeHart, *Trial of the Witnesses*, 47–48. I will return to this in the conclusion.
87. For an attempt at this, see Marshall, *Trinity and Truth*.

3. PREFIGURATION

1. Cf. Ricoeur, *The Conflict of Interpretations*, 3–11.
2. Cf. Rom 11:17–24. Don Ihde first made this argument for this construal of Ricoeur's dialectical pattern in *Hermeneutic Phenomenology*.
3. Greisch, *Le Cogito Herméneutique*, 27–28.
4. *TA*, 12.
5. *CC*, 23.
6. Ibid.
7. *CC*, 25.
8. Marcel, *Man against Mass Society*, 156–57.
9. Ibid., 1.
10. Marcel, *Tragic Wisdom and Beyond*, 235.
11. Marcel, *Man against Mass Society*, 155.
12. Ibid.

13. Ibid.

14. Marcel, *The Philosophy of Existentialism*.

15. Marcel, *Man against Mass Society*, 3.

16. Ricoeur notes that for Marcel, *mystery* does not mean "Do Not Touch!" but is rather an invitation to think more. "[S]i la pensée de Gabriel Marcel s'énonce elle-même comme pensée du mystère, ce terme, selon une remarque enjouée de l'auteur, n'équivaut pas a l'étiquette: défense de toucher! Il marque plutôt l'invitation à *penser plus*, comme le dit Kant du symbole dans la *Critique de la faculté de juger*." Ricoeur, *Lectures 2*, 47.

17. Ibid., 156.

18. See Alfred O. Schmitz, "Marcel's Dialectical Method," in Schilpp and Hahn, *The Philosophy of Gabriel Marcel*, 161–62.

19. Marcel, *Man against Mass Society*, 160.

20. Ibid., 159.

21. Marcel, "An Autobiographical Essay." He was even more vigorous in his rejection of the label "Christian existentialism," declaring, "I cannot protest enough against this way of putting the matter." See Marcel, *Tragic Wisdom and Beyond*, 237.

22. Ibid., 251.

23. Nabert's influence on Ricoeur has recently been emphasized. See Stefan Orth, "From Freedom to God? The Impact of Jean Nabert's Philosophy on Paul Ricoeur," in *BSS*, 120–30.

24. Ricoeur sees secondary reflection as his "ally" within Marcel's work, and uses it to question other concepts with which he has less affinity. See Ricoeur, "Gabriel Marcel and Phenomenology," 490–91.

25. *CC*, 24.

26. Marcel, *Metaphysical Journal*.

27. Husserl, *Ideas*.

28. Ricoeur, "Gabriel Marcel and Phenomenology," 471.

29. Ricoeur, *Gabriel Marcel et Karl Jaspers*, 369. Translation mine.

30. Ricoeur, *Freedom and Nature*, 15.

31. Spiegelberg, *The Phenomenological Movement*, 681.

32. It should be noted that Husserl objects, no less than Ricoeur, to the "hypostasizing" of essences, firmly rejecting the Platonic sense of "essence."

33. Merleau-Ponty, *Phenomenology of Perception*, xiv.

34. Ricoeur, "Intellectual Autobiography," 12.

35. Ricoeur, *Husserl*, 43.

36. Philip Buckley argues that Husserl's transcendental attitude is not opposed to hermeneutics, but is rather a natural partner. See Buckley, "Husserl and the 'Infinite Task' of Hermeneutics," in *BHD*, 66–80.

37. Ricoeur, *Freedom and Nature*, 4.

38. "The phenomenology elaborated in *Ideas I* is incontestably an idealism, even a transcendental idealism." See Ricoeur, *Husserl*, 24.

39. Spiegelberg, *The Phenomenological Movement*, 594.

40. Ricoeur, "Gabriel Marcel and Phenomenology," 474.

41. Merleau-Ponty, *The Phenomenology of Perception*. See also Raynova, "All That Gives Us to Think," 671.

42. Ricoeur, *Freedom and Nature*, 7.

43. Ricoeur, "Gabriel Marcel and Phenomenology," 489.

44. *TA*, 52.

45. As Walter Lowe puts it, "Husserlian phenomenology prevents existentialism, Marcellian or otherwise, from becoming self-enclosed; for it requires a careful description that proceeds by way of the object." See Lowe, "Introduction," in Ricoeur, Fallible Man, xv.

46. FS, 3.

47. Husserl, Idées directrice pour une phenomenology.

48. This appeared in English as Freedom and Nature: The Voluntary and Involuntary.

49. For a more detailed analysis of the limits of eidetics, see Bourgeois, Extension of Ricoeur's Hermeneutic, 10–27.

50. PPR, 15.

51. Jean Grondin, Le Tournant herméneutique de la phénoménologie.

52. PPR, 16.

53. Ibid.

54. Ricoeur, Symbolism of Evil, 351.

55. A hermeneutics oriented around symbol is ultimately limited, which will lead to Ricoeur's developing a theory of narrative. See Pellauer, "The Symbol Gave Rise to Thought."

56. For a stinging rejection of Ricoeur's hermeneutic treatment of Freud, see Grünbaum, "The Poverty of the Semiotic Turn in Psychoanalytic Theory and Therapy." For a more balanced reception, see Phillips, "Text, Interpretation, and the Unconscious in the Thought of Paul Ricoeur."

57. PPR, 21.

58. TA, 16.

59. This is perhaps Ricoeur's best-known phrase, although as Jervolino notes, it owes something to Emmanuel Mounier. See Domenico Jervolino, The Cogito and Hermeneutics, 160n44.

60. See Ricoeur, "Hermeneutics and the Critique of Ideology," in Hermeneutics and the Human Sciences, 62–99. See also TA, 270–308.

61. Ricoeur, Hermeneutics and the Human Sciences, 64.

62. Ibid.

63. Ibid., 88.

64. It is Gadamer himself who criticizes this most incisively: "where are the limits of this analogy? Where does the patient-relationship end and the social partnership in its unprofessional right begin? Most fundamentally: Over against what self-interpretation of the social consciousness (and all morality is such) is it in place to inquire behind that consciousness, and when is it not? Within the context of the purely practical, or of a universalized emancipatory reflection, these questions appear unanswerable." Gadamer, Philosophical Hermeneutics, 42.

65. Ricoeur, Hermeneutics and the Human Sciences, 95–96.

66. Ibid., 96.

67. Ibid., 99.

68. Ibid., 98.

69. Ibid., 64, 94, 99.

70. Ricoeur, "Structure, Word, Event," in The Conflict of Interpretations, 81–83.

71. Ibid., 83.

72. Ricoeur, "Intellectual Autobiography," 22.

73. Ricoeur, The Conflict of Interpretations, 86–88.

74. Ricoeur, "Intellectual Autobiography," 19.

75. This question is pursued further in Ricoeur, "Sign, Word and Symbol," in *The Conflict of Interpretations*, 236–66.

76. *OA*, 115n2.

77. Reagan, *Paul Ricoeur*, 133.

78. *OA*, 17; emphasis Ricoeur's.

79. *OA*, 32.

80. *OA*, 40.

81. This is an extension of the analysis first undertaken in the 1971 essay "The Model of the Text." See *TA*, 144–67.

82. There is in fact a third class, the "perlocutionary" act, but this does not enter into our discussion.

83. *OA*, 42.

84. *OA*, 43.

85. Ibid.

86. *OA*, 44.

87. *OA*, 57.

88. *OA*, 64–65.

89. *OA*, 72.

90. *OA*, 86.

91. For more detailed and illuminating discussion of Ricoeur's treatment of intentionality and action, see van den Hengel, "Can There Be a Science of Action?"

92. *OA*, 88.

93. *OA*, 89.

94. *OA*, 96.

95. *OA*, 110.

96. *OA*, 313.

97. Marcel, *Tragic Wisdom*, 247.

98. Marcel, *The Mystery of Being*, vol. 1, *Reflection and Mystery*, 103.

99. Marcel, *The Philosophy of Existentialism*, 96–97.

100. The ties are even stronger when Marcel argues that memory is "inseparable from witness." See Marcel, *Being and Having*, 97.

101. Marcel, *Creative Fidelity*, 168.

102. See Marcel, *Tragic Wisdom*, 238–39.

103. See Raynova, "Entre la Régression et l'Eschatologie."

104. *CC*, 24.

4. CONFIGURATION

1. Ricoeur, *Interpretation Theory*, 95.

2. *TN* 1, ix.

3. See Rentdorff, "Paul Ricoeur's Poetic Ontology."

4. *TN* 1, xi.

5. *TN* 1, x.

6. *TN* 1, ix.

7. Ibid.

8. Steven H. Clark, "Narrative Identity in Ricoeur's 'Oneself as Another,'" in Simms, *Critical Studies*, 2.

9. *TN* 1, 3.

10. *TN* 1, 53–54.

11. *TN* 1, 31.

12. Augustine, *Confessions*, 25:32.

13. *TN* 1, 83.

14. Augustine, *Confessions*, 27:36.

15. *TN* 1, 16.

16. *TN* 1, 21.

17. *TN* 1, 31.

18. I follow Ricoeur here in translating *muthos* as "emplotment" (*mise en intrigue*), but leaving "mimesis" as an untranslatable combination of representation and imitation.

19. *TN* 1, 33.

20. Aristotle, *Poetics*, 50a1.

21. *TN* 1, 54–55.

22. *TN* 1, 56.

23. *TN* 1, 58, 57.

24. Ricoeur rejects the notion that actions can be ethically neutral: "The very project of ethical neutrality presupposes the original ethical quality of action," which "is itself only a corollary of the major characteristic of action, that it is always symbolically mediated." *TN* 1, 59.

25. For a more extended discussion of this issue in a theological context, see Richard J. Severson, *Time, Death, and Eternity*.

26. Ricoeur accepts virtually all of Heidegger's arguments on time *except* the grounding of *Innerzeitigkeit* in *Sein zum Tode*: "Despite the desire to derive historicality and within-time-ness from radical temporality, a new dispersion of the notion of time will, in fact, emerge from the incommensurability of mortal time . . . and cosmic time, which within-time-ness leads to." *TN* 3, 67. Heidegger ultimately ends up with the same aporias as Augustine, unable to reconcile phenomenological and cosmic time. Only a historical, narrated time can bridge the gap, which opens the way (and in fact necessitates) a narrative identity.

27. *TN* 1, 63.

28. Heidegger, *Being and Time*, 460.

29. *TN* 1, 63.

30. *TN* 1, 64.

31. *TN* 1, 68.

32. Ricoeur begins his account of the *Confessions* with an apology for why he engages Augustine's reflections on time without situating them within Augustine's concern with eternity. He admits that this does some "violence to the text." See *TN* 1, 5.

33. *TN* 1, 65.

34. *TN* 1, 66.

35. *TN* 1, 67.

36. *TN* 1, 68.

37. *TN* 1, 69.

38. *TN* 1, 77.

39. Ricoeur actually addresses this final question first, but the argument does not build on this point, and addressing it last will smooth the transition into narrative identity. Because we are concerned here with narrative primarily as it relates to narrative identity (as opposed to temporality), I am also leaving out of this exposition Ricoeur's continued engagement of the phenomenology of time in Kant, Husserl, and Heidegger. He summarizes his position concisely in *TN* 3, 249–61.

Severson takes up this question in chapter 4, "Time and Narrative: A Theological Extension," in *Time, Death, and Eternity*, 131–56.

40. *TN* 1, 77.
41. *TN* 1, 78.
42. *TN* 1, 80.
43. *TN* 1, 82.
44. *TN* 1, 73.
45. *TN* 1, 74.
46. Toth, "The Graft, Residue, and Memory."
47. Reagan, *Paul Ricoeur*, 74.
48. *OA*, 1–3.
49. *OA*, 1.
50. *OA*, 8.
51. *OA*, 11.
52. *OA*, 15.
53. Friedrich Nietzsche, *Will to Power*, as quoted in *OA*, 14–15n23.
54. *OA*, 11.
55. *OA*, 16.
56. *OA*, 4.
57. *OA*, 21.
58. *OA*, 22.
59. *OA*, 23.
60. See Bourgeois, "Ricoeur and Marcel"; Bourgeois, "Hermeneutics and Deconstruction"; Lawlor, "A Note on Radical Alterity in Paul Ricoeur and Jacques Derrida"; Lawlor, *Imagination and Chance.*
61. *TN* 3, 248.
62. *OA*, 115.
63. *TN* 3, 241.
64. Ibid.
65. *TN* 3, 243.
66. *CC*, 89.
67. Paul Ricoeur, "Narrative Identity," in Wood, *On Paul Ricoeur*, 186–201.
68. *TN* 3, 246.
69. Ibid.
70. See Arendt, *The Human Condition.*
71. Ricoeur, "Narrative Identity," 188. See also *OA*, 114n1.
72. See Blamey, "Paul Ricoeur's *Durcharbeiten*."
73. Ricoeur, "Sorrows and the Making of Life-Stories," 323.
74. *TN* 3, 247.
75. Ibid., 248.
76. Ibid.
77. Ibid., 246.
78. Ricoeur, "Narrative Identity," 189.
79. *OA*, 116.
80. Parfit, *Reasons and Persons.*
81. Ibid., 255; from *OA*, 130.
82. Whether Ricoeur gives full credit to the positive power of "technomyths" is called into question by Don Ihde in "Literary and Science Fictions," 93.
83. *OA*, 137–38.

84. Welsen, "Personal Identity as Narrative Identity," 199.

85. *OA*, 136.

86. *OA*, 118.

87. Ricoeur, "Narrative Identity," 192.

88. *OA*, 118–19.

89. *OA*, 121.

90. *OA*, 122.

91. *OA*, 143.

92. For a nice illustration of this, using the children's tale of Jack and the Beanstalk, see Bontekoe, *Dimensions of the Hermeneutic Circle*, 174–75.

93. *OA*, 123.

94. Ibid.

95. *OA*, 121.

96. *OA*, 121.

97. *TN* 3, 249.

98. *OA*, 161–62.

99. *OA*, 115.

5. REFIGURATION

1. Ricoeur, "Ethics and Human Capability."

2. A condensed form of the three studies first appeared as "The Teleological and Deontological Structures of Action: Aristotle and/or Kant?" *Philosophy* 21 (1987): 99–111.

3. *OA*, 171.

4. *OA*, 170.

5. While Ricoeur expresses no concern with "Aristotelean orthodoxy," it remains that Aristotle offers more resources on ascription and agency than he takes up. See Latona, "Selfhood and Agency in Ricoeur and Aristotle."

6. *OA*, 172.

7. See MacIntyre, *After Virtue*.

8. *OA*, 176.

9. See "Symbolic Mediation," in chapter 4 above.

10. Ricoeur, "Life in Quest of Narrative," 32.

11. *OA*, 177.

12. *OA*, 180.

13. Ibid.

14. *OA*, 182.

15. Taylor, "Self-Interpreting Animals," and "Cross-Purposes: The Liberal-Communitarian Debate."

16. *OA*, 193.

17. *OA*, 194.

18. *OA*, 194.

19. Weber, *Economy and Society*.

20. See Arendt, *Crisis of the Republic*, 140–43.

21. Rawls, *A Theory of Justice*, 3. Ricoeur's treatment of Rawls will be addressed further in the section on the moral norm.

22. Morny Joy points out that the third-person treatment at each stage of the analysis is taken further by Ricoeur in *The Just*. See Joy, "Recognition in the Work of Paul Ricoeur," 518–30, esp. 521; Ricoeur, *The Just*.

23. Artistotle, *Ethics*, V.3, 1131a12–33.

24. *OA*, 202.
25. *OA*, 203.
26. *OA*, 204.
27. Ibid.
28. Aristotle, *Nicomachean Ethics*, II.7, 1107a31ff.
29. *OA*, 204.
30. Kant, *Grounding for the Metaphysics of Morals*, 4.
31. *OA*, 205.
32. *OA*, 206.
33. Kant, *Grounding for the Metaphysics of Morals*, 18.
34. *OA*, 210.
35. *OA*, 218.
36. *OA*, 219.
37. Ibid.
38. *OA*, 220.
39. Whether Ricoeur has fully appreciated the nuances of Kant's position is contestable. See Anderson, "Ricoeur's Reclamation of Autonomy."
40. *OA*, 226.
41. *OA*, 227.
42. *OA*, 228.
43. See Boucher and Kelly, *The Social Contract from Hobbes to Rawls*.
44. *OA*, 228.
45. *OA*, 229.
46. *OA*, 237–38.
47. *OA*, 236.
48. Baynes, *The Normative Grounds of Social Criticism*.
49. *OA*, 238.
50. *OA*, 239.
51. Ibid.
52. *OA*, 260.
53. Ricoeur does this at some length in *Time and Narrative*. See chapters 9 and 10, "Should We Renounce Hegel?" and "Towards a Hermeneutics of Historical Consciousness," in *TN* 3, 193–240.
54. *OA*, 290.
55. *OA*, 240. See Brito, "Hegel dans 'Soi-même comme une autre' de Paul Ricoeur."
56. *OA*, 249.
57. *OA*, 290.
58. *OA*, 250.
59. *OA*, 240–41.
60. Ricoeur, "Ethics and Human Capability," 287.
61. Birgit Schaff, "Toward a Logic of Tragic Conflict."
62. *OA*, 249.
63. Nussbaum, "Ricoeur on Tragedy," 273. Nussbaum raises a further point, whether in the case of conflicting duties, the one that practical wisdom chooses *against* requires some kind of compensatory action. This seems a necessity if the element of "tragedy" in the situation is to be respected. In this case, one would seek not only to find the wisest choice in the situation, but also to discover what could be done to prevent such conflicts in the future. See also Nussbaum, *The Fragility of Goodness*.

64. Ricoeur, "Ethics and Human Capability," 288.

65. "We can either modify our account of the initial situation or we can revise our existing judgments . . . by going back and forth, sometimes altering the conditions of the contractual circumstances, at others withdrawing our judgments and conforming them to principle, I assume that eventually we find a description of the initial situation that both expresses reasonable conditions and yields principles which match our considered judgments duly pruned and adjusted." Rawls, *A Theory of Justice*, 20.

66. *OA*, 252. See Walzer, *Spheres of Justice*.

67. *OA*, 258.

68. *OA*, 259; esp. n32.

69. *OA*, 259.

70. *OA*, 261.

71. Aristotle, *Nicomachean Ethics* V.10, 1137b12–24.

72. *OA*, 263.

73. Kant, *Grounding for the Metaphysics of Morals*, 63–67.

74. *OA*, 267.

75. Ibid.

76. Marcel, *Being and Having*, 46.

77. *OA*, 268.

78. *OA*, 266.

79. *OA*, 268.

80. See Fairfield, "Hans-Georg Gadamer, Paul Ricoeur, and Practical Judgment."

81. *OA*, 269.

82. *OA*, 273.

83. *OA*, 274.

84. *OA*, 275.

85. *OA*, 276.

86. *OA*, 277.

87. *OA*, 280n64.

88. As we saw in the first chapter, Ricoeur does not fully endorse Habermas's discourse ethics, but rather positions it within a hermeneutic model. He particularly objects to the strategy of "purifying" discourse of all "convention," which he sees as a social version of Kant's attempt to purify moral reasoning of all inclination. Cf. *OA*, 286. While discourse ethics has a clear relevance to autonomy, Ricoeur spends an inordinate amount of time and space on this discussion. One suspects that this section is one of those he was thinking of when he claimed that the study "still looks like an appendix."

89. David Kaplan rightly notes that Ricoeur's attribution of this argument-conviction dichotomy is not reflective of Habermas's more nuanced statements. See Kaplan, *Ricoeur's Critical Theory*, 121.

90. *OA*, 280.

91. *OA*, 289.

92. Kaplan, *Ricoeur's Critical Theory*, 113.

93. Ricoeur, "Les Paradoxes de L'Identité," 201–206.

94. Levinas, *Otherwise than Being*.

95. See *OA*, 332–41, esp. 338. This uncharacteristically harsh judgment has provoked several responses on both sides. There was a short but courteous exchange of letters between Levinas and Ricoeur; see Paul Ricoeur et al., *Ethique et*

Responsabilité, ed. Jean-Charles Aeschlimann (Neuchâtel: La Baconnière, 1994), 36–38. Patrick Bourgeois defends Ricoeur's position while Richard A. Cohen attacks it in *Ricoeur as Another*. See Bourgeois, "Ricoeur and Levinas," and Cohen, "Moral Selfhood," in Cohen and Marsh, *Ricoeur as Another*. See also Wallace, "The Summoned Self." Ricoeur refines his criticism of Levinas, and in so doing strengthens it, in *Autrement*. Richard Kearney presents a helpful selection of this "especially trenchant" criticism in "Between Oneself and Another," 149–150n17.

96. "[T]here is no contradiction in holding the movement from the Same toward the Other and that from the Other toward the Same to be dialectically complementary. The two movements do not annihilate one another to the extent that one unfolds in the gnoseological dimension of sense, the other in the ethical dimension of injunction." *OA*, 340–41.

97. *OA*, 296.

98. This is a recapitulation of Ricoeur's first treatment of recognition in the context of the self. See Ricoeur, *Fallible Man*, 122.

99. For purposes of this work, there is no need to develop this point further. Recognition as a concept, however, does turn out to be one of the *lacunae* that Ricoeur goes on to address in a later series of lectures given in Vienna. See *The Course of Recognition*.

100. *OA*, 295. Ricoeur feels that the issue of *memory*, central to responsibility to the past, was neglected in both *Time and Narrative* and *Oneself as Another*. See *CC*, 93–94. He begins to rectify this in Ricoeur, "Memory and Forgetting." This culminates in *Memory, History, Forgetting*.

101. *OA*, 295.

102. *OA*, 292.

103. *OA*, 302.

104. Raynova, "All That Gives Us to Think," 687–88.

105. *OA*, 355.

PART 3. RETURN

1. Habermas, "Transcendence from Within, Transcendence Within this World," 231.

2. Barth, *The Humanity of God*, 57.

6. CHALCEDONIAN HERMENEUTICS

1. See note 37 in chapter 2 above.

2. See Demson, *Hans Frei and Karl Barth*; see also Demson, "Inspiration as the Basis for Biblical Interpretation." For other "non-Yale" Barthians, see McCormack, *Barth's Critically Realist Dialectical Theology*; Torrance, *Karl Barth*; Webster, *Barth*.

3. See *SN*, 87–110.

4. The compatibility is not surprising to some. Frederick Lawrence tells of a lecture that Ricoeur gave at Boston University in the 1970s. A questioner, objecting to an argument of Ricoeur's, angrily denounced him as a "Barthian," and was deflated when Ricoeur merely responded: "Thank you."

5. *CD* I/2, 722–40.

6. Ricoeur, *Interpretation Theory*, 76.

7. Cf. Heidegger, *Being and Time*, esp. §32, "Understanding and Interpretation," 188–95. See also Gadamer, *Truth and Method*, 269–70.

8. See *SN*, 54.

9. *SN*, 53–54.

10. Ricoeur, "Philosophical Hermeneutics and Theological Hermeneutics," 19.

11. Ibid., 20.

12. *CD* I/2, 728.

13. "Everyone has some sort of philosophy, i.e., a particular view of the fundamental nature and relationship of things. . . . This is true even of the simplest Bible reader (and of him perhaps with particular force and tenacity)." Ibid.

14. *CD* I/2, 723.

15. *TA*, 37.

16. *CD* IV/2, 479; as quoted in *SN*, 51.

17. "Therefore, following the holy fathers, we all with one accord teach men to acknowledge one and the same Son, our Lord Jesus Christ, at once complete in Godhead and complete in manhood, truly God and truly man, consisting also of a reasonable soul and body, of one substance with the Father as regards his Godhead, and at the same time of one substance with us as regards his manhood; like us in all respects, apart from his sin; as regards his Godhead, begotten of the Father before the ages, but yet as regards his manhood begotten, for us men and for our salvation, of Mary the Virgin, the God-bearer; one and the same Christ, Son, Lord, Only-begotten, recognized IN TWO NATURES, WITHOUT CONFUSION, WITHOUT CHANGE, WITHOUT DIVISION, WITHOUT SEPARATION; the distinction of natures being in no way annulled by the union, but rather the characteristics of each nature being preserved and coming together to form one person and subsistence, not as parted or separated into two persons, but one and the same Son and Only-begotten God the Word, Lord Jesus Christ; even as the prophets from earliest times spoke of him, and our Lord Jesus Christ himself taught us, and the creed of the Fathers has handed down to us." Henry Bettenson, *Documents of the Christian Church* (New York: Oxford University Press, 1947), 73.

18. Hunsinger, "Karl Barth's Christology: Its Basic Chalcedonian Character," in *Disruptive Grace*, 131–47, esp. 132.

19. Ibid., 133.

20. Hunsinger, *How to Read Karl Barth*, 83.

21. *CD* III/2, 325, emphasis mine.

22. Hunsinger, *How to Read Karl Barth*, 186.

23. Ibid., 204.

24. *CD* IV/2, 494.

25. Ibid., 205.

26. *CD* I/1, 238.

27. *CD* I/1, 45.

28. *CD* II/2, 194.

29. *CD* I/1, 199.

30. *CD* I/1, 200.

31. *CD* IV/2, 740.

32. Hunsinger, *How to Read Karl Barth*, 287.

33. Ricoeur, *History and Truth*. While this was not the first book to go to press, the essays that are contained within this collection were among the first things Ricoeur wrote.

34. *CC*, 151.

35. Wallace addresses the anthropological issue first, which serves to place anthropology *before* Christology in the progression of the argument, a move that will inevitably distance him from Barth. To generate anthropological definitions

prior to Christological definitions would violate the rule of *asymmetry* in Barth's Chalcedonian pattern.

36. *CD* III/2, 3; as quoted in *SN*, 76. The exposition that follows is not a particularly fair reading of Barth. Ever the dialectician, Barth modifies this terse statement almost immediately: "Man is certainly not his only creation. Man is only *a* creature and not *the* creature. . . . Man is a creature in the midst of others which were directly created by God and exist independently of man. The Word of God itself sees man in this context and within these appointed limits." *CD* III/2, 3–4.

37. *SN*, 78.

38. Ibid.

39. *SN*, 78–80. See also *CD* II/1, 727.

40. *SN*, 78–82.

41. *CC*, 151.

42. One could, however, take the following as a concise summary: "In the face of its object, theology itself can only wish to be *ancilla*. That is why it cannot assign any other role to philosophy. Scripture alone can be the *domina*. Hence there is no real cause for disputes about prestige." *CD* I/2, 735.

43. Barth, *Ethics*, 19–45.

44. Ibid., 20–21.

45. Ibid., 21.

46. Ibid.

47. Ibid., 23

48. See chapter 1, n. 5, above.

49. Ibid., 24.

50. Ibid., 27. John van den Hengel, brilliant reader and interpreter of Ricoeur, labels Barth's entire theology as one of "diastasis," which leads him to overlook the compatibility. See J. van den Hengel, "From Text to Action in Theology," in *Memory, Narrativity, Self and the Challenge to Think God*, 120.

51. "[Theology] will not look on askance and bewail the omission of its own terminology when a philosophy of practical reason may perhaps in its own way, without ceasing to be philosophy, make fruitful instead of rejecting the superior knowledge that characterizes itself." Ibid.

52. Ibid., 33. He goes on to note that we have only to compare the Catholic union of Aristotle and Augustine with the "confusion" of Protestant conceptions, "and in this way be forced to acknowledge that it is a classical, and as, we might calmly say, one of the most grandiose achievements in the entire field." Ibid.

53. Ibid., 28.

54. Ibid., 32.

55. Ibid., 34–35.

56. Ibid., 36.

57. Ibid., 42.

58. Ibid., 39.

59. Ibid., 36.

60. When Richard Kearney, for example, argues for the ascendance of *posse* over *esse* in God, he does nothing to violate Barth's conception of what philosophy ought to do. Indeed Kearney (following Ricoeur) is attempting to oppose the "conceptual idolatry" that results from inscribing God within a metaphysics of Being, which Barth would heartily endorse. See Kearney, "The God of the Possible," 531–39, esp. 537, and *The God Who May Be: A Hermeneutics of Religion* (Bloomington:

Indiana University Press, 2001). If, however, this phenomenological investigation were used to judge the suitability of theological reflection, it would be a transgression of disciplines.

61. Barth, *Ethics*, 45.

62. See Dosse, *Paul Ricoeur,* esp. "Le Réveil Barthien," 220–30.

63. Ibid., 223.

64. Ricoeur, "Myth as the Bearer of Possible Worlds," 27.

65. Dosse, *Paul Ricoeur,* 225.

66. Raynova, "All That Gives Us to Think," 685.

67. *CC,* 150.

68. Ricoeur, "Reply to David Stewart," in *PPR,* 449.

69. *CC,* 151.

70. Raynova, "All That Gives Us to Think," 684.

71. *TA,* 99.

72. *FS,* 203.

73. *CD* I/2, 734.

74. Milbank would concur, rejecting the notion that "philosophy straightforwardly provides a foundation on which theology builds," on the grounds that such a model "at once accords too much autonomy to philosophy and too much superiority to theology." See Milbank, "Faith, Reason and Imagination," 9.

75. *FS,* 288.

7. THEOLOGICAL ANTHROPOLOGY

1. *BSS,* 679–80.

2. Barth, *The Humanity of God,* 57.

3. Marcel, *Man against Mass Society,* 155. See chapter 3 above.

4. See Jaspert and Bromiley, *Karl Barth—Rudolf Bultmann,* 38.

5. Barth, *CD* III/2, 231–242.

6. For an example of such an application in a different theological context, see van den Hengel, "Between Philosophy and Theology," 122–37.

7. *CD* III/2, 71.

8. Ibid., 133.

9. Ibid., 71.

10. Ibid., 68.

11. Ibid., 71.

12. Ibid.

13. Ibid., 134.

14. Jüngel, *Karl Barth,* 127.

15. Barth, *The Humanity of God,* 11. Note the implied criticism that any theological anthropology that is less committed to starting with the person of Christ is doomed to fall victim to abstraction (much like Marcel's "spirit of abstraction") *about God.* For Barth, the very possibility of a theology that is grounded in the concrete is bound up in this The-anthropological choice.

16. This has made Barth virtually unassailable by postmodern theology. The critique of master narratives, which would seem to apply a fortiori to Barth, does not apply at all because Barth does not ground his theology in a metaphysical system. This has made Barth a useful tool to the imperialist project of the "radical orthodoxy" movement. Committing a similar error as that of Frei and Wallace, Graham Ward argues for a natural affinity between Barth on one side and Derrida and Levinas on

the other. But in this once again we find a lack of respect for the distinction between philosophy and theology. While Wallace, following Tracy, allows theology to be colonized by philosophy, Ward wants to colonize philosophy with his theology. While Barth is a staunch defender of theological space, he is no theological imperialist. See Ward, *Barth, Derrida and the Language of Theology.*

17. *CD* III/2, 72–132. He also engages Emil Brunner's "theistic" anthropology, rooted in human morality. This is odd, as Barth claims to be engaging non-theological anthropologies, and he does not deny that it is an attempt at theological anthropology. Anthropologies that do not start with the person of Christ are not, it seems, theological anthropologies at all.

18. *CD* III/2, 120.

19. Ibid., 114.

20. Ibid., 127–28.

21. Ibid., 122.

22. *OA*, 355.

23. *TA*, 99.

24. *OA*, 313.

25. Ricoeur, *The Course of Recognition*, 105.

26. *FS*, 36.

27. An example of this would be the use of composite characters in biographical films. The point of the film is to tell about the main character. If that main character has three significant and revealing interactions with three different people at different points in his life, the filmmaker may well turn those three people into a single person for the film. This is less true factually, but the introduction of two new characters would clutter the narrative such that it would take away from the film's main point and diminish the truth (the disclosive power) of the narrative.

28. The craving for narrative anesthesia is not a mere desire but a *need* in the fullest sense, because our sense of self is at risk of being obliterated by the psychological pressure involved in telling the story of our suffering truly. See my *Broken Levees and Broken Narratives: A Hermeneutic Engagement of Post-Katrina New Orleans* (New Orleans: Loyola University Yamauchi Lectures in Religion, 2006).

29. *OA*, 121.

30. Ibid.

31. It is this duty of narrative to truth in the institutional sense that impels Ricoeur from *Oneself as Another* to *Memory, History, Forgetting.*

32. Kearney, *On Stories.*

33. *CD* III/2, 132.

34. Ibid., 157.

35. Ibid., 133.

36. Ibid., 157.

37. Ibid., 158.

38. *OA*, 121.

39. See Westphal, "Blind Spots: Christianity and Postmodern Philosophy," *Christian Century,* June 14, 2003; see also *Overcoming Ontotheology.*

40. Hauerwas, *A Community of Character,* 144. Don Browning notes the similarity between Ricoeur and Hauerwas (and MacIntyre) on this point in his *Christian Ethics and the Moral Psychologies* (Grand Rapids, Mich.: Eerdmans, 2006).

41. Hauerwas, *A Community of Character,* 148.

42. Ibid.

43. Galatians 2:20a, RSV.

44. *FS*, 249–61, esp. 257–58.

45. It is important here to note that meganarrative is not to be taken as a *monolithic* narrative, but rather as a collection of all the first-order narratives.

CONCLUSION

1. Fodor, "Postliberal Theology," 229–48.

2. Jüngel, *Karl Barth*, 129.

WORKS CITED

WORKS OF RICOEUR CITED

Ricoeur, Paul. *Autrement: Lecture D'autrement Qu'être Ou Au-Delà De L'essence D'emmanuel Levinas, Les Essais Du Collège International De Philosophie*. Paris: Presses Universitaires de France, 1997.

———. *The Conflict of Interpretations: Essays in Hermeneutics, Northwestern University Studies in Phenomenology and Existential Philosophy*. Evanston, Ill.: Northwestern University Press, 1974.

———. *The Course of Recognition*. Cambridge, Mass.: Harvard University Press, 2005.

———. *Critique and Conviction: Conversations with Francois Azouvi and Marc De Launay*. New York: Columbia University Press, 1998.

———. "Ethics and Human Capability." In *Paul Ricoeur and Contemporary Moral Thought*, ed. Wall, Schweiker, and Hall, 279–90.

———. *Fallible Man*. Ed. Paul Ricoeur. Rev. ed. New York: Fordham University Press, 1986.

———. *Freedom and Nature: The Voluntary and Involuntary*. Northwestern University Studies in Phenomenology and Existential Philosophy. Evanston, Ill.: Northwestern University Press, 1966.

———. *Freud and Philosophy: An Essay on Interpretation*. New Haven, Conn.: Yale University Press, 1970.

———. *From Text to Action: Essays in Hermeneutics 2*. Evanston, Ill.: Northwestern University Press, 1991.

———. "Gabriel Marcel and Phenomenology." In *The Philosophy of Gabriel Marcel*, ed. Schlipp and Hahn, 471–98.

———. *Gabriel Marcel et Karl Jaspers, Philosophie du Mystère et Philosophie du Paradoxe*. Paris: Editions du Temps Présent, 1948.

———. *Hermeneutics and the Human Sciences*. Trans. John B. Thompson. Ed. John B. Thompson. Cambridge: Cambridge University Press, 1981.

———. *History and Truth*. Trans. Charles A. Kelbey. Northwestern University Studies in Phenomenology and Existential Philosophy. Evanston, Ill.: Northwestern University Press, 1965.

———. *Husserl: An Analysis of His Phenomenology*. Northwestern University Studies in Phenomenology and Existential Philosophy. Evanston, Ill.: Northwestern University Press, 1967.

———. "Husserl and Wittgenstein on Language." In *Phenomenology and Existentialism*, ed. E. N. Lee and M. Mandelbaum, 207–17. London: Johns Hopkins Press, 1967.

———. "Intellectual Autobiography." In *The Philosophy of Paul Ricoeur*, ed. Lewis Edwin Hahn. Peru: Open Court, 1994.

———. *Interpretation Theory: Discourse and the Surplus of Meaning.* Fort Worth: Texas Christian University Press, 1976.

———. "Irrationality and the Plurality of Philosophical Systems." *Dialectica* 39 (1985): 297–319.

———. *The Just.* Trans. David Pellauer. Chicago: University of Chicago Press, 2000.

———. "La Pensée De Gabriel Marcel." *Bulletin de la Société Française de Philosophie* 78 (1984): 3–63.

———. "L'attribution de la mémoire à soi-même, aux proches et aux autres: un scheme pour la theologie philosophique?" *Archivo di filosofia* 69 (2001): 18–36.

———. *Lectures 2: La Contrée des Philosophes.* Paris: Seuil, 1992.

———. "Les Paradoxes de L'Identité." *Information Psychiatrique* 72, no. 3 (1996): 201–206.

———. "Life in Quest of Narrative." In *On Paul Ricoeur: Narrative and Interpretation,* ed. David Wood, 20–33. New York: Routledge, 1991.

———. "Memory and Forgetting." In *Questioning Ethics: Contemporary Debates in Philosophy,* ed. Richard Kearney and Mark Dooley, 5–11. London: Routledge, 1999.

———. *Memory, History, Forgetting.* Chicago: University of Chicago Press, 2004.

———. "Myth as the Bearer of Possible Worlds." In *Dialogues with Contemporary Continental Thinkers: The Phenomenological Heritage: Paul Ricoeur, Emmanuel Levinas, Herbert Marcuse, Stanislas Breton, Jacques Derrida,* ed. Richard Kearney. Manchester: Manchester University Press, 1984.

———. "Narrative Identity." In *On Paul Ricoeur: Narrative and Interpretation,* ed. David Wood, 188–99. New York: Routledge, 1991.

———. *Oneself as Another.* Chicago: University of Chicago Press, 1992.

———. "Religious Belief: The Difficult Path of the Religious." In *Narrative Transformations,* ed. B. Treanor and H. Venema. Bronx: Fordham University Press, forthcoming 2010.

———. "Philosophical Hermeneutics and Theological Hermeneutics." *Studies in Religion. Sciences religieuses* 5 (1975): 14–33.

———. *Réflexion Faite: Autobiographie Intellectuelle, Philosophie.* Paris: Editions Esprit, 1995.

———. "Reply to David Stewart." In *The Philosophy of Paul Ricoeur,* ed. Hahn, 443–49.

———. *The Rule of Metaphor: Multi-Disciplinary Studies of the Creation of Meaning in Language.* Toronto: University of Toronto Press, 1977.

———. *Soi-Même Comme Un Autre.* Paris: Seuil, 1990.

———. "Sorrows and the Making of Life-Stories." Trans. Boyd Blundell. *Philosophy Today* 47, no. 3 (2003): 322–24.

———. *The Symbolism of Evil.* New York: Harper and Row, 1967.

———. "The Teleological and Deontological Structures of Action: Aristotle and/or Kant?" *Philosophy* 21 (1987): 99–111.

———. *Time and Narrative.* Vol. 1. Chicago: University of Chicago Press, 1984.

———. *Time and Narrative.* Vol. 3. Chicago: University of Chicago Press, 1988.

Ricoeur, Paul, and Hans Georg Gadamer. "The Conflict of Interpretations." In *Phenomenology, Dialogues and Bridges,* ed. Ronald Bruzina, 299–320. Albany: SUNY Press, 1982.

Ricoeur, Paul, with André LaCocque. *Thinking Biblically: Exegetical and Hermeneutical Studies,* trans. David Pellauer. Chicago: University of Chicago Press, 1998.

Ricoeur, Paul, and Lewis Seymour Mudge. *Essays on Biblical Interpretation.* Philadelphia: Fortress Press, 1980.

Ricoeur, Paul, and John B. Thompson. *Hermeneutics and the Human Sciences: Essays on Language, Action, and Interpretation.* Cambridge, New York, Paris: Cambridge University Press; Editions de la Maison des sciences de l'homme, 1981.

Ricoeur, Paul, Pol Vandevelde, and Edmund Husserl. *A Key to Husserl's Ideas.* Vol. 1. Marquette Studies in Philosophy 10. Milwaukee, Wisc.: Marquette University Press, 1996.

Ricoeur, Paul, and Mark I. Wallace. *Figuring the Sacred: Religion, Narrative, and Imagination.* Minneapolis: Fortress Press, 1995.

Ricoeur, Paul, et al. *Ethique Et Responsabilité.* Ed. Jean-Christophe Aeschlimann. Neuchâtel: La Baconnière, 1994.

Carr, David, Charles Taylor, and Paul Ricoeur. "Ricoeur on Narrative." In *On Paul Ricoeur: Narrative and Interpretation,* ed. David Wood. New York: Routledge, 1991.

Dufrenne, Mikel, and Paul Ricoeur. *Karl Jaspers et la Philosophie de L'existence.* Collections "Esprit." La Condition Humaine. Paris: Éditions du Seuil, 1947.

Ihde, Don. *Hermeneutic Phenomenology: The Philosophy of Paul Ricoeur.* Northwestern University Studies in Phenomenology and Existential Philosophy. Evanston, Ill.: Northwestern University Press, 1971.

Kearney, Richard, and Paul Ricoeur. *Dialogues with Contemporary Continental Thinkers: The Phenomenological Heritage: Paul Ricoeur, Emmanuel Levinas, Herbert Marcuse, Stanislas Breton, Jacques Derrida.* Manchester, UK: Manchester University Press, 1984.

Lacocque, André, and Paul Ricoeur. *Thinking Biblically: Exegetical and Hermeneutical Studies.* Chicago: University of Chicago Press, 1998.

Levinas, Emmanuel, Jean-Christophe Aeschlimann, and Paul Ricoeur. *Répondre D'autrui Emmanuel Lévinas, Langages.* Neuchâtel: A la Baconnière, 1989.

Marcel, Gabriel, Paul Ricoeur, and Stephen Jolin. *Tragic Wisdom and Beyond; Including, Conversations between Paul Ricoeur and Gabriel Marcel.* Northwestern University Studies in Phenomenology and Existential Philosophy. Evanston, Ill.: Northwestern University Press, 1973.

Thompson, John B., Paul Ricoeur, and Jürgen Habermas. *Critical Hermeneutics: A Study in the Thought of Paul Ricoeur and Jürgen Habermas.* Cambridge: Cambridge University Press, 1981.

OTHER WORKS CITED

Anderson, Pamela Sue. *Ricoeur and Kant: Philosophy of the Will.* Atlanta, Ga.: Scholars Press, 1993.

———. "Ricoeur's Reclamation of Autonomy." In *Paul Ricoeur and Contemporary Moral Thought,* ed. Wall, Schweiker, and Hall, 15–31.

Arendt, Hannah. *Crisis of the Republic.* New York: Harcourt Brace Jovanovich, 1972.

———. *The Human Condition.* Trans. Margaret Canovan. Chicago: University of Chicago Press, 1998.

Aristotle. *Nicomachean Ethics.* Trans. and ed. Roger Crisp. Cambridge: Cambridge University Press, 2000.

———. *Poetics.* Trans. Kenneth McLeish. London: Nick Hern Books, 1999.

Augustine. *Confessions*. Trans. Henry Chadwick. Oxford: Oxford University Press, 1998.

Barth, Karl. *Church Dogmatics*. Ed. Geoffrey W. Bromiley and Thomas F. Torrance. Edinburgh: T&T Clark.

———. *Ethics*. Ed. Dietrich Braun. Trans. Geoffrey W. Bromiley. New York: Seabury Press, 1981.

———. *The Humanity of God*. Trans. T. Weiser and J. N. Thomas. Atlanta, Ga.: John Knox Press, 1960.

Baynes, Kenneth. *The Normative Grounds of Social Criticism: Kant, Rawls, and Habermas*. Albany: SUNY Press, 1992.

Blamey, Kathleen. "Paul Ricoeur's *Durcharbeiten*." In *Between Suspicion and Sympathy*, ed. Wiercinski, 575–84.

Bontekoe, Ronald. *Dimensions of the Hermeneutic Circle*. Atlantic Highlands, N.J.: Humanities Press, 1996.

Boucher, David, and Paul Kelly, eds. *The Social Contract from Hobbes to Rawls*. New York: Routledge, 1994.

Bouchindhomme, Christian, and Rainer Rochlitz. *Temps et Récit de Paul Ricoeur en débat*. Paris: Cerf, 1990.

Bourgeois, Patrick L. *Extension of Ricoeur's Hermeneutic*. The Hague: Martinus Nijhoff, 1975.

———. "Hermeneutics and Deconstruction: Paul Ricoeur in Postmodern Dialogue." In *Between Suspicion and Sympathy*, ed. Wiercinski, 333–50.

———. *Philosophy at the Boundary of Reason: Ethics and Postmodernity*. Albany: SUNY Press, 2001.

———. "Ricoeur and Levinas: Solicitude in Reciprocity and Solitude in Existence." In *Ricoeur as Another*, ed. Cohen and Marsh, 109–26.

———. "Ricoeur and Marcel: An Alternative to Postmodern Deconstruction." *Bulletin de la Société Américaine de Philosophie de la Langue Française* 7, no. 1–2 (1985): 164–75.

Brito, Emilio. "Hegel dans 'Soi-même comme un autre' de Paul Ricoeur." *Laval Theologique et Philosophique* 51, no. 2 (June 1995): 389–404.

Browning, Don S., and Francis Schüssler Fiorenza, eds. *Habermas, Modernity, and Public Theology*. Chicago: University of Chicago Press, 1992.

Buckley, R. Philip. "Husserl and the 'Infinite Task' of Hermeneutics." In *Between the Human and the Divine*, ed. Wiercinski, 66–80.

Clark, Steven. *Paul Ricoeur*. New York: Routledge, 1991.

Cohen, Richard A. "Moral Selfhood: A Levinasian Response to Ricoeur on Levinas." In *Ricoeur as Another*, ed. Cohen and Marsh, 109–60.

Cohen, Richard A., and James L. Marsh, eds. *Ricoeur as Another: The Ethics of Subjectivity*. Albany: SUNY, 2002.

Comstock, Gary. "Truth or Meaning: Ricoeur vs. Frei on Biblical Narrative." *Journal of Religion* 66, no. 2 (1986): 117–40.

D'Ambrosio, Francis, ed. *The Question of Christian Philosophy Today*. New York: Fordham University Press, 1999.

DeHart, Paul. *The Trial of the Witnesses: The Rise and Decline of Postliberal Theology*. Oxford: Blackwell, 2006.

Demson, David. *Hans Frei and Karl Barth: Different Ways of Reading Scripture*. Grand Rapids, Mich.: Eerdmans, 1997.

———. "Inspiration as the Basis for Biblical Interpretation: Karl Barth on Case Specific Hermeneutics." In *Between the Human and the Divine*, ed. Wiercinski, 184–91.

Dilthey, Wilhelm. *Selected Writings*. Ed. Hans P. Rickman. Cambridge: Cambridge University Press, 1976.

Dorrien, Gary. "The Future of Postliberal Theology." *Christian Century* (July 18–25, 2001): 22–29.

Dosse, François. *Paul Ricoeur: Le Sens d'une Vie*. Paris: La Découverte, 1997.

Douglass, Bruce, and David Hollenbach, eds. *Catholicism and Liberalism: Contributions to American Public Philosophy*. New York: Cambridge University Press, 1994.

Fairfield, Paul. "Hans-Georg Gadamer, Paul Ricoeur, and Practical Judgment." In *Between Suspicion and Sympathy*, ed. Wiercinski, 131–42.

Fodor, James. *Christian Hermeneutics: Paul Ricoeur and the Refiguring of Theology*. Oxford: Clarendon Press, 1995.

———. "Postliberal Theology." In *The Modern Theologians: An Introduction to Christian Theology since 1918*, ed. David F. Ford and Rachel Muers, 229–48. 3rd ed. Malden, Mass.: Blackwell, 2005.

Frei, Hans. *The Eclipse of Biblical Narrative: A Study in Eighteenth and Nineteenth Century Hermeneutics*. New Haven, Conn.: Yale University Press, 1974.

———. *Theology and Narrative: Selected Essays*. Ed. William C. Placher and George Hunsinger. New York: Oxford University Press, 1993.

———. *Types of Christian Theology*. New Haven, Conn.: Yale University Press, 1992.

Gadamer, Hans-Georg. *Philosophical Hermeneutics*. Trans. David Linge. Berkeley: University of California Press, 1976.

———. *Truth and Method*. Trans. Joel Weinsheimer and Donald G. Marshall. 2nd rev. ed. New York: Continuum, 1998.

Gagnon, Martin. "Ricoeur et la fiction de l'autonomie." *Eidos* 11, no. 1–2 (1993): 45–54.

Greisch, Jean, ed. *Paul Ricoeur: L'herméneutique à l'école de la phénoménologie*. Paris: Beauchesne, 1995.

———. *Le Cogito Herméneutique: L'Herméneutique philosophique et l'heritage cartésien*. Paris: J. Vrin, 2000.

Grondin, Jean. *Le Tournant herméneutique de la phénoménologie*. Paris: PUF, 2003.

Grünbaum, Adolf. "The Poverty of the Semiotic Turn in Psychoanalytic Theory and Therapy." In *Between Suspicion and Sympathy*, ed. Wiercinski, 602–19.

Gustafson, James M. "The Sectarian Temptation." *Proceedings of the Catholic Theological Society* 40 (1985): 83–94.

Habermas, Jürgen. *Moral Consciousness and Communicative Action*. Cambridge, Mass.: MIT Press, 1990.

———. "Transcendence from Within, Transcendence within this World." In *Habermas, Modernity, and Public Theology*, ed. Browning and Fiorenza, 236–48.

Hahn, Lewis Edwin, ed. *The Philosophy of Paul Ricoeur*. Chicago: Open Court, 1995.

Hauerwas, Stanley. *Against the Nations: War and Survival in a Liberal Society*. Minneapolis: Winston Press, 1985.

———. *A Community of Character: Toward a Constructive Christian Social Ethic*. Notre Dame, Ind.: University of Notre Dame Press, 1981.

Heidegger, Martin. *Being and Time*. Trans. Joan Stambaugh. Albany: SUNY Press, 1996.

Hick, John, and Paul Knitter, eds. *The Myth of Christian Uniqueness*. Maryknoll, N.Y.: Orbis, 1997.

Hunsinger, George. *Disruptive Grace: Studies in the Theology of Karl Barth.* Grand Rapids, Mich.: Eerdmans, 2000.

——. *How to Read Karl Barth: The Shape of His Theology.* Oxford: Oxford University Press, 1991.

Husserl, Edmund. *Ideas: General Introduction to Pure Phenomenology.* Trans. William R. Boyce Gibson. New York: Macmillan, 1952.

——. *Idées directrice pour une phenomenology.* Trans. Paul Ricoeur. Bibliothèque de philosophie. Paris: Gaillmard, 1950.

Ihde, Don. "Literary and Science Fictions: Philosophers and Technomyths." In *Ricoeur as Another,* ed. Cohen and Marsh, 93–105.

——. "Paul Ricoeur's Place in the Hermeneutic Tradition." In *The Philosophy of Paul Ricoeur,* ed. Hahn, 59–70.

Jaspert, Bernd, and Geoffrey W. Bromiley, eds. *Karl Barth—Rudolf Bultmann: Letters 1922–1966.* Trans. Geoffrey W. Bromiley. Edinburgh: T&T Clark, 1982.

Jeanrond, Werner. *Theological Hermeneutics: Development and Significance.* London: SCM Press, 1994.

Jervolino, Domenico, and Gordon Poole. *The Cogito and Hermeneutics: The Question of the Subject in Ricoeur.* Dordrecht: Kluwer, 1990.

Joy, Morny. "Recognition in the Work of Paul Ricoeur." In *Between Suspicion and Sympathy,* ed. Wiercinski, 518–30.

——, ed. *Ricoeur and Narrative: Context and Contestation.* Calgary: Calgary University Press, 1997.

Jüngel, E. *Karl Barth: A Theological Legacy.* Westminster: John Knox Press, 1986.

Kant, Immanuel. *Grounding for the Metaphysics of Morals, with, On a Supposed Right to Lie because of Philanthropic Concerns.* Trans. James Ellington, 3rd ed. Indianapolis: Hackett, 1993.

Kaplan, David M. *Ricoeur's Critical Theory.* Albany: SUNY Press, 2003.

Kearney, Richard. "Between Oneself and Another: Ricoeur's Diacritical Hermeneutics." In *Between Suspicion and Sympathy,* ed. Wiercinski, 149–60.

——. "The God of the Possible: Towards a New Hermeneutics of Religion." In *Between the Human and the Divine,* ed. Wiercinski, 531–39.

——. *The God Who May Be: A Hermeneutics of Religion.* Bloomington: Indiana University Press, 2001.

——. *On Stories.* London: Routledge, 2001.

——. *Poetics of Imagining: Modern to Post-Modern.* New York: Fordham University Press, 1998.

——, ed. *Paul Ricoeur: the Hermeneutics of Action.* London; Thousand Oaks, Calif.: Sage Publications, 1996.

Keenan, James F. "Proposing Cardinal Virtues." *Theological Studies* 56 (1995): 709–29.

Kerr, Fergus. *Theology after Wittgenstein.* 2nd. ed. London: SPCK Press, 1997.

Klemm, David E., and William Schweiker. *Meanings in Texts and Actions.* Charlottesville: University Press of Virginia, 1993.

Knitter, Paul. *Jesus and the Other Names.* Maryknoll, N.Y.: Orbis Books, 1996.

Latona, Max. "Selfhood and Agency in Ricoeur and Aristotle." *Philosophy Today* 45, no.2 (Summer 2001): 107–20.

Lawlor, Leonard. *Imagination and Chance: The Difference between the Thought of Ricoeur and Derrida.* Albany: SUNY Press, 1992.

——. "A Note on Radical Alterity in Paul Ricoeur and Jacques Derrida." In *Between Suspicion and Sympathy,* ed. Wiercinski, 351–56.

Levinas, Emmanuel. *Otherwise than Being*. Trans. Alphonso Lingis. The Hague; Boston: Kluwer, 1981.

Lindbeck, George. *The Nature of Doctrine: Religion and Theology in a Postliberal Age*. Philadelphia: Westminster Press, 1984.

Maan, Ajit K. *Internarrative Identity*. Lanham, Md.: University Press of America, 1999.

MacIntyre, Alasdair. *After Virtue: A Study in Moral Theory*. 2nd ed. Notre Dame, Ind.: University of Notre Dame Press, 1984.

Madison, Gary B. *The Hermeneutics of Post-Modernity: Figures and Themes*. Bloomington: Indiana University Press, 1989.

Manoussakis John, and Paul Gratton, eds. *Traversing the Imaginary*. Lanham, Md.: Rowan and Littlefield, 2003.

Marcel, Gabriel. "An Autobiographical Essay." In *The Philosophy of Gabriel Marcel*, ed. Schilpp and Hahn, 3–68.

——. *Being and Having: An Existentialist Diary*. Gloucester, Mass.: Peter Smith, 1976.

——. *Man against Mass Society*. Trans. George S. Fraser. Chicago: Henry Regnery, 1962.

——. *Metaphysical Journal*. Trans. Bernard Wall. Chicago: Henry Regnery, 1952.

——. *The Mystery of Being*. Vol. 1, *Reflection and Mystery*. Chicago: Henry Regnery: Gateway, 1960.

——. *The Philosophy of Existentialism*. Trans. Manya Harari. New York: Citadel Press, 1995.

——. *Tragic Wisdom and Beyond*. Evanston, Ill.: Northwestern University Press, 1973.

Marshall, B. *Trinity and Truth*. Cambridge: Cambridge University Press, 1999.

McCormack, Bruce. *Barth's Critically Realist Dialectical Theology*. Oxford: Oxford University Press, 1995.

Merleau-Ponty, Maurice. *Phenomenology of Perception*. Trans. Colin Smith. New York: Humanities Press, 1962.

Milbank, John. "Foreword." In James K. A. Smith, *Introducing Radical Orthodoxy: Mapping a Post-Secular Theology*. Grand Rapids, Mich.: Baker Academic, 2004.

Mudge, Lewis S. "Introduction." In Paul Ricoeur, *Essays on Biblical Interpretation*, ed. Lewis S. Mudge. Philadelphia: Fortress Press, 1980, 1–22.

Nussbaum, Martha. *The Fragility of Goodness: Luck and Ethics in Greek Tragedy and Philosophy*. Cambridge, Mass.: Cambridge University Press, 1986.

——. "Ricoeur on Tragedy." In *Paul Ricoeur and Contemporary Moral Thought*, ed. Wall, Schweiker, and Hall.

Ormiston, Gayle L., and Alan D. Schrift, eds. *The Hermeneutic Tradition: From Ast to Ricoeur*. Albany: SUNY Press, 1990.

Palmer, Richard E. "Heideggerian Ontology and Gadamer's Hermeneutics." In *Between the Human and the Divine*, ed. Wiercinski, 113–21.

Parfit, Derek. *Reasons and Persons*. Oxford: Clarendon Press, 1984.

Pecknold, C. C. *Transforming Postliberal Theology*. Edinburgh: TandT Clark, 2005.

Pellauer, David. "The Symbol Gave Rise to Thought." In *The Philosophy of Paul Ricoeur*, ed. Hahn, 99–122.

Phillips, James. "Text, Interpretation, and the Unconscious in the Thought of Paul Ricoeur." In *Between Suspicion and Sympathy*, ed. Wiercinski, 585–601.

Placher, William. *Unapologetic Theology*. Louisville, Ky.: Westminster; John Knox Press, 1989.

Plourde, Simonne. "Emmanuel Levinas: une ethique deconcertante." *Laval Theologique et Philosophique* 55, no. 2 (1999): 205–13.

Rawls, John. *A Theory of Justice*. Cambridge, Mass.: Belknap Press of Harvard University Press, 1971.

Raynova, Yvanka. "All That Gives Us to Think: Conversations with Paul Ricoeur." In *Between Suspicion and Sympathy*, ed. Wiercinski, 670–96.

———. "Entre la Régression et l'Eschatologie: Philosophie et Théologie dans la Phénoménologie herméneutique de Paul Ricoeur." In *Temps-Utopie-Eschatologie*, ed. Charlotte Meuthen, 65–80. Leuven: Peeters, 1999.

Reagan, Charles. *Paul Ricoeur: His Life and Work*. Chicago: University of Chicago Press, 1996.

Rentdorff, Jacob D. "Paul Ricoeur's Poetic Ontology: Metaphor as Tensional Resemblance." In *Between Suspicion and Sympathy*, ed. Wiercinski, 379–97.

Schaff, Birgit. "Toward a Logic of Tragic Conflict: Paul Ricoeur's *Antigone* Interpretation in *Oneself as Another*." In *Between Suspicion and Sympathy*, ed. Wiercinski, 437–46.

Schilpp, Paul Arthur, and Lewis Edwin Hahn, eds. *The Philosophy of Gabriel Marcel*. La Salle, Ill.: Open Court, 1984.

Schleiermacher, Friedrich. *Hermeneutics: The Handwritten Manuscripts*. Ed. Heinz Kimmerle, trans. James Duke and Jack Forstman. Missoula, Mont.: Scholar's Press, 1977.

Severson, Richard J. *Time, Death, and Eternity: Reflecting on Augustine's* Confessions *in Light of Heidegger's* Being and Time. Lanham, Md.: Scarecrow Press, 1995.

Simms, Karl, ed. *Critical Studies: Ethics and the Subject*. Amsterdam: Rodopi, 1997.

Spiegelberg, Herbert. *The Phenomenological Movement*. 3rd. rev. and enl. ed. The Hague: Martinus Nijhoff, 1982.

Stiver, Daniel J. *Theology after Ricoeur*. Louisville: Westminster John Knox, 2001.

Taylor, Charles, ed. *Philosophical Arguments*. Cambridge, Mass.: Harvard University Press, 1997.

———. "Self-Interpreting Animals." In *Human Agency and Language: Philosophical Papers 1*, ed. C. Taylor, 45–76. Cambridge: Cambridge University Press, 1985.

Thistleton, Anthony. *Interpreting God and the Postmodern Self: On Meaning, Manipulation and Promise*. Grand Rapids, Mich.: Eerdmans, 1995.

Thomas, Owen C. "Public Theology and Counter-Public Spheres." *Harvard Theological Review* 85, no. 4 (1992): 452–63.

Thompson, John B. *Critical Hermeneutics: A Study in the Thought of Paul Ricoeur and Jürgen Habermas*. Cambridge: Cambridge University Press, 1981.

Torrance, Thomas F. *Karl Barth: Biblical and Evangelical Theologian*. Edinburgh: T&T Clark, 1990.

Toth, Tamas. "The Graft, Residue, and Memory: Two Conversations with Tamas Toth." In *Between Suspicion and Sympathy*, ed. Wiercinski, 642–69.

Tracy, David. *The Analogical Imagination*. New York: Crossroad, 1981.

———. *Blessed Rage for Order: The New Pluralism in Theology*. New York: Seabury, 1975.

———. "Lindbeck's New Program for Theology: A Reflection." *Thomist* 49, no. 3 (July 1985): 460–72.

———. "Ricoeur's Philosophical Journey: Its Import for Religion." In *Paul Ricoeur: The Hermeneutics of Action*, ed. Kearney, 202–205.

———. "A Theological View of Philosophy: Revelation and Reason." In *The Question of Christian Philosophy Today,* ed. Francis D'Ambrosio. New York: Fordham University Press, 1999.

———. "Theology, Critical Social Theory, and the Public Realm." In *Habermas, Modernity, and Public Theology,* ed. Browning and Fiorenza.

———. "The Uneasy Alliance Reconceived: Catholic Theological Method, Modernity, and Postmodernity." *Theological Studies* 50 (1989): 548–70.

van den Hengel, John. "Between Philosophy and Theology: Ricoeur's Testimony of the Self." In *Between the Human and the Divine,* ed. Wiercinski, 122–37.

———. "Can There Be a Science of Action?" In *Ricoeur as Another,* ed. Cohen and Marsh, 71–92.

———. *The Home of Meaning: The Hermeneutics of the Subject of Paul Ricoeur.* Washington, D.C.: University Press of America, 1982.

———. *Memory, Narrativity, Self and the Challenge to Think God.* Ed. M. Junker-Kenny. Münster: Lit Verlag, 2004.

Vandevelde, Pol, Jacqueline Bouchard Spurlock, and Bond Harris. *Paul Ricoeur: A Key to Husserl's "Ideas I."* Milwaukee: Marquette University Press, 1996.

Vanhoozer, Kevin J. *Biblical Narrative in the Philosophy of Paul Ricoeur: A Study in Hermeneutics and Theology.* New York: Cambridge University Press, 1990.

Venema, Henry. *Identifying Selfhood: Imagination, Narrative and Hermeneutics in the Thought of Paul Ricoeur.* Albany: SUNY Press, 2000.

Wall, John, William Schweiker, and David Hall, eds. *Paul Ricoeur and Contemporary Moral Thought.* New York: Routledge, 2002.

Wallace, Mark I. *The Second Naïveté: Barth, Ricoeur, and the New Yale Theology.* 2nd. ed. Macon, Ga.: Mercer University Press, 1995.

———. "The Summoned Self: Ethics and Hermeneutics in Paul Ricoeur in Dialogue with Emmanuel Levinas." In *Paul Ricoeur and Contemporary Moral Thought,* ed. Wall, Schweiker, and Hall, 80–93.

Walzer, Michael. *Spheres of Justice: A Defense of Pluralism and Equality.* New York: Basic Books, 1983.

Ward, Graham. *Barth, Derrida and the Language of Theology.* Cambridge: Cambridge University Press, 1999.

Weber, Max. *Economy and Society: An Outline of Interpretive Sociology.* Ed. Guenther Roth and Claus Wittich. Berkeley: University of California Press, 1978.

Webster, John. *Barth.* London: Continuum, 2000.

Welsen, Peter. "Personal Identity as Narrative Identity." In *Between Suspicion and Sympathy,* ed. Wiercinski, 192–202.

Westphal, Merold. "Hermeneutical Finitude from Schleiermacher to Derrida." In *Between the Human and the Divine,* ed. Wiercinski, 50–65.

———. *Overcoming Ontotheology: Toward a Postmodern Christian Faith.* New York: Fordham University Press, 2001.

———. "Review of *Oneself as Another.*" *American Philosophical Quarterly* 34 (1994): 385–86.

Wiercinski, Andrzej, ed. *Between the Human and the Divine: Philosophical and Theological Hermeneutics.* Toronto: Hermeneutic Press, 2002.

———. *Between Suspicion and Sympathy: Paul Ricoeur's Unstable Equilibrium.* Toronto: Hermeneutic Press, 2003.

———. *Inspired Metaphysics: Gustav Siewerth's Hermeneutic Reading of the Onto-Theological Tradition.* Toronto: Hermeneutic Press, 2003.

———. "Introduction: Celebrating the Confusion of Voices and the Fusion of Hermeneutic Horizons." In *Between Suspicion and Sympathy,* ed. Wiercinski, ix–xiv.

———. "Seeking Understanding: Philosophical and Theological Hermeneutics." In *Between the Human and the Divine,* ed. Wiercinski, xiv–xvi.

Williams, Bernard. *Ethics and the Limits of Philosophy.* Cambridge, Mass.: Harvard University Press, 1985.

Wood, David, ed. *On Paul Ricoeur: Narrative and Interpretation.* New York: Routledge, 1991.

INDEX

Boyd Blundell is assistant professor of ethics in the Department of Religious Studies at Loyola University, New Orleans.

Printed and bound by CPI Group (UK) Ltd, Croydon, CR0 4YY

13/04/2025

14656544-0001